The Foundations of Modern Austrian Economics

Edited with an Introduction by
Edwin G. Dolan

SHEED & WARD, INC.
Subsidiary of Universal Press Syndicate
Kansas City

This edition is cosponsored by the Institute for Humane Studies, Inc., Menlo Park, California.

Library of Congress Cataloging in Publication Data
Main entry under title: ⸦

The Foundations of modern Austrian economics. ℮

(Studies in economic theory)
Proceedings of a conference sponsored by the Institute for Humane Studies and held at Royalton College, South Royalton, Vt., in June 1974.
Bibliography: p.
Includes index.
1. Austrian school of economists — Congresses.
I.   Dolan, Edwin G.   II.   Institute for Humane Studies.   III.   Series.
HB98.F68   330'.09436   76-5894
ISBN 0-8362-0653-3
ISBN 0-8362-0654-1 pbk.

CONTENTS

PART 3   APPLICATIONS

PART 4   CONCLUSION

PREFACE

In June 1974 the Institute for Humane Studies sponsored the first of a series of conferences on Austrian economics. This conference was held at Royalton College in South Royalton, Vermont, and attracted some fifty participants from all regions of the United States and three continents abroad. The conferees came to hear Israel M. Kirzner, Ludwig M. Lachmann, and Murray N. Rothbard survey the fundamentals of modern Austrian economics and thereby challenge the Keynesian-neoclassical orthodoxy, which has dominated economic science since World War II.

Each lecturer addressed himself to two general questions: What is the distinctive Austrian contribution to economic theory? And what are the important problems and new directions for Austrian economics today? By answering these questions, the papers collected in this volume become more than just a set of conference proceedings—they take on the character of a manifesto and provisional textbook as well.

The enthusiastic response to the South Royalton conference suggests that the century-old Austrian tradition is now entering a new era of increasing influence. Both the Austrian school and its orthodox competitor trace their origins to the restructuring of economic science that took place in the 1870s. The marginalist revolution of that period, which marked the breakdown of the classical economics established by Adam Smith, David Ricardo, and John Stuart Mill, was followed by the appearance of a number of new schools of economics in England and on the Continent. The greatest of the English economists of this period was Alfred Marshall. The so-called neoclassical school of Marshall and his followers soon became the new orthodoxy. In the process it absorbed the contributions of two other major schools that had arisen independently—one associated with William

vii

Stanley Jevons in England and the other with Léon Walras in Switzerland.

Meanwhile in Vienna the marginalist revolution was proceeding on another front. In 1871 Carl Menger published his *Grundsätze der Volkswirtschaftslehre* and, soon joined by Friederich von Wieser and Eugen von Böhm-Bawerk, established the Austrian school. The Austrian school, although failing to achieve dominance in the international profession, retained its own identity and did not become wholly absorbed into neoclassicism. Throughout the remainder of the nineteenth century and into the twentieth, it continued to attract a small but vigorous stream of adherents, among whom the most distinguished were Ludwig von Mises and Friedrich A. Hayek.

During the Great Depression neoclassical economics was deeply shaken. The depth and duration of the economic crisis exceeded the expectations of orthodox theorists. Government policymakers were unable to find adequate guidance in the textbooks of the day, and members of the economics profession cast about for a new theoretical insight. The two major candidates for the leadership role were Hayek, the Austrian theoretician, and John Maynard Keynes, the most prominent of Marshall's pupils. By the end of the decade of the thirties, the Keynesian system had attracted the greatest number of adherents, and the Austrian school, after a brief period of prominence, was left to pursue an independent course in relative obscurity.

In the early postwar period neoclassicism proved its resilience and adaptability by gradually coalescing with the Keynesian school. The work of Keynes, which at the time seemed so radical, was modified until today economists like Paul Samuelson and Milton Friedman, once thought leaders of irreconcilable camps, share a common theoretical basis for their research.

The Kennedy-Johnson years were the heyday of the Keynesian-neoclassical synthesis in the United States. Keynesian and leading neoclassical economists were installed to head advisory posts in Washington, D.C., and were confident of their ability to "fine tune" the economy and render it free of depression forevermore. Now, in the inflationary recession of the seventies, new doubts are raised, and new questions are being asked. The papers in this volume are addressed to these doubts and questions, and economists of all academic persuasions will profit from their reading.

A number of institutions and individuals have contributed to the success of the conference and the publication of the proceedings. First, thanks must go to the Institute for Humane Studies for providing the necessary funding for both the conference and the preparation of this volume. George Pearson and Kenneth Templeton of the Institute for Humane Studies were the prime movers of the conference from start to finish, and I am grateful to them for naming me conference director and editor of the proceedings.

Much of the credit for the success of the week-long conference must go to Royalton College, which as conference host bore the burden of all local arrangements. College president Anthony N. Doria together with Kilby Dewitt and Athena Jacobi of the college staff worked tirelessly to put the facilities of the college at the disposal of the conferees. Neighboring Dartmouth College also merits thanks for making auxiliary local arrangements.

I would also like to acknowledge the gracious cooperation of the conference contributors for preparing their manuscripts according to schedule and granting me permission to include them in this volume. Gerald P. O'Driscoll, Jr., and Sudha R. Shenoy attended the conference and participated in the discussions at the end of each session. I am grateful to them for agreeing to prepare a special paper for inclusion in this volume on the Austrian theory of the business cycle and its application to the modern-day problem of stagflation. Finally, I am indebted to Laurence S. Moss, editor of the series Studies in Economic Theory, of which this volume is a part, for his support and assistance in the preparation of the manuscript.

Edwin G. Dolan
South Royalton, Vermont
June 1975

PART 1
INTRODUCTION

Austrian Economics as Extraordinary Science

Edwin G. Dolan

Thomas Kuhn in *The Structure of Scientific Revolutions* (Chicago: University of Chicago Press, 1970) made a distinction between *normal* and *extraordinary* science. Normal science is the day-to-day research activity of a community of scholars working and communicating with one another on the basis of certain shared principles and methods embodied in what Kuhn called a "paradigm" for that science. From time to time such a science may undergo revolutionary change, in the course of which the prevailing paradigm is replaced by a new one. Work involved in the search for and establishment of a new paradigm, as opposed to work proceeding within the framework of an accepted paradigm, is called extraordinary science.

We need not, on this occasion, enter the debate about the strict applicability of Kuhn's analysis to the social sciences. It is enough for the moment to use his work as a source of useful analogy and metaphor. Taking this approach, we find that in contemporary economics, normal science is represented by work within the framework of the Keynesian-neoclassical synthesis. We can easily list many features characteristic of normal science. Communication among economists is primarily by means of journal articles presenting incremental contributions to knowledge rather than by means of books concerned with first principles. There is a well-established textbook tradition, and students are exposed to the original works of classical and contemporary economists only briefly and at a relatively advanced stage in their training. Economists go about their day-to-day work of establish-

3

ing significant empirical facts, matching facts with theory, and extending applications of theory to new areas with little explicit attention to such fundamental questions as what constitutes a *valid* problem or a valid solution in economic analysis. Disputes arise, but underlying the disputes is fundamental agreement as to the kind of evidence or debate on which the dispute is, in principle, to be resolved.

In contrast to the majority of economists, the contributors to this volume on Austrian economics talk and act like people who are doing extraordinary science. They produce relatively more books and contribute fewer articles to established journals. They do not write textbooks; their students learn directly from the masters. They are very much concerned with methodological and philosophical fundamentals. And what makes the label *extraordinary* most applicable to their work is that they share a conviction that orthodox economics is at the point of breakdown, that it is unable to provide a coherent and intelligible analysis of the present-day economic world.

Students of contemporary economic thought ought not, however, allow the status of modern Austrian economics as extraordinary science to be settled entirely on the basis of the Austrian economist's self-image. Others have seen things differently, among them Milton Friedman, a leading articulator of the orthodox paradigm. Speaking informally at the South Royalton conference, Friedman startled his audience with the bold assertion that "there is no Austrian economics — only good economics, and bad economics." His intention, he went on to explain, was not to condemn Austrian economics as bad economics but rather to declare that the truly valuable and original contributions of Austrian-school economists (he was speaking of Friedrich A. Hayek in particular) could be smoothly incorporated into the mainstream of economic theory.

It seems to me that the question of the status of Austrian economics is not incapable of resolution and that, in fact, the papers presented here represent a sufficient sample on which to base such a conclusion. The question is whether or not Austrian economics possesses a paradigm truly distinct from that of the

Keynesian-neoclassical orthodoxy. For, as Kuhn emphasized, an extraordinary science must not simply be critical of the established normal science paradigm; it must also present an alternative.

In analyzing the Austrian paradigm, I shall focus on three particular functions that, according to Kuhn, a paradigm must perform. First, a paradigm must tell the investigator what types of entities the world does and does not contain. Second, a paradigm must define what constitutes a legitimate problem for the science at hand. Third, it must specify the methods by which legitimate solutions to these problems may be reached.

The methodological principle about which Austrian-school writers are most insistent is that the basic building block of economic theory must be the individual human action. As Murray N. Rothbard put it, the whole of Austrian economic theory is the working out of the logical implications of the fact that human beings do engage in purposeful action (Rothbard, "Praxeology" [references to papers included in this volume are in abbreviated form]).

The term *action*, as used by Austrian theorists, takes on a precise technical sense that is perhaps best understood by contrasting actions with events. An event may be thought of as something that "just happens" — a change that takes place in the state of the world, such as a rock falling from a cliff and killing Smith. An action, in contrast, is something that happens as a result of purposeful intervention in the "natural" course of events; for example, Jones pushes a rock off a cliff for the purpose of murdering Smith, who is standing below. An action may be thought of as consisting of two components. The first component is the event, that the rock fell killing Smith. The second is the implied counterfactual proposition that if Jones had not intervened in the situation in order to carry out his purpose of murder, the rock would not have fallen, and Smith would be alive.

Orthodox economists, influenced by positivist and behaviorist methodological principles, are uncomfortable with the concept of action because the second, counterfactual component is not directly observable. As a consequence, orthodox theories tend to be couched exclusively in terms of observable events and the so-called empirical relationships among events. The Austrians, in marked contrast to the orthodox thinkers, believe that an economic explanation in terms of events alone cannot tell the whole story, because it necessarily omits an important component of reality — the concept of purposive action (see Kirzner, "On the Method").

At the same time the Austrian economists criticize orthodox writers for omitting the concept of purposive action from their set of basic entities, they criticize them for admitting certain illegitimate constructs into their economic theories. Austrian writers are characteristically critical of the use of macroeconomic aggregates, especially when these appear as arguments in mathematical formulations that imply functional and/or causal relationships between aggregates. The concept of the quantity of capital is especially singled out for criticism in this regard (see Lachmann, "Toward a Critique").

The question of what constitutes a legitimate problem for analysis receives careful attention in Kirzner's paper on the methodology of Austrian economics (see his "On the Method," below). Kirzner noted that the Austrian tradition assigns two tasks to economics. The first is that of "making the world intelligible in terms of human action." The second is "to explain how conscious, purposeful human action can generate unintended consequences through social interaction" and to trace these unintended consequences. These tasks are both more and less ambitious than the tasks undertaken by orthodox economics. The Austrian-type explanation is more ambitious than the orthodox explanation in the sense that a picture painted in terms of human purposes is more complete than one painted only in terms of events. The Austrian enterprise is also more ambitious because it insists on laying bare the true causal relationships at work in the social world and is not content to simply establish empirical regularities among dubious statistical aggregates.

At the same time, Austrian explanatory systems are less ambitious precisely because they do not seek to establish quantitative relationships among economic magnitudes. The Austrians are, in fact, quite insistent about the exclusion of such quantitative determinations from the range of legitimate economic problems. As Ludwig von Mises put it, in a passage quoted approvingly by Rothbard in his essay "Praxeology":

> The impracticability of measurement is not due to the lack of technical methods for the establishment of measure. It is due to the absence of constant relations . . . . Economics is not, as . . . positivists repeat again and again, backward because it is not "quantitative." It is not quantitative and does not measure because there are no constants (Ludwig von Mises, *Human Action: A Treatise on Economics* [New Haven: Yale University Press, 1963], pp. 55-56).

The nature of the problems the Austrians undertake to solve and the entities which they employ determine the permissible methods of solving problems under the Austrian paradigm. The Austrian method, simply put, is to spin out by verbal deductive reasoning the logical implications of a few fundamental axioms. First among the axioms is the fact of purposeful human action. Supplementary axioms are that human beings are diverse in tastes and abilities, that all action takes place through time, and that people learn from experience. The epistemological status of these axioms is a matter of some dispute among Austrians, but Rothbard's position — that they are in the last analysis empirical — appears to be the most acceptable (see his essay "Praxeology," below).

Acceptance of the Austrian paradigm entails a radical rejection of econometrics as a tool of economic theory. It is easy to see why Austrians find econometrics useless as a tool for discovering or establishing economic laws. First, since the axioms from which economic laws are deduced are taken to be apodictically true (barring logical errors in the deductive process), the theories themselves must also be true and consequently cannot and need not be subjected to falsification by statistical methods. Second, Austrian theories are formulated in terms of action, and action, as was argued above, contains a counterfactual element, which is in principle not subject to direct observation or confirmation.

Finally, the absence of constants in economic life makes any attempt at econometric determination of such constants futile.

In the abstract, such are the characteristics of the paradigm the Austrians, as would-be scientific revolutionaries, hold out as an alternative to the Keynesian-neoclassical orthodoxy. Whether this paradigm is to remain an empty program or has the substance for an alternative normal science tradition depends on its application to concrete analytical problems. With this in mind, let us briefly look at recent contributions of the Austrian school to the theory of prices and markets, of capital, and of money and economic fluctuations, as presented in the essays in this volume.

In the subject area orthodox theorists refer to as "microeconomics," Israel Kirzner has made several recent and important contributions. In his book *Competition and Entrepreneurship* (Chicago: University of Chicago Press, 1974) and again in his essay "Equilibrium versus Market Process" (see below), Kirzner criticized neoclassical economics for devoting too much attention to the elaboration of the formal conditions for general equilibrium, and too little to an understanding of actual market processes through which resources are moved from lower to higher valued uses during periods of market disequilibrium. (Lachmann in his paper "On the Central Concept" went further than Kirzner and rejected the practical relevance of the concept of equilibrium altogether.) To understand market process, according to Kirzner, two types of economic decision making must be differentiated. The first is what he called "Robbinsian economizing," that is, using known available resources in the most efficient manner to achieve given purposes with the object of allocating these resources so that no transfer of a marginal unit from one use to another can promise a net benefit. The second is entrepreneurial decision making, that is, being alert to previously unknown opportunities for buying low and selling high in situations where the planned activities of Robbinsian economizers are imperfectly coordinated. A theory couched purely in terms of Robbinsian economizing can at best identify the price-quantity configurations necessary to sustain an equilibrium. But it is only by introducing the concept of entrepreneurial action that one can explain how systematic changes in the information and expectations upon which market participants act lead them in the direction of the postulated equilibrium price and quantity relationships.

By contrasting the theory of general equilibrium with the theory of market process, we can understand more clearly the differences between the orthodox and the Austrian paradigm. The theory of general equilibrium poses a number of attractive puzzles for neoclassical economists, particularly those wishing to display their virtuosity in mathematical analysis. The variables of a general equilibrium model are all, in principle at least, empirically observable, and the types of decisions made by Robbinsian economizers can be neatly and accurately expressed in functional notation. But from the point of view of an Austrian theorist bent on making the world intelligible in terms of human action, the puzzles of general equilibrium are simply not the whole story. Far from being deterred by the fact that the decision-making processes of the entrepreneur are not easily expressed in mathematical notation, a writer like Kirzner is able to exercise his own virtuosity at verbal-deductive analysis and produce a variety of useful insights.

Lest it be thought that the matter of equilibrium versus market process is of no practical significance, the reader's attention is directed to Kirzner's discussion of the role of advertising. Neoclassical economics, with its emphasis on decision making based on given information and under perfect competition, has had difficulty finding a place for advertising in the economic world. Frequently, this theoretical untidiness has led the neoclassical economist to become critical of advertising on the policy level. Kirzner's analysis, which at last makes advertising an integral part of the entrepreneurial role in the market process, provides the basis for a rather different and more supportive attitude toward advertising.

Turning now to recent Austrian work on capital theory, let us single out for attention the issue of the nature and measurability of an economy's stock of capital. Sir John Hicks (in his paper "Capital Controversies: Ancient and Modern," *American*

Economic Review 64(May 1974): 307-16; and discussed by Kirzner, "The Theory of Capital") divided economists into two broad
groupings according to their definition of capital. According to
Hicks, the "materialists" contend that the stock of capital is
nothing more than an inventory of the stock of physical capital
goods in an economy. This view has as a corollary that, in any two
economies with identical physical stocks of capital goods, the
economic measure of capital must be identical. To the "fundists," on the other hand, capital is something other than mere
physical goods, and the measure of capital must be a *value*
measure derived in some way from the flow of future output.

According to Kirzner, Austrian economists can accept neither
the materialist nor the fundist position on the question of the
nature and measurement of capital. Materialism is rejected out
of hand on the grounds that the physical heterogeneity of capital
goods prohibits simply adding them up. The fundist point of
view receives somewhat more sympathy, because it at least recognizes that the nature of capital goods is intimately bound up
with valuation, that is, with future plans for the production of
output. Nonetheless, Kirzner denied that there is any legitimate
way of adding together these streams of future output to provide
a meaningful measure of a nation's capital stock. One problem,
often discussed in the literature on capital theory, is that it is hard
to find a unit of measurement for capital that is invariant to
changes in relative prices. Equally important is the problem that
at a given moment the plans of various individual economic
agents, of which existing capital goods form a part, may well be
incompatible. Suppose, for example, that individual A builds a
house with the intention of living in it, and individual B builds a
bomb for the purpose of blowing up A's house. A counts on a
future stream of housing services having a certain determinate
value, and B counts on a future stream of destruction services
also having a certain determinate value. But surely these two
future value streams cannot legitimately be added together to
get a measure of the economy's current stock of capital, because
it is logically impossible that both could be realized simultaneously. Thus, any attempt at adding up (future) value streams to get a

measure of capital necessarily overstates the quantity of capital to the extent that current plans are imperfectly coordinated, which is equivalent to saying that a consistent measure of capital is possible only when the economy is in full equilibrium. The Austrian economists, of course, emphasize that it never is in full equilibrium.

In the controversy over the measurability of capital, the differences between the Austrian and the orthodox paradigm are once again evident. Neoclassical theorists, intent on constructing mathematical models of economic reality, are unable to proceed without grasping some single number, or "index," and calling it the "quantity of capital." Since they cannot dispense with such a number, they brush aside all theoretical objections and resort when pressed to such contrivances as the single product economy. To the Austrian economists, such constructions are the most arid of formalisms and do more to mask the true nature of economic reality than to provide useful insight. Instead, they prefer a concept of capital that identifies capital goods as physical objects directed toward specific purposes by individual agents, even if this approach means abandoning the possibility of measuring a nation's capital stock altogether.

As our third illustration, let us look at the nature of Austrian-school contributions to the theory of money and economic fluctuations. The Austrian economists are characteristically averse to using the term *macroeconomics* when referring to this area of study. This very term smacks of illegitimate aggregates and the type of methodological holism they seek to avoid. From the earliest days, the hallmark of Austrian work in this area has been a microeconomic approach to macroeconomic problems. Ludwig von Mises's *Theory of Money and Credit* (first German edition 1912; English edition, New Haven: Yale University Press, 1963), a pioneering contribution, identified the lack of coordination between individual expectations and the supply of money and credit as a prime cause of economic disturbance. Later work by Hayek extended the Misesian analysis and integrated the theory of the business cycle with the Austrian theory of production. Let us take a brief look at Hayek's contribution in this area, as updated and applied by Gerald P. O'Driscoll, Jr., and Sudha R. Shenoy in their paper "Inflation, Recession and Stagflation" included in this volume.

O'Driscoll and Shenoy, together with other modern Austrian economists, hold that the major anomaly facing orthodox economics and defying explanation is the seemingly intractable inflationary stagnation that has beset the major industrial countries in the seventies. In their view, orthodox theories, Keynesian and monetarist alike, are formulated at too high a level of aggregation and are thus blind to the distorting effects of overexpansionary monetary policy on relative prices and the capital structure. In barest outline, their argument is that expansionary policies inject money into the economy, not uniformly, but at a specific point. The injection of new money creates a monetary "pull" on relative prices at this point. As a result of the effect of monetary expansion on relative prices, some businesses make profits that otherwise would have made losses, and some workers find jobs in places where there would otherwise have been none. If the injection of new money is by way of commercial bank loans to businessmen, the capital goods industries, and among them firms producing specific capital goods suitable for use in processes of relatively low labor intensity, are built up first. However, the expansion of these industries cannot be sustained without a concomitant decline in the fraction of current output consumed. Barring a fortuitous shift in consumption habits, the injection of new money must be continued. Because expectations adjust to any constant rate of injection, the needed degree of monetary pull on relative prices requires an accelerating rate of monetary expansion. This leaves policymakers in a dilemma. Either they must inflate without limit, or when they cease inflating, they must face the unemployment and drop in output that will inevitably accompany the liquidation of the unjustified investments made earlier. To use Hayek's metaphor, the policymakers have a tiger by the tail.

Here again we see how the Austrian paradigm, with its principled rejection of aggregative analysis, has produced insights that in recent years orthodox economists have been quick to overlook. In the case of business cycle theory, however, the possibility is greater than in our previous examples that the essentials of Austrian theory can be co-opted into orthodox analysis. Orthodox theorists may well wish to recast Hayek's theories in a form that would make them subject to econometric evaluation. If they are pleased with the results, one can easily imagine Hayek's relative-price mechanism being spliced onto existing Keynesian or monetarist models, just as has happened to other microeconomic insights such as the theory of job search and the theory of inflationary expectations. If this takes place, the Austrian paradigm may not succeed in replacing that of the Keynesian-neoclassical orthodoxy.

Despite the fact that the gap between Austrian and orthodox economics may be narrower in the area last discussed than elsewhere, I think the evidence indicates that the modern Austrian school does present a truly distinct paradigm against the alternative of a distinction only between good economics and bad economics. The possession of a distinct paradigm may be thought of as necessary for a successful scientific revolution. It goes without saying, however, that it is not a sufficient condition. In concluding our analysis of Austrian economics as extraordinary science, let us consider some remarks Kuhn made regarding the nature of the debate between advocates of alternative paradigms:

The choice between competing paradigms regularly raises questions that cannot be resolved by the criteria of normal science. To the extent, as significant as it is incomplete, that two scientific schools disagree about what is a problem and what is a solution, they will inevitably talk through each other when debating the relative merits of their respective paradigms. In the partially circular arguments that regularly result, each paradigm will be shown to satisfy more or less the criteria that it dictates for itself and to fall short of a few of those dictated by its opponent. There are other reasons, too, for the incompleteness of logical contact that consistently characterizes paradigm debates. For example, since no paradigm ever solves all the problems it defines and since no two paradigms leave all the same problems unsolved, paradigm debates always involve the question: Which problems is it more significant to have solved? [Kuhn, *Structure*, pp. 109-10.]

The tendency of the advocates of alternative paradigms to talk through, rather than to, each other may be seen in the various Austrian critiques of mathematical economics and econometrics. In their attack on mathematical economics, at least two separate arguments can be discerned. One is that mathematical economics does not really achieve greater theoretical precision; instead it requires the translation of simple concepts into mathematical language followed by arduous retranslation into English (see Rothbard's discussion in "Praxeology," below). This line of criticism is not found only among Austrian economists; it was given a most eloquent expression by Alfred Marshall. The other strand of the Austrian critique of mathematical economics is the contention that those problems most amenable to mathematical treatment — general equilibrium theory, formal growth models, and the like — are in principle not interesting or legitimate economic problems. The problems important to Austrian theorists (for example, the puzzle of the nature of entrepreneurship) neither can be nor need be dealt with mathematically.

In the critique of econometrics, the tendency to talk through the opposition is perhaps more evident than anywhere else. Here again we can distinguish two strands of thought in Austrian writing. One, already discussed, concerns the absence of constants in human action and the absurdity of subjecting valid deductions from true axioms to superfluous empirical tests.

The other strand of the Austrian critique concerns the definition of the legitimate boundaries of economics as a science. At one point in discussing Austrian methodology, Rothbard (see his paper "Praxeology") distinguished among three branches of intellectual inquiry. Economics is the discipline devoted to the logical implications of the axiom of human action. Technology deals with the choice of certain means for the achievement of certain ends. History deals with ends adopted in the past and means used (to try) to achieve them. Now, from these definitions, it is immediately clear that econometrics can serve no purpose in economics per se. That is the substance of the previously mentioned line of criticism. Yet this argument leaves open the possibility that econometrics could be a legitimate tool of technology and history. In collecting statistics on, say, past fluctuations in the prices and quantities of cotton, econometricians are not measuring constants in human behavior or testing economic theory, and they delude themselves if they think they are. Nonetheless, in principle the econometricians' work, properly interpreted, may be valuable to noneconomists. For example, a historian trying to interpret patterns of economic activity in the southern United States might want to know the approximate ex post elasticity relationships in the cotton market in certain periods. Alternatively, a textile manufacturer, seeking profit maximization by the best means available, might employ an econometrician as a technologist to advise him concerning inventory strategy. In short, if econometricians would stop insisting that they were engaging in the discovery of economic laws, a variety of purely instrumentalist justifications for their work could be found without forcing a head-on confrontation with Austrian doctrine.

PART 2
THEORY AND
METHOD

Praxeology:
The Methodology of
Austrian Economics

Murray N. Rothbard

Praxeology is the distinctive methodology of the Austrian school. The term was first applied to the Austrian method by Ludwig von Mises, who was not only the major architect and elaborator of this methodology but also the economist who most fully and successfully applied it to the construction of economic theory.[1] While the praxeological method is, to say the least, out of fashion in contemporary economics — as well as in social science generally and in the philosophy of science — it was the basic method of the earlier Austrian school and also of a considerable segment of the older classical school, in particular of J. B. Say and Nassau W. Senior.[2]

Praxeology rests on the fundamental axiom that individual human beings *act*, that is, on the primordial fact that individuals engage in conscious actions toward chosen goals. This concept of action contrasts to purely *reflexive*, or knee-jerk, behavior, which is not directed toward goals. The praxeological method spins out by verbal deduction the logical implications of that primordial fact. In short, praxeological economics is the structure of logical implications of the *fact* that individuals act. This structure is built on the fundamental axiom of action, and has a few subsidiary axioms, such as that individuals vary and that human beings regard leisure as a valuable good. Any skeptic about deducing from such a simple base an entire system of economics, I refer to Mises's *Human Action*. Furthermore, since praxeology begins

19

with a true axiom, A, all the propositions that can be deduced from this axiom must also be true. For if A implies B, and A is true, then B must also be true.

Let us consider some of the immediate implications of the action axiom. Action implies that the individual's behavior is purposive, in short, that it is directed toward goals. Furthermore, the fact of his action implies that he has consciously chosen certain means to reach his goals. Since he wishes to attain these goals, they must be valuable to him; accordingly he must have values that govern his choices. That he employs means implies that he believes he has the technological knowledge that certain means will achieve his desired ends. Let us note that praxeology does not assume that a person's choice of values or goals is wise or proper or that he has chosen the technologically correct method of reaching them. All that praxeology asserts is that the individual actor adopts goals and believes, whether erroneously or correctly, that he can arrive at them by the employment of certain means.

All action in the real world, furthermore, must take place through time; all action takes place in some present and is directed toward the future (immediate or remote) attainment of an end. If all of a person's desires could be instantaneously realized, there would be no reason for him to act at all.[3] Furthermore, that a man acts implies that he believes action will make a difference; in other words, that he will prefer the state of affairs resulting from action to that from no action. Action therefore implies that man does not have omniscient knowledge of the future; for if he had such knowledge, no action of his would make any difference. Hence, action implies that we live in a world of an uncertain, or not fully certain, future. Accordingly, we may amend our analysis of action to say that a man chooses to employ means according to a technological plan in the present because he expects to arrive at his goals at some future time.

The fact that people act necessarily implies that the means employed are scarce in relation to the desired ends; for, if all means were not scarce but superabundant, the ends would already have been attained, and there would be no need for action.

Stated another way, resources that are superabundant no longer function as means, because they are no longer objects of action. Thus, air is indispensable to life and hence to the attainment of goals; however, air being superabundant is not an object of action and therefore cannot be considered a *means*; but rather what Mises called a "general condition of human welfare." Where air is not superabundant, it may become an object of action, for example, where cool air is desired and warm air is transformed through air conditioning. Even with the absurdly unlikely advent of Eden (or what a few years ago was considered in some quarters to be an imminent "postscarcity" world), in which all desires could be fulfilled instantaneously, there would still be at least one scarce means: the individual's time, each unit of which if allocated to one purpose is necessarily not allocated to some other goal.[4]

Such are some of the immediate implications of the axiom of action. We arrived at them by deducing the logical implications of the existing fact of human action, and hence deduced true conclusions from a true axiom. Apart from the fact that these conclusions cannot be "tested" by historical or statistical means, there is no *need* to test them since their truth has already been established. Historical fact enters into these conclusions only by determining which branch of the theory is applicable in any particular case. Thus, for Crusoe and Friday on their desert island, the praxeological theory of money is only of academic, rather than of currently applicable, interest. A fuller analysis of the relationship between theory and history in the praxeological framework will be considered below.

There are, then, two parts to this axiomatic-deductive method: the process of deduction and the epistemological status of the axioms themselves. First, there is the process of deduction; why are the means verbal rather than mathematical logic?[5] Without setting forth the comprehensive Austrian case against mathematical economics, one point can immediately be made: let the reader take the implications of the concept of action as developed so far in this paper and try to place them in mathematical form. And even if that could be done, what would have been accomplished except a drastic loss in meaning at each step of the deductive process? Mathematical logic is appropriate to physics—the science that has become the model science, which modern positivists and empiricists believe all other social and physical sciences should emulate. In physics the axioms and therefore the deductions are in themselves purely formal and only acquire meaning "operationally" insofar as they can explain and predict given facts. On the contrary, in praxeology, in the analysis of human action, the axioms themselves are known to be true and meaningful. As a result, each verbal step-by-step deduction is also true and meaningful; for it is the great quality of verbal propositions that each one is meaningful, whereas mathematical symbols are not meaningful in themselves. Thus Lord Keynes, scarcely an Austrian and himself a mathematician of note, leveled the following critique at mathematical symbolism in economics:

It is a great fault of symbolic psuedo-mathematical methods of formalising a system of economic analysis, that they expressly assume strict independence between the factors involved and lose all their cogency and authority if this hypothesis is disallowed: whereas, in ordinary discourse, where we are not blindly manipulating but know all the time what we are doing and what the words mean, we can keep "at the back of our heads" the necessary reserves and qualifications and the adjustments which we shall have to make later on, in a way in which we cannot keep complicated partial differentials "at the back" of several pages of algebra which assume that they all vanish. Too large a proportion of recent "mathematical" economics are mere concoctions, as imprecise as the initial assumptions they rest on, which allow the author to lose sight of the complexities and interdependencies of the real world in a maze of pretentious and unhelpful symbols.[6]

Moreover, even if verbal economics could be successfully translated into mathematical symbols and then retranslated into English so as to explain the conclusions, the process makes no sense and violates the great scientific principle of Occam's Razor of avoiding unnecessary multiplication of entities.[7]

Furthermore, as political scientist Bruno Leoni and mathematician Eugenio Frola pointed out,

It is often claimed that translation of such a concept as the maximum from ordinary into mathematical language, involves an improvement in the logical accuracy of the concept, as well as wider opportunities for its use. But the lack of mathematical precision in ordinary language reflects precisely the behavior of individual human beings in the real world. . . . We might suspect that translation into mathematical language by itself implies a suggested transformation of human economic operators into virtual robots.[8]

Similarly, one of the first methodologists in economics, Jean-Baptiste Say, charged that the mathematical economists

have not been able to enunciate these questions into analytical language, without divesting them of their natural complication, by means of simplifications, and arbitrary suppressions, of which the consequences, not properly estimated, always essentially change the condition of the problem, and pervert all its results.[9]

More recently, Boris Ischboldin has emphasized the difference between verbal, or "language," logic ("the actual analysis of thought stated in language expressive of reality as grasped in common experience") and "construct" logic, which is "the application to quantitative (economic) data of the constructs of mathematics and symbolic logic which constructs may or may not have real equivalents."[10]

Although himself a mathematical economist, the mathematician son of Carl Menger wrote a trenchant critique of the idea that mathematical presentation in economics is necessarily more precise than ordinary language:

Consider, for example, the statements (2) *To a higher price of a good, there corresponds a lower (or at any rate not a higher) demand.*

(2′) *If p denotes the price of, and q the demand for, a good, then*

$$q = f(p) \text{ and } \frac{dq}{dp} = f'(p) \leq 0.$$

Those who regard the formula (2′) as more precise or "more mathematical" than the sentence (2) are under a complete misapprehension. . . . The only difference between (2) and (2′) is this: since

(2′) is limited to functions which are differentiable and whose graphs, therefore, have tangents (which from an economic point of view are not more plausible than curvature), the sentence (2) is *more general*, but it is by no means less precise: it is *of the same mathematical precision as* (2′).[11]

Turning from the deduction process to the axioms themselves, what is their epistemological status? Here the problems are obscured by a difference of opinion within the praxeological camp, particularly on the nature of the fundamental axiom of action. Ludwig von Mises, as an adherent of Kantian epistemology, asserted that the concept of action is a priori to all experience, because it is, like the law of cause and effect, part of "the essential and necessary character of the logical structure of the human mind."[12] Without delving too deeply into the murky waters of epistemology, I would deny, as an Aristotelian and neo-Thomist, any such alleged "laws of logical structure" that the human mind necessarily imposes on the chaotic structure of reality. Instead, I would call all such laws "laws of reality," which the mind apprehends from investigating and collating the facts of the real world. My view is that the fundamental axiom and subsidiary axioms are derived from the experience of reality and are therefore in the broadest sense empirical. I would agree with the Aristotelian realist view that its doctrine is radically empirical, far more so than the post-Humean empiricism which is dominant in modern philosophy. Thus, John Wild wrote:

It is impossible to reduce experience to a set of isolated impressions and atomic units. Relational structure is also given with equal evidence and certainty. The immediate data are full of determinate structure, which is easily abstracted by the mind and grasped as universal essences or possibilities.[13]

Furthermore, one of the pervasive data of all human experience is existence; another is consciousness, or awareness. In contrast to the Kantian view, Harmon Chapman wrote that

conception is a kind of awareness, a way of apprehending things — or comprehending them — and not an alleged subjective manipulation of so-called generalities or universals solely "mental" or "logical" in their provenience and non-cognitive in nature.

That in thus penetrating the data of sense, conception also synthesizes these data is evident. But the synthesis here involved, unlike the synthesis of Kant, is not a prior condition of perception, an anterior process of constituting both perception and its object, but rather a cognitive synthesis *in* apprehension, that is, a uniting or "comprehending" which is one with the apprehending itself. In other words, perception and experience are not the results or end products of a synthetic process a priori, but are themselves synthetic or comprehensive apprehensions whose structured unity is prescribed solely by the nature of the real, that is, by the intended objects in their togetherness and not by consciousness itself whose (cognitive) nature is to apprehend the real — as it is.[14]

If, in the broad sense, the axioms of praxeology are radically empirical, they are far from the post-Humean empiricism that pervades the modern methodology of social science. In addition to the foregoing considerations, (1) they are so broadly based in common human experience that once enunciated they become self-evident and hence do not meet the fashionable criterion of "falsifiability"; (2) they rest, particularly the action axiom, on universal *inner* experience, as well as on external experience, that is, the evidence is *reflective* rather than purely physical; and (3) they are therefore a priori to the complex historical events to which modern empiricism confines the concept of "experience".[15]

Say, perhaps the first praxeologist, explained the derivation of the axioms of economic theory as follows:

Hence the advantage enjoyed by every one who, from distinct and accurate observation, can establish the existence of these general facts, demonstrate their connection and deduce their consequences. They as certainly proceed from the nature of things as the laws of the material world. We do not imagine them; they are results disclosed to us by judicious observation and analysis. . . .

Political economy . . . is composed of a few fundamental principles, and of a great number of corollaries or conclusions, drawn from these principles . . . that can be admitted by every reflecting mind.[16]

Friedrich A. Hayek trenchantly described the praxeological

method in contrast to the methodology of the physical sciences, and also underlined the broadly empirical nature of the praxeological axioms:

The position of man . . . brings it about that the essential basic facts which we need for the explanation of social phenomena are part of common experience, part of the stuff of our thinking. In the social sciences it is the elements of the complex phenomena which are known beyond the possibility of dispute. In the natural sciences they can only be at best surmised. The existence of these elements is so much more certain than any regularities in the complex phenomena to which they give rise, that it is they which constitute the truly empirical factor in the social sciences. There can be little doubt that it is this different position of the empirical factor in the process of reasoning in the two groups of disciplines which is at the root of much of the confusion with regard to their logical character. The essential difference is that in the natural sciences the process of deduction has to start from some hypothesis which is the result of inductive generalizations, while in the social sciences it starts directly from known empirical elements and uses them to find the regularities in the complex phenomena which direct observations cannot establish. They are, so to speak, empirically deductive sciences, proceeding from the known elements to the regularities in the complex phenomena which cannot be directly established.[17]

Similarly, J. E. Cairnes wrote:

The economist starts with a knowledge of ultimate causes. He is already, at the outset of his enterprise in the position which the physicist only attains after ages of laborious research. . . . For the discovery of such premises no elaborate process of induction is needed . . . for this reason, that we have, or may have if we choose to turn our attention to the subject, direct knowledge of these causes in our consciousness of what passes in our own minds, and in the information which our senses convey . . . to us of external facts.[18]

Nassau W. Senior phrased it thus:

The physical sciences, being only secondarily conversant with mind, draw their premises almost exclusively from observation or hypothesis. . . . On the other hand, the mental sciences and the mental arts draw their premises principally from consciousness. The subjects with which they are chiefly conversant are the workings of the human mind. [These premises are] a very few general propositions, which are the result of observation, or consciousness, and which almost every man, as soon as he hears them, admits, as familiar to this thought, or at least, included in his previous knowledge.[19]

Commenting on his complete agreement with this passage, Mises wrote that these "immediately evident propositions" are "of aprioristic derivation . . . unless one wishes to call aprioristic cognition inner experience."[20] To which Marian Bowley, the biographer of Senior, justly commented:

The only fundamental difference between Mises' general attitude and Senior's lies in Mises' apparent denial of the possibility of using any general empirical data, i.e., facts of general observation, as initial premises. This difference, however, turns upon Mises' basic ideas of the nature of thought, and though of general philosophic importance, has little special relevance to economic method as such.[21]

It should be noted that for Mises it is only the fundamental axiom of action that is a priori; he conceded that the subsidiary axioms of the diversity of mankind and nature, and of leisure as a consumers' good, are broadly empirical.

Modern post-Kantian philosophy has had a great deal of trouble encompassing self-evident propositions, which are marked precisely by their strong and evident truth rather than by being testable hypotheses, that are, in the current fashion, considered to be "falsifiable". Sometimes it seems that the empiricists use the fashionable analytic-synthetic dichotomy, as the philosopher Hao Wong charged, to dispose of theories they find difficult to refute by dismissing them as necessarily *either* disguised definitions *or* debatable and uncertain hypotheses.[22] But what if we subject the vaunted "evidence" of modern positivists and empiricists to analysis? What is it? We find that there are two types of such evidence to either confirm or refute a proposition: (1) if it violates the laws of logic, for example, implies that $A = -A$; or (2) if it is confirmed by empirical facts (as in a laboratory) that can be checked by many persons. But what is the nature of such "evidence" but the bringing, by various means, of propositions hitherto cloudy and obscure into clear and evident view, that is, evident to the scientific observers? In short, logical or laboratory processes serve to make it evident to the "selves" of the various observers that the propositions are either confirmed or refuted, or, to use unfashionable terminology, either true or false. But in that case propositions that are *immediately* evident to the selves of the observers have at least as good scientific status as the other and currently more acceptable forms of evidence. Or, as the Thomist philosopher John J. Toohey put it,

Proving means *making evident* something which is not evident. If a truth or proposition is self-evident, it is useless to attempt to prove it; to attempt to prove it would be to attempt to make evident something which is already evident.[23]

The action axiom, in particular, should be, according to Aristotelian philosophy, unchallengeable and self-evident since the critic who attempts to refute it finds that he must use it in the process of alleged refutation. Thus, the axiom of the existence of human consciousness is demonstrated as being self-evident by the fact that the very act of denying the existence of consciousness must itself be performed by a conscious being. The philosopher R. P. Phillips called this attribute of a self-evident axiom a "boomerang principle," since "even though we cast it away from us, it returns to us again."[24] A similar self-contradiction faces the man who attempts to refute the axiom of human action. For in doing so, he is ipso facto a person making a conscious choice of means in attempting to arrive at an adopted end: in this case the end, or goal, of trying to refute the axiom of action. He employs action in trying to refute the notion of action.

Of course, a person may *say* that he denies the existence of self-evident principles or other established truths of the real world, but this mere saying has no epistemological validity. As Toohey pointed out,

A man may *say* anything he pleases, but he cannot *think* or *do* anything he pleases. He may say he saw a round square, but he cannot *think* he saw a round square. He may say, if he likes, that he saw a horse riding astride its own back, but we shall know what to think of him if he says it.[25]

The methodology of modern positivism and empiricism comes a cropper even in the physical sciences, to which it is much better suited than to the sciences of human action; indeed, it particularly fails where the two types of disciplines interconnect. Thus, the phenomenologist Alfred Schutz, a student of Mises at Vienna, who pioneered in applying phenomenology to the social sciences, pointed out the contradiction in the empiricists' insistence on the principle of empirical verifiability in science, while at the same time denying the existence of "other minds" as unverifiable. But *who* is supposed to be doing the laboratory verification if not these selfsame "other minds" of the assembled scientists? Schutz wrote:

It is . . . not understandable that the same authors who are convinced that no verification is possible for the intelligence of other human beings have such confidence in the principle of verifiability itself, which can be realized only through cooperation with others.[26]

In this way, the modern empiricists ignore the necessary presuppositions of the very scientific method they champion. For Schutz, knowledge of such presuppositions is "empirical" in the broadest sense,

provided that we do not restrict this term to sensory perceptions of objects and events in the outer world but include the experiential form, by which common-sense thinking in everyday life understands human actions and their outcome in terms of their underlying motives and goals.[27]

Having dealt with the nature of praxeology, its procedures and axioms and its philosophical groundwork, let us now consider what the relationship is between praxeology and the other disciplines that study human action. In particular, what are the differences between praxeology and technology, psychology, history, and ethics — all of which are in some way concerned with human action?

In brief, *praxeology* consists of the logical implications of the universal formal fact that people act, that they employ means to try to attain chosen ends. *Technology* deals with the contentual problem of *how* to achieve ends by the adoption of means. *Psychology* deals with the question of *why* people adopt various ends and *how* they go about adopting them. *Ethics* deals with the question of what ends, or values, people *should* adopt. And *history* deals with ends adopted in the past, what means were used to try to achieve them—and what the consequences of these actions were.

Praxeology, or economic theory in particular, is thus a unique discipline within the social sciences; for, in contrast to the others, it deals not with the *content* of men's values, goals, and actions— not with what they have done or how they have acted or how they should act—but purely with the fact that they *do* have goals and act to attain them. The laws of utility, demand, supply, and price apply regardless of the type of goods and services desired or produced. As Joseph Dorfman wrote of Herbert J. Davenport's *Outlines of Economic Theory* (1896):

The ethical character of the desires was not a fundamental part of his inquiry. Men labored and underwent privation for "whiskey, cigars, and burglars' jimmies," he said, "as well as for food, or statuary or harvest machinery." As long as men were willing to buy and sell "foolishness and evil," the former commodities would be economic factors with market standing, for utility, as an economic term, meant merely adaptability to human desires. So long as men desired them, they satisfied a need and were motives to production. Therefore economics did not need to investigate the origin of choices.[28]

Praxeology, as well as the sound aspects of the other social sciences, rests on methodological individualism, on the fact that only individuals feel, value, think, and act. Individualism has always been charged by its critics—and always incorrectly—with the assumption that each individual is a hermetically sealed "atom," cut off from, and uninfluenced by, other persons. This absurd misreading of methodological individualism is at the root of J. K. Galbraith's triumphant demonstration in *The Affluent Society* (Boston: Houghton Mifflin Co., 1958) that the values and choices of individuals are influenced by other persons, and therefore—supposedly—that economic theory is invalid. Galbraith also concluded from his demonstration that these choices, because influenced, are artificial and illegitimate. The fact that praxeological economic theory rests on the universal fact of individual values and choices means, to repeat Dorfman's summary of Davenport's thought, that economic theory does "not need to investigate the origin of choices." Economic theory is not based on the absurd assumption that each individual arrives at his values and choices in a vacuum, sealed off from human influence. Obviously, individuals are continually learning from and influencing each other. As F. A. Hayek wrote in his justly famous critique of Galbraith, "The Non Sequitur of the 'Dependence Effect' ":

Professor Galbraith's argument could be easily employed, without any change of the essential terms, to demonstrate the worthlessness of literature or any other form of art. Surely an individual's want for literature is not original with himself in the sense that he would experience it if literature were not produced. Does this then mean that the production of literature cannot be defended as satisfying a want because it is only the production which provokes the demand?[29]

That Austrian-school economics rested firmly from the beginning on an analysis of the fact of individual subjective values and choices unfortunately led the early Austrians to adopt the term *psychological school*. The result was a series of misdirected criticisms that the latest findings of psychology had not been incorporated into economic theory. It also led to misconceptions such as that the law of diminishing marginal utility rests on some psychological law of the satiety of wants. Actually, as Mises firmly pointed out, that law is praxeological rather than psychological and has nothing to do with the *content* of wants, for example, that the tenth spoonful of ice cream may taste less pleasurable than the ninth spoonful. Instead, it is a praxeological truth, derived from the nature of action, that the first unit of a good will be allocated to its most valuable use, the next unit to the next most valuable, and so on.[30] On one point, and on one point alone, however, praxeology and the related sciences of human action take a stand in philosophical psychology: on the proposition that the human mind, consciousness, and subjectivity exist, and therefore action exists. In this it is opposed to the philosophical base of behaviorism and related doctrines and joined with all branches of classical philosophy and with phenomenology. On all other questions, however, praxeology and psychology are distinct and separate disciplines.[31]

A particularly vital question is the relationship between economic theory and history. Here again, as in so many other areas of Austrian economics, Ludwig von Mises made the outstanding contribution, particularly in his *Theory and History*.[32] It is especially curious that Mises and other praxeologists, as alleged "a priorists", have commonly been accused of being "opposed" to history. Mises indeed held not only that economic theory does not need to be "tested" by historical fact but also that it *cannot* be so tested. For a fact to be usable for testing theories, it must be a simple fact, homogeneous with other facts in accessible and repeatable classes. In short, the theory that one atom of copper, one atom of sulfur, and four atoms of oxygen will combine to form a recognizable entity called copper sulfate, with known properties, is easily tested in the laboratory. Each of these atoms is homogeneous, and therefore the test is repeatable indefinitely. But each historical event, as Mises pointed out, is not simple and repeatable; each event is a complex resultant of a shifting variety of multiple causes, none of which ever remains in constant relationships with the others. Every historical event, therefore, is heterogeneous, and therefore historical events cannot be used either to test or to construct laws of history, quantitative or otherwise. We can place every atom of copper into a homogeneous class of copper atoms; we cannot do so with the events of human history.

This is not to say, of course, that there are no similarities among historical events. There are many similarities, but no homogeneity. Thus, there were many similarities between the presidential election of 1968 and that of 1972, but they were scarcely homogeneous events, since they were marked by important and inescapable differences. Nor will the next election be a repeatable event to place in a homogeneous class of "elections".

Hence no scientific, and certainly no quantitative, laws can be derived from these events.

Mises's radically fundamental opposition to econometrics now becomes clear. Econometrics not only attempts to ape the natural sciences by using complex heterogeneous historical facts as if they were repeatable homogeneous laboratory facts; it also squeezes the qualitative complexity of each event into a quantitative number and then compounds the fallacy by acting as if these quantitative relations rémain constant in human history. In striking contrast to the physical sciences, which rest on the empirical discovery of quantitative constants, econometrics, as Mises repeatedly emphasized, has failed to discover a single constant in human history. And given the ever-changing conditions of human will, knowledge, and values and the differences among men, it is inconceivable that econometrics·can ever do so.

Far from being opposed to history, the praxeologist, and not the supposed admirers of history, has profound respect for the irreducible and unique facts of human history. Furthermore, it is the praxeologist who acknowledges that individual human beings cannot legitimately be treated by the social scientist as if they were not men who have minds and act upon their values and expectations, but stones or molecules whose course can be scientifically tracked in alleged constants or quantitative laws. Moreover, as the crowning irony, it is the praxeologist who is truly empirical because he recognizes the unique and heterogeneous nature of historical facts; it is the self-proclaimed "empiricist" who grossly violates the facts of history by attempting to reduce them to quantitative laws. Mises wrote thus about econometricians and other forms of "quantitative economists":

There are, in the field of economics, no constant relations, and consequently no measurement is possible. If a statistician determines that a rise of 10 per cent in the supply of potatoes in Atlantis at a definite time was followed by a fall of 8 per cent in the price, he does not establish anything about what happened or may happen with a change in the supply of potatoes in another country or in another time. He has not "measured" the "elasticity of demand" of potatoes. He has established a unique and individual historical fact. No intelligent man can doubt that the behavior of men with regard to potatoes and every other commodity is variable. Different individuals value the same things in a different way, and valuations change with the same individuals with changing conditions. . . .

The impracticability of measurement is not due to the lack of technical methods for the establishment of measure. It is due to the absence of constant relations. . . . Economics is not, as . . . positivists repeat again and again, backward because it is not "quantitative." It is not quantitative and does not measure because there are no constants. Statistical figures referring to economic events are historical data. They tell us what happened in a nonrepeatable historical case. Physical events can be interpreted on the ground of our knowledge concerning constant relations established by experiments. Historical events are not open to such an interpretation. . . .

Experience of economic history is always experience of complex phenomena. It can never convey knowledge of the kind the experimenter abstracts from a laboratory experiment. Statistics is a method for the presentation of historical facts. . . . The statistics of prices is economic history. The insight that, *ceteris paribus,* an increase in demand must result in an increase in prices is not derived from experience. Nobody ever was or ever will be in a position to observe a change in one of the market data *ceteris paribus.* There is no such thing as quantitative economics. All economic quantities we know about are data of economic history. . . . Nobody is so bold as to maintain that a rise of *a* percent in the supply of any commodity must always—in every country and at any time—result in a fall of *b* per cent in price. But as no quantitative economist ever ventured to define precisely on the ground of statistical experience the special conditions producing a definite deviation from the ratio *a: b,* the futility of his endeavors is manifest.[33]

Elaborating on his critique of constants Mises added:

The quantities we observe in the field of human action . . . are manifestly variable. Changes occurring in them plainly affect the result of our actions. Every quantity that we can observe is a historical event, a fact which cannot be fully described without specifying the time and geographical point.

The econometrician is unable to disprove this fact, which cuts the ground from under his reasoning. He cannot help admitting that there are no "behavior constants." Nonetheless, he wants to introduce some numbers, arbitrarily chosen on the basis of a historical fact, as "unknown *behavior constants.*" The sole excuse he advances is that his hypotheses are "saying only that these unknown numbers remain reasonably constant through a period of years."[34] Now whether such a period of supposed constancy of a definite number is still lasting or whether a change in the number has already occurred can only be established later on. In retrospect it may be possible, although in rare cases only, to declare that over a (probably rather short) period an approximately stable ratio—which the econometrician chooses to call a "reasonably" constant ratio—prevailed between the numerical values of two factors. But this is something fundamentally different from the constants of physics. It is the assertion of a historical fact, not of a constant that can be resorted to in attempts to predict *future events*.[35] The highly praised equations are, insofar as they apply to the future, merely equations in which all quantities are unknown.[36]

In the mathematical treatment of physics the distinction between constants and variables makes sense; it is essential in every instance of technological computation. In economics there are no constant relations between various magnitudes. Consequently all ascertainable data are variables, or what amounts to the same thing, *historical* data. The mathematical economists reiterate that the plight of mathematical economics consists in the fact that there are a great number of variables. The truth is that there are only variables and no constants. It is pointless to talk of variables where there are no invariables.[37]

What, then, is the proper relationship between economic theory and economic history or, more precisely, history in general? The historian's function is to try to explain the unique historical facts that are his province; to do so adequately he must employ all the relevant theories from all the various disciplines that impinge on his problem. For historical facts are complex resultants of a myriad of causes stemming from different aspects of the human condition. Thus, the historian must be prepared to use not only praxeological economic theory but also insights from physics, psychology, technology, and military strategy along with an interpretive understanding of the motives and goals of individuals. He must employ these tools in understanding both the goals of the various actions of history and the consequences of such actions. Because understanding diverse individuals and their interactions is involved, as well as the historical context, the historian using the tools of natural and social science is in the last analysis an "artist", and hence there is no guarantee or even likelihood that any two historians will judge a situation in precisely the same way. While they may agree on an array of factors to explain the genesis and consequences of an event, they are unlikely to agree on the precise weight to be given each causal factor. In employing various scientific theories, they have to make judgments of relevance on which theories applied in any given case; to refer to an example used earlier in this paper, a historian of Robinson Crusoe would hardly employ the theory of money in a historical explanation of his actions on a desert island. To the economic historian, economic law is neither confirmed nor tested by historical facts; instead, the law, where relevant, is applied to help explain the facts. The facts thereby *illustrate* the workings of the law.

The relationship between praxeological economic theory and the understanding of economic history was subtly summed up by Alfred Schutz:

No economic act is conceivable without some reference to an economic actor, but the latter is absolutely anonymous; it is not you, nor I nor an entrepreneur, nor even an "economic man," as such, but a pure universal "one." This is the reason why the propositions of theoretical economics have just that "universal validity" which gives them the ideality of the "and so forth" and "I can do it again." However, one can study the economic actor as such and try to find out what is going on in his mind; of course, one is not then engaged in theoretical economics but in economic history or economic sociology. . . . However, the statements of these sciences can claim no universal validity, for they deal either with the economic sentiments of particular historical individuals or with types of economic activity for which the economic acts in question are evidence. . . .

In our view, pure economics is a perfect example of an objective meaning-complex about subjective meaning-complexes, in other words, of an objective meaning-configuration stipulating the typical and invariant subjective experiences of anyone who acts within an economic framework. . . . Excluded from such a scheme would have to be any consideration of the uses to which the "goods" are to be put after they are acquired. But once we do turn our attention to the subjective meaning of a real individual person, leaving the anonymous "anyone" behind, then of course it makes sense to speak of behavior that is atypical. . . . To be sure, such behavior is irrelevant from the point of view of economics, and it is in this sense that economic principles are, in Mises' words, "not a statement of what usually happens, but of what necessarily must happen."[38]

NOTES

1.   See in particular Ludwig von Mises, *Human Action: A Treatise on Economics* (New Haven: Yale University Press, 1949); also see idem, *Epistemological Problems of Economics,* trans. George Reisman (Princeton: D. Van Nostrand, 1960).

2.   See Murray N. Rothbard, "Praxeology as the Method of Economics," in *Phenomenology and the Social Sciences,* ed. Maurice Natanson, 2 vols. (Evanston: Northwestern University Press, 1973), 2: 323-35; also see Marian Bowley, *Nassau Senior and Classical Economics* (New York: Augustus M. Kelley, 1949), pp 27-65; and T.W. Hutchison, "Some Themes from *Investigations into Method,*" in *Carl Menger and the Austrian School of Economics,* ed. J. R. Hicks and Wilhelm Weber (Oxford: Clarendon Press, 1973), pp. 15-31.

3.   In answer to the criticism that not all action is directed to some future point of time, see Walter Block, "A Comment on 'The Extraordinary Claim of Praxeology' by Professor Gutierrez," *Theory and Decision* 3(1973): 381-82.

4.   See Mises, *Human Action,* pp. 101-2; and esp., Block, "Comment," p. 383.

5.   For a typical criticism of praxeology for not using mathematical logic, see George J. Schuller, "Rejoinder," *American Economic Review* 41(March 1951):188.

6.   John Maynard Keynes, *The General Theory of Employment, Interest, and Money* (New York: Harcourt, Brace & Co., 1936), pp. 297-98.

7.   See Murray N. Rothbard, "Toward a Reconstruction of Utility and Welfare Economics," in *On Freedom and Free Enterprise,* ed. M. Sennholz (Princeton: D. Van Nostrand, 1956), p. 227; idem, *Man, Economy and State,* 2 vols. (Princeton: D. Van Nostrand, 1962), 1:65-66. On mathematical logic as being subordinate to verbal logic, see René Poirier, "Logique," in *Vocabulaire technique et critique de la philosophie,* ed. André Lalande, 6th ed. rev. (Paris: Presses Universitaires de France, 1951), pp. 574-75.

8.   Bruno Leoni and Eugenio Frola, "On Mathematical Thinking in Economics" (unpublished manuscript privately distributed), pp. 23-24; the Italian version of this article is "Possibilita di applicazione della matematiche alle discipline economiche," *Il Politico* 20(1955).

9.   Jean-Baptiste Say, *A Treatise on Political Economy* (New York: Augustus M. Kelley, 1964), p. xxvi n.

10.   Boris Ischboldin, "A Critique on Econometrics," *Review of Social Economy* 18(September 1960): 11 n.; Ischboldin's discussion is based on the construction of I. M. Bochenski, "Scholastic and Aristotelian Logic," *Proceedings of the American Catholic Philosophical Association* 30(1956):112-17.

11.   Karl Menger, "Austrian Marginalism and Mathematical Economics," in *Carl Menger*, p.41.

12.   Mises, *Human Action*, p. 34.

13.   John Wild, "Phenomenology and Metaphysics," in *The Return to Reason: Essays in Realistic Philosophy*, ed. John Wild (Chicago: Henry Regnery, 1953), pp. 48, 37-57.

14.   Harmon M. Chapman, "Realism and Phenomenology," in *Return to Reason*, p. 29. On the interrelated functions of sense and reason and their respective roles in human cognition of reality, see Francis H. Parker, "Realistic Epistemology," ibid., pp. 167-69.

15.   See Murray N. Rothbard, "In Defense of 'Extreme Apriorism,' " *Southern Economic Journal* 23(January 1957): 315-18. It should be clear from the current paper that the term *extreme apriorism* is a misnomer for praxeology.

16.   Say, *Treatise*, pp. xxv-xxvi, xlv.

17.   Friedrich A. Hayek, "The Nature and History of the Problem," in *Collectivist Economic Planning*, ed. F. A. Hayek (London: George Routledge & Sons, 1935), p. 11.

18.   John Elliott Cairnes, *The Character and Logical Method of Political Economy*, 2d ed. (London: Macmillan & Co., 1875), pp. 87-88 (Cairnes's italics).

19.   Bowley, *Nassau Senior*, pp. 43, 56.

20.   Mises, *Epistemological Problems*, p. 19.

21.   Bowley, *Nassau Senior*, pp. 64-65.

22.   Hao Wong, "Notes on the Analytic-Synthetic Distinction," *Theoria* 21(1955):158; see also John Wild and J. L. Cobitz, "On the Distinction between the Analytic and the Synthetic," *Philosophy and Phenomenological Research* 8(June 1948):651-67.

23.   John J. Toohey, *Notes on Epistemology*, rev. ed. (Washington, D.C.: Georgetown University, 1937), p. 36 (Toohey's italics).

24.   R. P. Phillips, *Modern Thomistic Philosophy* (Westminster, Md.: Newman Bookshop, 1934-35) 2:36-37; see also Murray N. Rothbard, "The Mantle of Science," in *Scientism and Values*, ed. Helmut Schoeck and J. W. Wiggins (Princeton: D. Van Nostrand, 1960), pp. 162-65.

25.   Toohey, *Notes on Epistemology*, p. 10 (Toohey's italics).

26.   Alfred Schutz, *Collected Papers of Alfred Schutz*, vol. 2, *Studies in Social Theory*, ed. A. Brodersen (The Hague: Nijhoff, 1964), p. 4; see also Mises, *Human Action*, p. 24.

27.   Ibid., vol. 1, *The Problem of Social Reality*, p. 65. On the philosophical presuppositions of science, see Andrew G. Van Melsen, *The Philosophy of Nature* (Pittsburgh: Duquesne University Press, 1953), pp. 6-29. On common sense as the groundwork of philosophy, see Toohey, *Notes on Epistemology*, pp. 74, 106-13. On the application of a

similar point of view to the methodology of economics, see Frank H. Knight, "'What is Truth' in Economics," in *On the History and Method of Economics* (Chicago: University of Chicago Press, 1956), pp. 151-78.

28. Joseph Dorfman, *The Economic Mind in American Civilization*, 5 vols. (New York: Viking Press, 1949) 3:376.

29. Friedrich A. Hayek, "The Non Sequitur of the 'Dependence Effect,' " in *Studies in Philosophy, Politics, and Economics*, ed. Friedrich A. Hayek (Chicago: University of Chicago Press, 1967), pp. 314-15.

30. Mises, *Human Action*, p. 124.

31. See Rothbard, "Toward a Reconstruction," pp. 230-31.

32. Ludwig von Mises, *Theory and History* (New Haven: Yale University Press, 1957).

33. Mises, *Human Action*, pp. 55-56, 348.

34. Cowles Commission for Research in Economics, *Report for Period, January 1, 1948-June 30, 1949* (Chicago: University of Chicago Press, 1949), p. 7, quoted in Mises, *Theory and History*, pp. 10-11.

35. Ibid., pp. 10-11.

36. Ludwig von Mises, "Comments about the Mathematical Treatment of Economic Problems" (unpublished manuscript), p. 3; the German language version of this essay is "Bemerkungen über die mathematische Behandlung nationalökonomischer Probleme," *Studium Generale* 6 (1953): 662-65.

37. Mises, *Theory and History*, pp. 11-12; see also Leoni and Frola, "On Mathematical Thinking," pp. 1-8; and Leland B. Yeager, "Measurement as Scientific Method in Economics," *American Journal of Economics and Sociology* 16(July 1957): 337-46.

38. Alfred Schutz, *The Phenomenology of the Social World* (Evanston: Northwestern University Press, 1967), pp. 137, 245; also see Ludwig M. Lachmann, *The Legacy of Max Weber* (Berkeley, Calif.: The Glendessary Press, 1971), pp. 17-48.

On the Method of Austrian Economics

Israel M. Kirzner

One of the areas in which disagreement among Austrian economists may seem to be nonexistent is that of methodology. Yet I shall attempt to point out that even with respect to method there are differences of opinion among individual thinkers. Some light may be cast on these differences by drawing attention to two distinct strands of thought that run through the writings of Austrian economists on the question of method. By separating these strands and then focusing on each in turn, we may discover and define different perspectives on economic method and perhaps more clearly understand how these different perspectives grow out of the unique view of method shared by all Austrian economists.

The general outline of the Austrian position on methodology is well known. Austrian economists are subjectivists; they emphasize the purposefulness of human action; they are unhappy with constructions that emphasize equilibrium to the exclusion of market processes; they are deeply suspicious of attempts to apply measurement procedures to economics; they are skeptical of empirical "proofs" of economic theorems and consequently have serious reservations about the validity and importance of a good deal of the empirical work being carried on in the economics profession today. These are the general features of the position that we know very well; yet within this general view we can distinguish two independent strands of argument. It is upon this debate that I should like to focus my attention in this paper.

TWO TASKS FOR ECONOMIC EXPLANATIONS

It will be helpful to cite two statements — by prominent Austrian economists — about what economics as a discipline is supposed to achieve. The first is by Friedrich A. Hayek, and the other is by Ludwig M. Lachmann. Hayek in his *Counter-revolution of Science* contended that the function of social science, and by implication economics, is to explain how conscious, purposeful human action can generate unintended consequences through social interaction.[1] The emphasis here is on the unintended consequences of individual human decisions. To explain phenomena that are not the unintended consequences of human decision making is outside the scope of the social sciences in general and economics in particular. Hayek's position was cited by Alexander Gerschenkron in his contribution to the Akerman *Festschrift*, and I think Gerschenkron was perceptive in focusing on exactly what is, in Hayek's view, the fundamental task of economic explanation.[2]

Let us contrast the Hayek view with one expressed by Lachmann. Lachmann's position on the purpose of economic explanations is dealt with at length in his contribution to the Hayek *Festschrift*, *Roads to Freedom*.[3] Here, however, I shall quote from a more recent statement of his position that appeared in his review of John R. Hicks's *Capital and Time*:

Economics has two tasks. The first is to make the world around us intelligible in terms of human action and the pursuit of plans. The second is to trace the unintended consequences of such action. Ricardian economics emphasized the second task, the "subjective revolution" of the 1870s stressed the urgency of the first, and the Austrian school has always cherished this tradition.[4]

Thus, we have here two tasks for economics. Besides the task that Hayek emphasized — the tracing out of the unintended consequences of action — we have the requirement that it make the world around us intelligible in terms of human action.

It is worth reminding ourselves that the two tasks Lachmann identified are to be found in Carl Menger's writings. In the third

part of his 1884 book on methodology Menger pointed out that
actions do have unintended consequences, and he made it very
clear, as Hayek had done, that economics is the science that is
able to explain how these unintended consequences emerge in
the market place.[5] But Menger was also aware of the other task
Lachmann emphasized. In a letter Menger wrote Léon Walras,
cited by T. W. Hutchison in several of his writings,[6] Menger
insisted that the economist is not merely after the relationships
between quantities, but the *essence* of economic phenomena: "the
essence of value, the essence of land rent, the essence of entrepreneurs' profits, the essence of the division of labor."[7] This view
is what Kauder meant when he described Menger as holding that
economics deals with social essences,[8] and what Hutchison called
"methodological essentialism."[9]

TWO BASIC AUSTRIAN TENETS

I have asserted that two distinct strands of thought may be
identified in the writings of Austrian economists with regard to
the meaning and purpose of economic explanation. I would now
like to distinguish two distinct insights about the economic world
that receive varying emphasis and are not often adequately
differentiated. First, there is the insight that *human action is
purposeful*, and, second, there is the insight that *there is an indeterminacy and unpredictability inherent in human preferences, human
expectations, and human knowledge*. Now these two insights are
really quite distinct, because one does not encompass the other in
any logical or epistemological sense. That human action is purposeful is an insight by itself, and that human knowledge and
expectations are largely unpredictable is another. Nor is the
truth of these two propositions equally obvious. The purposefulness of human action is something we arrive at by introspection. In this sense it is "obviously" true. On the other hand, the
insight that men's preferences are inherently unpredictable —
that we cannot discover consistent patterns in what men prefer
and that we cannot postulate that there are consistent patterns in

what men know and expect to happen — cannot be arrived at by introspection. The truth claimed for this last insight depends on our observations of our fellow men, that we do as a matter of fact find them to be unpredictable in their actions and expectations about future states of the world.

To me, the different emphasis Austrian economists attach to these basic insights is largely responsible for their different attitudes regarding the purpose of economic explanation. The recognition of purposefulness is, of course, fundamental to our definition of economics as the logic of choice. We are able to use our logic to simulate the actions of other human beings only because we share the logic that other men's purposes lead them to harness in their own interests. The recognition of purposefulness is essential to our positive conception of economics as the logic of choice and to our enterprise of studying the consequences of purposeful action. But if we consider those aspects of the Austrian approach that are used, not to derive economic laws, but to criticize other areas of contemporary economic thought, then the second of these basic tenets comes into prominence. Our dissatisfaction with empirical work and our suspicion of measurement rest on the conviction that empirical observations of past human choices will not yield any regularities or any consistent pattern that may be safely extrapolated beyond the existing data at hand to yield scientific theorems of universal applicability.

THE SIGNIFICANCE OF PURPOSEFULNESS

Let us try to understand the role these basic tenets of Austrian economics play in the Lachmann-Hayek discussions concerning what economic explanation is all about. In 1938 T. W. Hutchison published *The Significance and Basic Postulates of Economic Theory*.[10] The book received a blistering Austrian-like critique from the pen of Frank H. Knight, who was on most other issues, such as capital theory, not in sympathy with the Austrian school. In that article Knight conveyed some brilliant insights about the relationship of economics to the study of human action. Knight noted that "the whole subject of conduct — interests and motivation — constitutes a different realm of reality from the external world." In addition to the external world, with which the natural sciences are conversant, there is a different realm of reality, a realm no less real than the external world, but nevertheless different from it. This other realm is that of human conduct, which Knight identified as interests, motivation, and purpose.

The first fact to be recorded is that this realm of reality exists or "is there." This fact cannot be proved or argued or "tested." If anyone denies that men have interests or that "we" have a considerable amount of valid knowledge about them, economics and all its works will simply be to such a person what the world of color is to the blind man. But there would still be one difference: a man who is physically, ocularly blind may still be rated of normal intelligence and in his right mind.[11]

Here, surely, we have the first of the basic tenets of Austrian theory, that there is a realm of reality constituted of human motives, interests, and purposes, and that, although purposes cannot be seen or touched, they are nonetheless "there."

When Lachmann called upon economists to make the world intelligible in terms of human decisions and purposes, I take it that he was telling us the following: *It is the task of science to describe and explain reality. If reality consists of more than the external world, then a science that is confined to the facts of the external world is simply incomplete. It does not account for everything that is there.* The Austrian approach insists that there is something besides the facts of the external world and the relationships that may be postulated between these bare facts. What is that something else? It is the realm of reality that Knight pointed to, the realm of purposes. And even if one were able to explain the facts of the external world in terms of similar facts, without regard to the human purposes underlying these facts, one would not have explained everything there is to be explained, not have set forth everything there is to set forth. One would have failed to make the world intelligible in terms of human action, that is, in terms of human purposes. Thus, even if the second Austrian tenet (that there are no constants in human behavior) were false, even if one were able to postulate consistent chains of cause and effect that depend only on externally observable phenomena, still one has failed to fulfill one's scientific obligation. There is a realm of reality called purposes. It is there, and if we fail to point it out, then we fail in the task of making the world intelligible in terms of human action.

Let us consider a simple example. Suppose a man from Mars is doing research for his doctorate and, after focusing his telescope on a particular location on Earth, discovers a certain regularity. Through his telescope he observes a set of boxes lined up in a row. He further discovers that a smaller box moves past these boxes every day at 7:30 A.M., comes to a stop at one of the boxes, and then, after a short stay, moves on. Moreover the investigator discovers something else; out of one of these boxes a body emerges every morning, and when the moving box makes its daily stop, the body is swallowed up by the moving box. Discovering this regularity, the researcher postulates a definite law, the law of moving boxes and bodies. As he goes on with the research, however, he discovers that sometimes the box moves away before the body has entered it, leaving the body behind altogether; while sometimes the body moves at an unusually rapid speed, arriving at the daily moving-box stop just in time to be swallowed up before the box moves on. Now this Martian researcher may be able to predict just when the person is going to miss the box and when he is going to catch it. He may even be able to explain the movements of the body and the box entirely without reference to the fact that someone is trying to catch the bus because he wants to get to work on time. But if he does so, he has not told us everything there is to be learned about this situation. A theory of moving bodies and boxes that does not draw attention to the dimension of purpose gives a truncated picture of the real world. *This* is what economics, in the Austrian view, is all about. Economics has to make the world intelligible in terms of human motives. It is more than simply moving boxes or changing economic quantities. This is the task to which Lachmann drew our attention when he insisted that we must make the world intelligible in terms of human purpose.

A memorable passage in Hayek's *Counter-revolution* is the one in which he explained that objects useful to human beings are simply not objective facts.

In fact most of the objects of social or human action are not "objective facts" in the special narrow sense in which this term is used by the [natural] Sciences . . . they cannot be defined in physical terms. . . . Take the concept of a "tool" or "instrument," or of any particular tool such as a hammer or a barometer. It is easily seen that these concepts cannot be interpreted to refer to "objective facts," i.e. to things irrespective of what people think about them.[12]

Pursuing this point Hayek asserted (in a footnote reference to the work of Ludwig von Mises) that every important advance in economic theory in the preceding century had been a result of the consistent application of subjectivism.[13] Lachmann's advice to economists paralleled Hayek's. According to Hayek, when we deal with artifacts — with tools and instruments or other products of human beings — we have not exhausted the description of what it is that we are describing if we stubbornly confine ourselves to their physical entities. We have not described a hammer until we have drawn attention to its purpose. Lachmann, similarly, instructed us that when we deal with broader questions, with institutions and regularities in economic affairs, we have not completed our task if we have not called attention to the purposes and motives and interests that underlie these phenomena. A hammer is more than a handle with a metal head; so is a price more than a number, milk consumption more than a number of gallons, and its relationship to price more than a simple functional relationship. A whole world of interests and motives is "there," is real, and it is surely our responsibility as scientists to make it clear.

Critics of Austrian methodology often argue that since praxeology deals with unobservables, it is inherently incapable of telling us anything scientific about observables. The latest (and perhaps the clearest and most sympathetic) statement of this argument was by James Buchanan, in his contribution to the Hayek *Festschrift*,[14] when he drew attention to the distinction between (1) the logic of choice (what he called the abstract science of economic behavior) and (2) the predictive science of human behavior. Buchanan argued that if we treat economics as the logic of choice, it cannot in principle lead to refutable hypotheses because no particular preference ordering has been specified, and to that extent it cannot tell us anything about the real world.

In answer to Buchanan, our discussion indicates that the truth is the other way around. We are not only able to say something about the real world; we are also able to say a great deal about a large and important area of human experience about which other disciplines are necessarily silent — the realm of purpose. This needs to be stated and restated, emphasized and re-emphasized, again and again! The real world is more than the external world; the real world includes a whole range of matters beyond the scope of the measuring instruments of the econometrician. Economic science must be able to encompass this realm.

It is helpful in pursuing this strand of thought in Austrian methodology to constrast the Austrian use of purpose with the rationality hypothesis often employed by economists. For many non-Austrian economists this hypothesis is invoked with apologies and is considered something of a necessary evil. It is used to get theoretical results and is justified on the grounds that these results seem to fit the facts of the outside world although the hypothesis is philosophically suspect. Thus we find Gary Becker eager to demonstrate how certain fundamental theorems of economics do not require the rationality hypothesis — that rather embarrassing piece of excess baggage.[15] For Austrian economists, on the other hand, the notion of purposefulness is not merely a useful tool to obtain results but an essential element of economic reality that cannot be omitted. Making reference to human plans and motivations is an essential part of the economist's scientific task.

THE UNPREDICTABILITY OF KNOWLEDGE: A DILEMMA

Let us turn to the second basic tenet of Austrian methodology, the proposition that there is an inherent unpredictability and indeterminacy with regard to human preferences, expectations, and knowledge. I have already pointed out that this proposition does not have the same introspectively obvious ring of truth that the idea of human purposefulness does. Are we really so certain that human wants and human preference-orderings and the manner in which they undergo modification are inherently unpredictable? In fact, I wish to suggest that asserting this creates something of a dilemma for the Austrian economist.

There is a passage in an essay by Hayek that deals with this very question. In that essay Hayek discussed the concept of equilibrium and raised the problem of whether or not there is a tendency toward equilibrium in the economic world. Hayek remarked:

It is clear that, if we want to make the assertion that, under certain conditions, people will approach that state, we must explain by what process they will acquire the necessary knowledge. Of course, any assumption about the actual acquisition of knowledge in the course of this process will also be of a hypothetical character. But this does not mean that all such assumptions are equally justified. We have to deal here with assumptions about causation, so that what we assume must not only be regarded as possible . . . but must also be regarded as likely to be true; and it must be possible, at least in principle, to demonstrate that it is true in particular cases. The significant point here is that it is these apparently subsidiary hypotheses or assumptions that people do learn from experience, and about how they acquire knowledge, which constitute the empirical content of our propositions about what happens in the real world.[16]

Hayek, then, asserted that when postulating a tendency toward equilibrium, we do have to resort to a particular empirical proposition. Moreover, the empirical proposition in question would seem to contradict the other idea that there are an inherent unpredictability and an indeterminacy about human preferences and human knowledge. If we are to be able to say anything about the process of equilibration, especially if we are to say something about the course by which human decisions lead to unintended consequences, we shall have to rely upon the particular empirical proposition that men learn from market experience in a systematic manner. This is inconsistent with the second tenet underlying Austrian economics that there is an inherent indeterminacy in the way by which human knowledge changes.

Hayek's argument is straightforward. In disequilibrium man's knowledge is imperfect, some people are making mistakes; equilibrium is the situation in which nobody is making mistakes. A movement from disequilibrium to equilibrium must therefore be one in which men gradually learn to avoid mistakes, so that their actions become more and more coordinated. Where do we derive our confidence that this type of learning in fact takes place? Hayek stated very clearly that this is an empirical hypothesis. If we reject this hypothesis, then we reject the basis for viewing the market process as an equilibrating mechanism— that is, reject the claim that economics can tell us anything definite about the unintended market consequences of human actions. We may still be able to make the world intelligible—that is, we may explain that what happens happens because human beings pursue their purposes. We can assert that their interacting decisions generate certain changes in knowledge, but we shall no longer be able to say in which particular directions knowledge changes, and we can no longer postulate a determinate process toward equilibrium. We shall, to put the matter succinctly, not be able to go beyond the first Lachmann task in order to pursue the program advanced by Hayek. If, however, we confine ourselves to the enormously important task of making the world intelligible in terms of human purposes, we need not accept Hayek's empirical proposition about the coordination of plans and the progressive elimination of mistakes. But if we are to explain the unintended consequences of human action, that is, if we are to assert that there is a tendency for entrepreneurial profits to be eliminated, or for prices to move in one direction rather than another, we must be able to say something about the manner in which human knowledge and human expectations undergo modification. If one accepts this particular empirical hypothesis, one has surely weakened, perhaps irreparably, the second basic tenet underlying Austrian methodology.

CONCLUSION

We have identified two requirements of economic explanations that Austrian economists consider important. We have also identified two basic tenets that seem fundamental to Austrian methodology. It turns out, however, that while one of these basic tenets, that of human purposefulness, is sufficient to sustain one of these two requirements (that of making the world intelligible in terms of human action), the second, which asserts the unpredictability of human knowledge, is inconsistent with the requirement that economic explanations trace the unintended consequences of human action. It seems therefore that the future progress of the Austrian school in applying its basic methodological tenets requires some decision about the extent to which the second tenet about the inconstancy of human purposes and knowledge can be upheld as a general proposition.

NOTES

1.   Friedrich A. Hayek, *The Counter-revolution of Science: Studies on the Abuse of Reason* (Glencoe, Ill.: Free Press, 1955), p. 39.
2.   Alexander Gerschenkron, "Reflection on Ideology as a Methodological and Historical Problem," in *Money, Growth, and Methodology,* ed. Hugo Hegeland (Lund: C. W. K. Gleerup, 1961), p. 180.
3.   Ludwig M. Lachmann, "Methodological Individualism and the Market Economy," in *Roads to Freedom: Essays in Honour of Friedrich A. von Hayek,* ed. Erich Streissler et al. (London: Routledge & Kegan Paul, 1969), pp. 93-104.

4. Ludwig M. Lachmann, "Sir John Hicks as a Neo-Austrian," *South African Journal of Economics* 41(September 1973): 204.

5. Carl Menger, *Problems of Economics and Sociology*, trans. Francis J. Nock, ed. L. Schneider (Urbana: University of Illinois, 1963). The title of the 1884 German edition of the work is *Untersuchungen über die Methode der Socialwissenschaften und der Politischen Oekonomieinsbesondere*, and it is therefore sometimes referred to as *Investigations into Method*, which more correctly indicates the character of its contents.

6. T. W. Hutchison, *A Review of Economic Doctrines, 1870-1929* (Oxford: Clarendon Press, 1954), p. 148; idem, "Some Themes from *Investigations into Method*," in *Carl Menger and the Austrian School of Economics*, ed. J. R. Hicks and Wilhelm Weber (Oxford: Clarendon Press, 1974), p. 17 n.

7. This letter was composed in 1884; see the reference to it in W. Jaffé, "Unpublished Papers and Letters of Léon Walras," *Journal of Political Economy* 43(April 1935): 187-207; also see Léon Walras, *Correspondence of Léon Walras and Related Papers*, ed. W. Jaffe, 2 vols. (Amsterdam: North-Holland Publishing Co., 1965), 2:3.

8. Emil Kauder, *A History of Marginal Utility Theory* (Princeton: Princeton University Press, 1965), p. 97.

9. Hutchison, "Some Themes," p. 18; Hutchison explained that the source of this term is in Karl Popper, *The Poverty of Historicism* (New York: Harper & Row, 1961), pp. 28-38.

10. T. W. Hutchison, *The Significance and Basic Postulates of Economic Theory* (London: Macmillan & Co., 1938).

11. Frank H. Knight, " 'What is Truth' in Economics," in *On the History and Method of Economics*, ed. Frank H. Knight (Chicago: University of Chicago Press, 1956), p. 160.

12. Hayek, *The Counter-revolution*, pp. 26-27.

13. Ibid., pp. 24, 31, 209-10.

14. James M. Buchanan, "Is Economics the Science of Choice?" in *Roads to Freedom: Essays in Honour of Friedrich A. von Hayek*, ed. Erich Streissler et al. (London: Routledge & Kegan Paul, 1969), pp. 47-65; see also James M. Buchanan, *Cost and Choice* (Chicago: Markham Publishing Co., 1970).

15. Gary S. Becker, "Irrational Behavior and Economic Theory," *Journal of Political Economy* 70(February 1962): 1-13.

16. Friedrich A. Hayek, "Economics and Knowledge," in *Individualism and Economic Order* (London: Routledge & Kegan Paul, 1952), p. 46.

New Light
on the Prehistory
of the Austrian School

Murray N. Rothbard

The most notable development in the historiography of the Austrian school in the post-World War II era has been the drastic reevaluation of what might be called its prehistory and, as a corollary, a fundamental reconsideration of the history of economic thought itself. This reevaluation may be summarized by briefly outlining the orthodox prewar paradigm of the development of economic thought before the advent of the Austrian school. The Scholastic philosophers were brusquely dismissed as medieval thinkers who totally failed to understand the market, and who believed on religious grounds that the just price was one that covered either the cost of production or the quantity of labor embodied in a product. After briefly outlining the bullionist and antibullionist discussion among the English mercantilists and lightly touching on a few French and Italian economists of the eighteenth century, the historian of economic thought pointed with a flourish to Adam Smith and David Ricardo as the founders of economic science. After some backing and filling in the mid-nineteenth century, marginalism, including the Austrian school, arrived in another great burst in the 1870s. Apart from the occasional mention of one or two English precursors of the Austrians, such as Samuel Bailey in the early nineteenth century, this completed the basic picture. Typical was the encyclopedic text of Lewis Haney: the Scholastics were described as medieval, dismissed as hostile to trade, and declared

52

believers in the labor and cost-of-production theories of the just price.[1] It is no wonder that in his famous phrase, R. H. Tawney could call Karl Marx "the last of the Schoolmen."[2]

The remarkably contrasting new view of the history of economic thought burst upon the scene in 1954 in the monumental, though unfinished, work of Joseph Schumpeter.[3] Far from mystical dunderheads who should be skipped over to get to the mercantilists, the Scholastic philosophers were seen as remarkable and prescient economists, developing a system very close to the Austrian and subjective-utility approach. This was particularly true of the previously neglected Spanish and Italian Scholastics of the sixteenth and seventeenth centuries. Virtually the only missing ingredient in their value theory was the marginal concept. From them filiations proceeded to the later French and Italian economists. In the Schumpeterian view, the English mercantilists were half-baked, polemical pamphleteers rather than essential milestones on the road to Adam Smith and the founding of economic science. In fact, the new view saw Smith and Ricardo, not as founding the science of economics, but as shunting economics onto a tragically wrong track, which it took the Austrians and other marginalists to make right. Until then, only the neglected anti-Ricardian writers kept the tradition alive. As we shall see, other historians, such as Emil Kauder, further demonstrated the Aristotelian (and hence Scholastic) roots of the Austrians amidst the diverse variants of the marginalist school. The picture is almost the reverse of the earlier orthodoxy.

It is not the purpose of this paper to dwell on Schumpeter's deservedly well-known work, but rather to assess the contributions of writers who carried the Schumpeterian vision still further and who remain neglected by most economists, possibly from a failure to match Schumpeter in constructing a general treatise. The best development of the new history must be sought in fugitive articles and brief pamphlets and monographs.

The other relatively neglected contributions began contemporaneously with Schumpeter. One of the most important, and probably the most neglected, was *The School of Salamanca* by

Marjorie Grice-Hutchinson, who suffered in the economics profession from being a professor of Spanish literature. Moreover,
the book bore the burden of a misleadingly narrow subtitle:
Readings in Spanish Monetary Theory.[4] In fact, the book was a
brilliant discovery of the pre-Austrian subjective-value-and-
utility views of the late sixteenth-century Spanish Scholastics.
But first Grice-Hutchinson showed that the works of even earlier
Scholastics as far back as Aristotle contained a subjective-value
analysis based on consumer wants alongside the competing objective conception of the just price based on labor and costs. In
the early Middle Ages, Saint Augustine (354-430) developed the
concept of the subjective-value scales of each individual. By the
High Middle Ages, the Scholastic philosophers had largely
abandoned the cost-of-production theory to adopt the view that
the market's reflection of consumer demand really sets the just
price. This was particularly true of Jean Buridan (1300-58),
Henry of Ghent (1217-93), and Richard of Middleton (1249-
1306). As Grice-Hutchinson observed:

Medieval writers viewed the poor man as consumer rather than producer. A cost-of-production theory would have given merchants an
excuse for over-charging on the pretext of covering their expenses,
and it was thought fairer to rely on the impersonal forces of the market
which reflected the judgment of the whole community, or, to use the
medieval phrase, the "common estimation." At any rate, it would seem
that the phenomena of exchange came increasingly to be explained in
psychological terms.[5]

Even Henry of Langenstein (1325-83), who of all the Scholastics was the most hostile to the free market and advocated government fixing of the just price on the basis of status and cost,
developed the subjective factor of utility as well as scarcity in his
analysis of price. But it was the sixteenth-century Spanish
Scholastics who developed the purely subjective and profree-
market theory of value. Thus, Luis Saravía de la Calle (c. 1544)
denied any role to cost in the determination of price; instead the
market price, which is the just price, is determined by the forces
of supply and demand, which in turn are the result of the

common estimation of consumers on the market. Saravia wrote that, "excluding all deceit and malice, the just price of a thing is the price which it commonly fetches at the time and place of the deal." He went on to point out that the price of a thing will change in accordance with its abundance or scarcity. He proceeded to attack the cost-of-production theory of just price:

> Those who measure the just price by the labour, costs, and risk incurred by the person who deals in the merchandise or produces it, or by the cost of transport or the expense of travelling ... or by what he has to pay the factors for their industry, risk, and labour, are greatly in error, and still more so are those who allow a certain profit of a fifth or a tenth. For the just price arises from the abundance or scarcity of goods, merchants, and money ... and not from costs, labour, and risk. If we had to consider labour and risk in order to assess the just price, no merchant would ever suffer loss, nor would abundance or scarcity of goods and money enter into the question. Prices are not commonly fixed on the basis of costs. Why should a bale of linen brought overland from Brittany at great expense be worth more than one which is transported cheaply by sea? ... Why should a book written out by hand be worth more than one which is printed, when the latter is better though it costs less to produce? ... The just price is found not by counting the cost but by the common estimation.[6]

Similarly the Spanish Scholastic Diego de Covarrubias y Leiva (1512-77) a distinguished expert on Roman law and a theologian at the University of Salamanca, wrote that the "value of an article" depends "on the estimation of men, even if that estimation be foolish." Wheat is more expensive in the Indies than in Spain "because men esteem it more highly, though the nature of the wheat is the same in both places." The just price should be considered not at all with reference to its original or labor cost but only with reference to the common market value where the good is sold, a value, Covarrubias pointed out, that will fall when buyers are few and goods are abundant and that will rise under opposite conditions.[7]

The Spanish Scholastic Francisco García (d. 1659) engaged in a remarkably sophisticated analysis of the determinants of value and utility. The valuation of goods, García pointed out, depends on several factors. One is the abundance or scarcity of the supply of goods, the former causing a lower estimation and the latter an increase. A second is whether buyers or sellers are few or many. Another is whether "money is scarce or plentiful," the former causing a lower estimation of goods and the latter a higher. Another is whether "vendors are eager to sell their goods." The influence of the abundance or the scarcity of a good brought Garcia almost to the brink, but not over it, of a marginal utility analysis of valuation.

For example, we have said that bread is more valuable than meat because it is more necessary for the preservation of human life. But there may come a time when bread is so abundant and meat so scarce that bread is cheaper than meat.[8]

The Spanish Scholastics also anticipated the Austrian school in applying value theory to money, thus beginning the integration of money into general value theory. It is generally believed, for example, that in 1568 Jean Bodin inaugurated what is unfortunately called "the quantity theory of money" but which would more accurately be called the application of supply-and-demand analysis to money. Yet he was anticipated twelve years earlier by the Salamanca theologian the Dominican Martín de Azpilcueta Navarro (1493-1587), who was inspired to explain the inflation brought about by the importation of gold and silver by the Spaniards from the New World. Citing previous Scholastics, Azpilcueta declared that "money is worth more where it is scarce than where it is abundant." Why? Because "all merchandise becomes dearer when it is in great demand and short supply, and that money, in so far as it may be sold, bartered, or exchanged by some other form of contract, is merchandise and therefore also becomes dearer when it is in great demand and short supply." Azpilcueta noted that "we see by experience that in France, where money is scarcer than in Spain, bread, wine, cloth, and labour are worth much less. And even in Spain, in times when money was scarcer, saleable goods and labour were given for very much less than after the discovery of the Indies, which flooded the country with gold and silver. The reason for this is that money is worth more where and when it is scarce than where and when it is abundant."[9]

Furthermore, the Spanish Scholastics went on to anticipate the classical-Mises-Cassel purchasing-power parity theory of exchange rates by proceeding logically to apply the supply-and-demand theory to foreign exchanges, an institution that was highly developed by the early modern period. The influx of specie into Spain depreciated the Spanish escudo in foreign exchange, as well as raised prices within Spain, and the Scholastics had to deal with this startling phenomenon. It was the eminent Salamanca theologian the Dominican Domingo de Soto (1495-1560) who in 1553 first fully applied the supply-and-demand analysis to foreign exchange rates. De Soto noted that "the more plentiful money is in Medina the more unfavourable are the terms of exchange, and the higher the price that must be paid by whoever wishes to send money from Spain to Flanders, since the demand for money is smaller in Spain than in Flanders. And the scarcer money is in Medina the less he need pay there, because more people want money in Medina than are sending it to Flanders."[10] What de Soto was saying is that as the stock of money increases, the utility of each unit of money to the population declines and vice versa; in short, only the great stumbling block of failing to specify the concept of the marginal unit prevented him from arriving at the doctrine of the diminishing marginal utility of money. Azpilcueta, in the passage quoted above, applied the de Soto analysis of the influence of the supply of money on exchange rates, at the same time that he set forth a theory of supply and demand in determining the purchasing power of money within a country.

The de Soto-Azpilcueta analysis was spread to the merchants of Spain by the Dominican friar Tomás de Mercado (d. 1585), who in 1569 wrote a handbook of commercial morality in Spanish, in contrast to the Scholastic theologians, who invariably wrote in Latin. It was followed by García and endorsed at the end of the sixteenth century by the Salamanca theologian the Dominican Domingo de Bañez (1527-1604) and by the great Portuguese Jesuit Luís de Molina (1535-1600). Writing near the turn of the century, Molina set forth the theory in an elegant and comprehensive manner:

There is another way in which money may be worth more in one place than in another; namely, because it is scarcer there than elsewhere. Other things being equal, wherever money is most abundant, there will it be least valuable for the purpose of buying goods and comparing things other than money.

Just as an abundance of goods causes prices to fall (the quantity of money and number of merchants being equal), so does an abundance of money cause them to rise (the quantity of goods and number of merchants being equal). The reason is that the money itself becomes less valuable for the purpose of buying and comparing goods. Thus we see that in Spain the purchasing-power of money is far lower, on account of its abundance, than it was eighty years ago. A thing that could be bought for two ducats at that time is nowadays worth 5, 6, or even more. Wages have risen in the same proportion, and so have dowries, the price of estates, the income from benefices, and other things.

We likewise see that money is far less valuable in the New World (especially in Peru, where it is most plentiful), than it is in Spain. But in places where it is scarcer than in Spain, there will it be more valuable. Nor will the value of money be the same in all other places, but will vary: and this will be because of variations in its quantity, other things being equal. ... Even in Spain itself, the value of money varies: it is usually lowest of all in Seville, where the ships come in from the New World and where for that reason money is most abundant.

Wherever the demand for money is greatest, whether for buying or carrying goods, . . . or for any other reason, there its value will be highest. It is these things, too, which cause the value of money to vary in course of time in one and the same place.[11]

The outstanding revisionist work on the economic thought of the medieval and later Scholastics is that of Raymond de Roover. Basing his work in part on the Grice-Hutchinson volume, de Roover published his first comprehensive discussion in 1955.[12] For the medieval period, de Roover particularly pointed to the early fourteenth-century French Ockhamite Scholastic Jean Buridan and to the famous early fifteenth-century Italian preacher San Bernardino of Siena (1380-1444). Buridan insisted that value is measured by the human wants of the community of individuals, and that the market price is the just price.

Furthermore, he was perhaps the first to make clear in a pre-Austrian manner that voluntary exchange demonstrates subjective preferences, since he stated that the "person who exchanges a horse for money would not have done so, if he had not preferred money to a horse."[13] He added that workers hire themselves out because they value the wages they receive higher than the labor they have to expend.[14]

De Roover then discussed the sixteenth-century Spanish Scholastics, centered at the University of Salamanca, the queen of the Spanish universities of the period. From Salamanca the influence of this school of Scholastics spread to Portugal, Italy, and the Low Countries. In addition to summarizing Grice-Hutchinson's contribution and adding to her bibliography, de Roover noted that both de Soto and Molina denounced as "fallacious" the notion of the late thirteenth-century Scholastic John Duns Scotus (1266-1308) that the just price is the cost of production plus a reasonable profit; instead that price is the common estimation, the interaction of supply and demand, on the market. Molina further introduced the concept of competition by stating that competition among buyers will drive prices up, while a scarcity of purchasers will pull them down.[15]

In a later article, de Roover elaborated on his researches into the Scholastic theory of the just price. He found that the orthodox view of the just price as a station-in-life, cost-of-production price was based almost solely on the views of fourteenth-century Viennese Scholastic Henry of Langenstein. But Langenstein, de Roover pointed out, was a follower of the minority views of William of Ockham and outside the dominant Thomist tradition; Langenstein was rarely cited by later Scholastic writers. While some of their passages are open to a conflicting interpretation, de Roover demonstrated that Albertus Magnus (1193-1280) and his great pupil Thomas Aquinas (1226-74) held the just price to be the market price. In fact, Aquinas considered the case of a merchant who brings wheat to a country where there is a great scarcity; the merchant happens to know that more wheat is on the way. May he sell his wheat at the existing price, or must he announce to everyone the imminent arrival of new supplies and suffer a fall in price? Aquinas unequivocally answered that he may justly sell the wheat at the current market price, even though he added as an afterthought that it would be more virtuous of him to inform the buyers. Furthermore, de Roover pointed to the summary of Aquinas's position by his most distinguished commentator, the late fifteenth-century Scholastic Thomas de Vio, Cardinal Cajetan (1468-1534). Cajetan concluded that for Aquinas the just price is "the one, which at a given time, can be gotten from the buyers, assuming common knowledge and in the absence of all fraud and coercion."[16]

The cost-of-production theory of just price held by the Scotists was trenchantly attacked by the later Scholastics. San Bernardino of Siena, de Roover pointed out, declared that the market price is fair regardless of whether the producer gains or loses, or whether it is above or below cost. The great early sixteenth-century jurist Francisco de Vitoria (c. 1480-1546), founder of the school of Salamanca, as well as his followers insisted that the just price is set by supply and demand regardless of labor costs or expenses; inefficient producers or inept speculators must bear the consequences of their incompetence and poor forecasting. Furthermore, de Roover made clear that the general Scholastic emphasis on the justice of "common estimation" (*communis aestimatio*) is identical to "market valuation" (*aestimatio fori*), since the Scholastics used these two Latin expressions interchangeably.[17]

De Roover noted, however, that this acceptance of market price did not mean that the Scholastics adopted a laissez-faire position. On the contrary, they were often willing to accept governmental price fixing instead of market action. A few prominent Scholastics, however, led by Azpilcueta and including Molina, opposed all price fixing; as Azpilcueta put it, price controls are unnecessary in times of plenty and ineffective or positively harmful in times of dearth.[18]

In a comment on de Roover's paper, David Herlihy noted that, in the northern Italian city-states of the twelfth and thirteenth centuries, the birthplace of modern commercial capitalism, the market price was generally considered just because it was "true" and "real," if it was "established or utilized without deceit or fraud." As Herlihy summed it up, the just price of an object is its "true value as determined by one of two ways: for objects that were unique, by honest negotiation between seller and purchaser; for staple commodities by the consensus of the marketplace established in the absence of fraud or conspiracy."[19]

John W. Baldwin's definitive account of the theories of just price during the High Middle Ages of the twelfth and thirteenth centuries amply confirmed de Roover's revisionist insight. Baldwin pointed out that there were three important and influential groups of medieval writers: the theologians (whom we have been examining), the Roman lawyers, and the canon lawyers. For their part, the Romanists, joined by the canonists, held staunchly to the principle of Roman private law that the just price is whatever is arrived at by free bargaining between buyers and sellers. Baldwin demonstrated that even the theologians of the High Middle Ages before Aquinas accepted the current market price as the just price.[21]

Several years later, de Roover turned to the views of the Scholastics on the broader issue of trade and exchange.[22] He conceded the partial validity of the older view that the medieval Church frowned on trade as endangering personal salvation; or rather that, while trade *can* be honest, it presents great temptation for sin. However, he pointed out that, as trade and commerce grew after the tenth century, the Church began to adapt to the idea of the merits of trade and exchange. Thus, while it is true that the twelfth-century Scholastic Peter the Lombard (c. 1100-60) denounced trade and soldiering as sinful occupations per se, a far more benevolent view of trade was set forth during the thirteenth century by Albertus Magnus and his student Thomas Aquinas, as well as by Saint Bonaventure (1221-74) and Pope Innocent V (1225-76). While trade presents occasions for sin, it is not sinful per se; on the contrary, exchange and the division of labor are beneficent in satisfying the wants of the citizens. Moreover, the early fourteenth-century Scholastic Richard of Middleton developed the idea that both the buyer and the seller gain by exchange, since each demonstrates that he prefers what he receives in exchange to what he gives up. Middleton also applied this idea to international trade, pointing out that both countries benefit by exchanging their surplus products. Since the merchants and citizens of each country benefit, neither party is exploiting the other.

At the same time, Aquinas and other theologians denounced "covetousness" and love of profit, mercantile gain being only justifiable when directed toward the "good of others"; furthermore, Aquinas attacked "avarice" as attempting to improve one's "station in life." But, as de Roover pointed out, the great early sixteenth-century Italian Thomist Cardinal Cajetan corrected this view by demonstrating that, if this were true, every person would have to be frozen in his current occupation and income. On the contrary, asserted Cajetan, people with unusual ability should be able to rise in the world. In contrast to such northern Europeans as Aquinas, Cajetan was quite familiar with the commerce and upward social mobility in the Italian cities. Furthermore, even Aquinas explicitly rejected the idea that prices should be determined by one's station in life, pointing out that the selling price of any good tends to be the same whether the entrepreneur is poor or wealthy.

De Roover hailed the early fifteenth-century Scholastic San Bernardino of Siena as being the only theologian who dealt in detail with the economic function of the entrepreneur. San Bernardino wrote of the uncommon qualities and abilities of the successful entrepreneur, including effort, diligence, knowledge of the market, and calculation of risks, with profit on invested capital justifiable as compensation for the risk and effort of the entrepreneur. The acceptance of profit was immortalized in a motto in a thirteenth-century account book: "In the name of God and of profit."[23]

De Roover's final work in this area was a booklet on San Bernardino and his contemporary Sant' Antonino (1389-1459) of Florence.[24] In San Bernardino's views of trade and the entrepreneur, the occupation of trade may lead to sin, but so may all other occupations, including that of bishops. As for the sins of traders, they consist of such illicit activity as fraud, misrepresentation of products, the sale of adulterated products, and the use of false weights and measures, as well as keeping creditors waiting for their money after a debt is due. As to trade, there are several kinds of useful merchants, according to San Bernardino: importer-exporters, warehousemen, retailers, and manufacturers.

San Bernardino described the rare qualities and virtues that go into the making of successful businessmen. One is efficiency (*industria*), which includes knowledge of qualities, prices, and costs and the ability to assess risks and estimate profit opportunities, which, he declared, "indeed very few are capable of doing." Entrepreneurial ability therefore includes the willingness to assume risks (*pericula*). Businessmen must be responsible and attentive to detail, and trouble and toil are also necessary. The rational and orderly conduct of business, also necessary to success, is another virtue lauded by San Bernardino, as are business integrity and the prompt settlement of accounts.

Turning again to the Scholastic view of value and price, de Roover pointed out that, as early as Aquinas, prices were treated as determined, not by their philosophic rank in nature, but by the degree of the usefulness or utility of the respective products to man and to human wants. As de Roover wrote of Aquinas, "These passages are clear and unambiguous; value depends upon utility, usefulness, or human wants. There is nowhere any mention of labor as the creator or the measure of value."[25] A century before the Spanish Scholastics and a century and a half before the sophisticated formulation of Francisco García, San Bernardino had demonstrated that price is determined by scarcity (*raritas*), usefulness (*virtuositas*), and pleasurability or desirability (*complacibilitas*). Greater abundance of a good will cause a drop in its value and greater scarcity a rise. To have value, furthermore, a good must have usefulness, or what we may call "objective utility"; but within that framework, the value is determined by the *complacibilitas*, or "subjective utility," that it has to individual consumers. Again, only the marginal element is lacking for a full-scale pre-Austrian theory of value. Coming to the brink of the later Austrian solution to the classical economists' "paradox of value," San Bernardino noted that a glass of water to a man dying of thirst would be so valuable as to be almost priceless, but fortunately water, though absolutely necessary to human life, is ordinarily so abundant that it commands either a low price or even no price at all.

Correcting Schumpeter's ascription of the founding of subjective utility to Sant' Antonino and observing that he had derived it from San Bernardino, de Roover showed further that recent scholarship demonstrates that Bernardino derived his own analysis almost word for word from a late thirteenth-century Provençal Scholastic, Pierre de Jean Olivi (1248-98). Apparently, Bernardino did not give credit to Olivi because the latter, coming from another branch of the Franciscan order, was at that time suspected of heresy.[26]

Turning to the concept of the "just price," de Roover made it clear that San Bernardino, following Olivi, held that price of a good or service to be "the estimation made in common by all the citizens of the community." This he held explicitly to be the valuation of the market, since he defined the just price as "the one which happens to prevail at a given time according to the estimation of the market, that is, what the commodities for sale are then commonly worth in a certain place."[27]

Wages were treated by the two Italian friars as equivalent to the prices of goods. For San Bernardino, "The same rules which apply to the prices of goods also apply to the price of services with the consequence that the just wage will also be determined by the forces operating in the market or, in other words, by the demand for labor and the available supply." An architect is paid more than a ditchdigger, asserted Bernardino, because "the former's job requires more intelligence, greater ability, and longer training and that, consequently, fewer qualify. ... Wage differentials are thus to be explained by scarcity because skilled workers are less numerous than unskilled and high positions require even a very unusual combination of skills and abilities."[28] And Sant' Antonino concluded that the wage of a laborer is a price which, like any other, is properly determined by the common estimation of the market in the absence of fraud.

During and after the sixteenth century, the Roman Catholic

church and Scholastic philosophy came under increasingly virulent attack, first from Protestants and then from rationalists, but the result was not so much to eliminate any influence of Scholastic philosophy and economics as to mask that influence, since their proclaimed enemies would often fail to cite their writings. Thus, the great early seventeenth-century Dutch Protestant jurist Hugo Grotius (1583-1645) adopted much of Scholastic doctrine, including the emphasis on want and utility as the major determinant of value, and the importance of the common estimation of the market in determining price. Grotius, in fact, explicitly cited the Spanish Scholastics Azpilcueta Navarro and Covarrubias. Even more explicitly following the Spanish Scholastics of the sixteenth century were the Jesuit theologians of the following century, including the highly influential Flemish Jesuit Leonardus Lessius (1554-1623), a friend of Luís de Molina, and the even more influential Spanish Jesuit Cardinal Juan de Lugo (1583-1660), whose treatise was originally published in 1642 and was reprinted many times in the next three centuries. Also explicitly following the Scholastics and the Salamanca school in the seventeenth century was the Genoese philosopher and jurist Sigismundo Scaccia (c. 1618), whose treatise was widely reprinted, as well as Antonio de Escobar (c. 1652), author of a moral manual.

To return to what would be the dominant Protestant trend for later economic thought, Grotius's legal and economic doctrines were followed closely in the later seventeenth century by the Swedish Lutheran jurist Samuel Pufendorf (1632-94). While Pufendorf followed Grotius on utility and scarcity and the common estimation of the market in determining value and price, and while he certainly consulted the writings of the Spanish Scholastics, it is the rationalist Pufendorf who dropped all citations to these hated Scholastic influences upon his teacher. Hence, when Grotian doctrine was brought to Scotland by the early eighteenth-century professor of moral philosophy at Glasgow Gershom Carmichael (1672-1729), who translated Pufendorf into English, knowledge of Scholastic influences was lost. Hence, with Carmichael's great student and successor Francis

Hutcheson, utility began to be weakened by labor and cost-of-production theories of value, until finally by the time Hutcheson's student Adam Smith (1723-90) wrote the *Wealth of Nations*, pre-Austrian Scholastic influence had unfortunately dropped out altogether. Hence the view of Schumpeter, de Roover, and others that Smith and later Ricardo shunted economics onto a wrong track, which the later marginalists (including the Austrians) had to correct.

Scholastic doctrine had a more lasting influence on economists on the Continent, particularly in Catholic countries. Thus, the brilliant mid-eighteenth-century Italian the Abbé Ferdinando Galiani (1728-87) is often credited by historians with inventing full-blown the concept of utility and scarcity as the determinants of price. No one wished to stress Scholastic writings in that rationalistic age, but strong Scholastic influence is detectable in Galiani's work, whose section on value even contains an explicit citation to the Salamanca Scholastic Diego Covarrubias y Leiva. Galiani's uncle Celestino, who brought up the youthful economist, had been professor of moral theology before becoming an archbishop and was therefore undoubtedly familiar with the Scholastic literature on the subject, which filled the Italian libraries of the eighteenth century. Galiani's contemporary Italian economist Antonio Genovesi (1712-69) was also directly influenced by Scholastic thought; he had served as professor of ethics and moral philosophy at the University of Naples.

From Galiani the central role of utility, scarcity, and the common estimation of the market spread to France, to the late eighteenth-century French abbé Étienne Bonnot de Condillac (1714-80), as well as to that other great abbé Robert Jacques Turgot (1727-81). Knowing only Galiani as his predecessor, Turgot echoed the Salamanca school in holding the prices of goods and the value of money, as the result of the "common estimation" of the market, to be built up out of the subjective valuations of individuals in that market. François Quesnay (1694-1774) and the eighteenth-century French physiocrats—often considered to be the founders of economic science—were also heavily influenced by the Scholastics, both in their natural law theory and in their emphasis on consumption and subjective value. Scholastic doctrine even appears in the fiercely anti-Catholic *Encyclopedie*, including the doctrine of natural law, as well as the analysis of price as determined by the current common estimation of the market. Even during the nineteenth century strong traces of Condillac and Turgot appear in Jean Baptiste Say (1767-1832), who upheld a utility model for the future.[29]

At about the same time as Schumpeter, Grice-Hutchinson, and de Roover published their researches, Emil Kauder set forth a similar revisionist viewpoint. Kauder traced the connection between the Scholastics and Galiani, first to the mid-sixteenth-century Italian politician Gian Francesco Lottini (1512-72).[30] He showed that Lottini first worked out a rudimentary concept of time preference: that people estimate present wants higher than future. The next link was the late sixteenth-century Italian merchant Bernardo Davanzati (1529-1606), who applied subjective-value theory to money in 1588. Indeed, Schumpeter was soon to point out that Davanzati also solved the "paradox of value," that water is very useful but not valuable on the market because it is highly abundant. Whether or not Davanzati was influenced by San Bernardino is not known.[31] He was followed almost a century later by the Italian mathematics professor Geminiano Montanari (1633-87). Galiani was then definitely influenced by Davanzati.

Kauder then developed in an original way the great contributions of Galiani. For not only did Galiani comprehensively set forth the familiar theory of utility and scarcity as determinants of price—which lacked only the marginal principle to arrive at the Austrian theory—but he also went on to apply the utility theory to the value of labor and other factors of production. For the value of labor is, in turn, determined by the utility and scarcity of the particular kind of labor being considered. The highly skilled are paid much more than the common laborer, since nature produces only a small number of able men. But not only that; for Galiani it is not labor costs that determine value, but value—and consumer choice—that determines labor cost. Furthermore,

Galiani touched on a pre-Böhm-Bawerk theory of interest, with interest being the difference between present and future money.[32] Turgot then anticipated the Austrians in applying Galiani's utility theory to a detailed analysis of isolated exchange, showing that both parties benefit in utility from the exchange. Turgot, furthermore, as Schumpeter pointed out, developed a time analysis of production and worked out a pre-Austrian general analysis of the law of eventually diminishing returns that was not to be matched until the end of the nineteenth century. Quite justly Schumpeter wrote that "it is not too much to say that analytic economics took a century to get where it could have got in twenty years after the publication of Turgot's treatise had its content been properly understood and absorbed by an alert profession."[33] Instead, as Kauder pointed out, it was left to Condillac to offer a last-ditch and neglected defense of Galiani's utility theory against the rising tide of British cost theory. In Condillac's trenchant phrase, "A thing does not have value because it costs, as people suppose; instead it costs because it has a value."[34]

In a fascinating companion article, Kauder speculated on the persistence of utility-and-subjective-value theory on the Continent, as compared to the rise and dominance of a quantity-of-labor-and-cost-of-production theory in Great Britain.[35] He was particularly intrigued by the fact that the pre-nineteenth-century French and Italian subjectivists were all Catholics (and, of course, he might have added the medieval and sixteenth-century Scholastics as well), while the British economists were all Protestants, or, more precisely, Calvinists. Kauder speculated that it was their Calvinist training that led John Locke and particularly Adam Smith to reject the Continental tradition (Smith knew Turgot and read Grotius) and to emphasize a labor theory of value. The Calvinists believed that work or labor was divine; could not this imprint have led Smith and the others to adopt a labor theory of economic value? Furthermore, Kauder pointed out that until the middle of the eighteenth century the French and Italian universities were dominated by Aristotelian philosophy, particularly as transmitted by the Jesuits and other religious orders. Kauder added that, in contrast to Calvinism, Aristotelian-Thomist philosophy did not glorify work or labor per se as divine; work may be necessary, but "moderate pleasure-seeking and happiness"—in short, utility—"form the center of economic actions." Kauder concluded that "if pleasure in a moderate form is the purpose of economics, then following the Aristotelian concept of the final cause, all principles of economics including valuation must be derived from it."[36]

Kauder admitted that his is a conjecture that cannot be proved, and also that it does not particularly hold for the nineteenth century. However, he did offer an intriguing explanation for Alfred Marshall's failure to adopt the full marginal utility theory and, instead, his shunting of the theory aside in favor of a recrudescence of Ricardo's objective cost-of-production theory. That explanation lies in Marshall's undoubtedly strong Evangelical and Calvinist background.[37]

Finally, Emil Kauder convincingly demonstrated the direct influence of Aristotelian philosophy on the founders of the Austrian school and contrasted the result with the other marginalist schools of the late nineteenth century. First, in contrast to Jevons and Walras, who believed that economic laws are hypotheses dealing with social quantities, Carl Menger and his followers held that economics investigates, not the quantities of phenomena, but the underlying essences of such real entities as value, profit, and the other economic categories. The belief in underlying essences inherent in superficial appearances is Aristotelian, and Kauder pointed out that Menger studied and cited Aristotle extensively in his methodological work. He also noted the similarities discovered by Oskar Kraus between the Austrian and the Aristotelian theories of imputation. Kauder also pointed out that Menger applied the fundamental Aristotelian distinction between matter and form to economic theory: economic theory deals with the underlying form of events, while history and statistics deal with the concrete matter. The concrete historical cases are the exemplifications of general regularities, the Aristotelian matter that contains potentialities, while the economic laws "are the Aristotelian forms which actualize the potential, i.e., they provide the laws and concepts valid for all times and places."[38]

Secondly, Menger held, in contrast to Jevons and Walras, that economic laws as expressed in mathematical equations are only arbitrary statements; on the contrary, genuine economic laws are "exact," in Menger's terminology meaning fixed laws that describe sequences invariable to time and place. Thus, Menger and the Austrians build up an "eternal structure of economics... stripped of all historical peculiarities." In short, Menger and, following him, Böhm-Bawerk were Aristotelian social ontologists, maintaining the absolute and apodictic reality of economic laws. Kauder perceptively pointed out that in contemporary economics, "only von Mises, the most faithful student of the three [Austrian] pioneers, maintains the ontological character of economic laws. His theory of human action . . . is a 'reflection about the essence of action.' Economic laws provide 'ontological facts.' "[39]

Finally, the Jevons-Walras mathematical method necessarily deals with "functions of interdependent phenomena," whereas, for Menger and the Austrians, economic laws are genetic and causal, proceeding from the utility and the action of the consumer to the market result. As Kauder put it:

For Marshall, value and cost, supply and demand are interdependent factors whose functional connection can be explained in an equation or a geometrical figure. For Wieser, Menger, and especially for Böhm-Bawerk the wants of the consumer are the beginning and the end of the causal nexus. The purpose and the cause of economic action are identical. There is no difference between causality and teleology, claims Böhm-Bawerk. He knew the Aristotelian origin of his argument.[40]

Kauder also pointed out that the characteristically Austrian method of proceeding by words from a Robinson Crusoe model and then proceeding step by step to a fully developed economy accords with the Aristotelian concept of entelechy, in which "the motion from the potentiality to the actualization determines not only the structure of the system but also the presentation of the thoughts."[41]

In attempting to explain the Austrian choice among all the marginalists for philosophical realism and social ontology, Kauder pointed to the late nineteenth-century influences on the Austrian intellectual climate of Aristotle, Thomas Aquinas, and other schools of realistic philosophy. Most influential was Aristotle, who was studied carefully down to the middle of the nineteenth century, and who was often taught in the secondary schools in Austria. And while realism gave way to empiricism in the Austrian schools by the turn of the twentieth century, "the Viennese *Schottengymnasium*, the intellectual nursery of many famous Austrians including Wieser, required, even after 1918, the students to read Aristotle's metaphysics in the original Greek."[42] In contrast, of course, the influence of Aristotelian philosophy in Britain or even France during the nineteenth century was virtually nil.

In recent decades, the revisionist scholars have clearly altered our knowledge of the prehistory of the Austrian school of economics. We see emerging a long and mighty tradition of proto-Austrian Scholastic economics, founded on Aristotle, continuing through the Middle Ages and the later Italian and Spanish Scholastics, and then influencing the French and Italian economists before and up till the day of Adam Smith. The achievement of Carl Menger and the Austrians was not so much to found a totally new system on the framework of British classical political economy as to revive and elaborate upon the older tradition that had been shunted aside by the classical school.

NOTES

1. Lewis H. Haney, *History of Economic Thought*, 4th ed. (New York: Macmillan Co., 1949), pp. 106-8.
2. R. H. Tawney, *Religion and the Rise of Capitalism* (New York: New American Library, 1954), pp. 38-39.

72 The Foundations of Modern Austrian Economics

3. Joseph A. Schumpeter, *A History of Economic Analysis* (New York: Oxford University Press, 1954).

4. Marjorie Grice-Hutchinson, *The School of Salamanca: Readings in Spanish Monetary Theory, 1544-1605* (Oxford: Clarendon Press, 1952).

5. Ibid., p. 27.

6. Luis Saravia de la Calle, *Instruccion de mercaderes* (1544), in Grice-Hutchinson, *School of Salamanca*, pp.79-82.

7. Ibid., p. 48.

8. Francisco García, *Tratado utilisimo y muy general de todos los contractos* (1583), in Grice-Hutchinson, *School of Salamanca*, pp. 104-5.

9. Martín de Azpilcueta Navarro, *Comentario resolutorio de usuras* (1556), in Grice-Hutchinson, *School of Salamanca*, pp. 94-95.

10. Domingo de Soto, *De Justitia et Jure* (1553), in Grice-Hutchinson, *School of Salamanca*, p. 55.

11. Luís de Molina, *Disputationes de Contractibus* (1601), in Grice-Hutchinson, *School of Salamanca*, pp. 113-14; Tomás de Mercado, *Tratos y contratos de mercaderes* (1569), ibid., pp. 57-58 and; Domingo de Bañez, *De Justitia et Jure* (1594), ibid., pp. 96-103.

12. Raymond de Roover, "Scholastic Economics: Survival and Lasting Influence from the Sixteenth Century to Adam Smith," *Quarterly Journal of Economics* 69(May 1955): 161-90; reprinted in idem, *Business, Banking, and Economic Thought* (Chicago: University of Chicago Press, 1974), pp. 306-35.

13. Ibid., p. 309.

14. Raymond de Roover, "Joseph A. Schumpeter and Scholastic Economics," *Kyklos* 10(1957):128. De Roover traced the concept of mutual benefit as exhibited in exchange back to Aquinas, who wrote that "buying and selling seem to have been instituted for the mutual advantage of both parties, since one needs something that belongs to the other, and conversely" (ibid., p. 128).

15. De Roover, *Business*, pp. 312-14. Elsewhere de Roover noted that the Scotists were a small minority among medieval and later Scholastics, whereas the Scholastics discussed here were in the mainstream of Thomist tradition.

16. Raymond de Roover, "The Concept of the Just Price: Theory and Economic Policy," *Journal of Economic History* 18(December 1958):422-23.

17. De Roover, "Just Price," p. 424.

18. Ibid., p. 426.

19. David Herlihy, "The Concept of the Just Price: Discussion," *Journal of Economic History* 18(December 1958):437.

20. John W. Baldwin, *The Medieval Theories of the Just Price, Transactions of the American Philosophical Society* (Philadelphia: July 1959); see

also the review of Baldwin by A. R. Bridbury, *Economic History Review* 12(April 1960): 512-14.

21. In particular, the theologians at the great center at the University of Paris in the early thirteenth century: Alexander of Hales and Aquinas's teacher, Albertus Magnus (ibid., p. 71). Baldwin further pointed out that theological treatment of such practical questions as the just price in the Middle Ages only began with the development of university centers at the end of the twelfth century (ibid., p. 9).

22. Raymond de Roover, "The Scholastic Attitude toward Trade and Entrepreneurship," *Explorations in Entrepreneurial History* 2(1963):76-87; reprinted in idem, *Business*, pp. 336-45.

23. De Roover, here and in his other writings, pointed to the great deficiency in Scholastic analysis of the market: the belief that any interest on a pure loan (a *mutuum*) constituted the sin of usury. The reason is that while the Scholastics understood the economic functions of risk and opportunity cost, they never arrived at the concept of time preference. On the Scholastics and usury, see the magisterial work of John T. Noonan, Jr., *The Scholastic Analysis of Usury* (Cambridge: Harvard University Press, 1957); see also Raymond de Roover, "The Scholastics, Usury, and Foreign Exchange," *Business History Review* 41(1967):257-71.

24. Raymond de Roover, *San Bernardino of Siena and Sant' Antonino of Florence: The Two Great Economic Thinkers of the Middle Ages* (Boston: Kress Library of Business and Economics, 1967).

25. Ibid., p. 17.

26. On the originality of Olivi, see ibid., p. 19.

27. Ibid., p. 20.

28. Ibid., pp. 23-24.

29. On the later influence of the Scholastics, see Schumpeter, *History*, pp. 94-106; Grice-Hutchinson, *School of Salamanca,* pp. 59-78; de Roover, *Business*, pp. 330-35; and de Roover, "Joseph Schumpeter," p. 128-29.

30. Emil Kauder, "Genesis of the Marginal Utility Theory: From Aristotle to the End of the Eighteenth Century," *Economic Journal* 63(September 1953):638-50.

31. Schumpeter, *History*, p. 300.

32. Kauder, "Genesis," p. 645.

33. Schumpeter, *History*, p. 249; see also ibid., pp. 259-61, 332-33.

34. In Kauder "Genesis," p. 647. Kauder and Schumpeter also noted the early eighteenth-century French mathematician Daniel Bernoulli (1738), who outside the stream of economic thought developed a mathematical version of the diminishing marginal utility of money (ibid., pp. 647-50: Schumpeter, *History*, pp. 302-5).

35. Emil Kauder, "The Retarded Acceptance of the Marginal Util-

ity Theory," *Quarterly Journal of Economics* 67(November 1953):564-75.

36.   Ibid., p. 569.

37.   Ibid., pp. 570-71. These two articles are essentially represented in Emil Kauder, *A History of Marginal Utility Theory* (Princeton: Princeton University Press, 1965), pp. 3-29.

38.   Emil Kauder, "Intellectual and Political Roots of the Older Austrian School," *Zeitschrift für Nationalökonomie* 17(December 1957):411-25.

39.   Ibid., p. 417.

40.   Ibid., p. 418.

41.   Ibid.

42.   Ibid., p. 420; see also Kauder, *History of Marginal Utility*, pp. 90-100. On Menger as Aristotelian, also see T. W. Hutchison, "Some Themes from *Investigations into Method*," in *Carl Menger and the Austrian School of Economics*, ed. J. R. Hicks and Wilhelm Weber (Oxford: Clarendon Press, 1973), pp. 17-20.

Philosophical and Ethical Implications of Austrian Economics

Israel M. Kirzner

The title of this paper contains an apparent paradox: it assumes that Austrian economic theory *can* have philosophical and ethical implications, while the tradition within Austrian economics has been strongly in support of *Wertfreiheit* as a cardinal precept of scientific propriety. A good deal of what I have to say in this paper relates to the resolution of this paradox. Let us first rapidly review the history of the doctrine of value-freedom in economics.

WERTFREIHEIT: *A THUMBNAIL SKETCH*

In his 1884 *Untersuchungen* Carl Menger included an appendix that briefly but very clearly criticized the tendency of the German "historical" economists to confuse ethical positions with the conclusions of economics.[1] At that time holders of chairs of economics at the German universities considered themselves social reformers. They fused their economics with their personal views on social justice and morality. In their lectures they reportedly permitted their emotions free rein. Adolf Wagner, for example, would shake his fist at imaginary opponents of his proposals. Other professors would lecture as if addressing preelection meetings, to the cheers of their students.[2] It was with this style of economic discussion that Menger was expressing his disenchantment.

In subsequent decades the figure to mount a vigorous cam-
paign for *Wertfreiheit* in the social sciences was, of course, Max
Weber. He described the fusion of ethical and scientific statements as "the work of the devil."[3] The issue was heatedly debated
at the 1909 meeting of the *Verein für Sozialpolitik* in what
Schumpeter described as almost amounting to a row.[4] In Weber's
opinion, when a scientist combines his scientific conclusions
with his ethical views, he may mislead the layman into supposing
that these views carry with them the authority of science. For
science to be interpersonally valid, it must not depend on the
personal views of any one scholar. Any departure from an aus-
tere neutrality on the part of the scientist qua scientist with
respect to judgments of value must be denounced. Weber not
only stated value-freedom to be a canon of scientific procedure
to be jealously guarded but also defended the possibility of
pursuing this procedure in economics. Others argued that since
economics and social science in general deal with material per-
meated with ethical content—values, interests, and motives—it is
impossible to engage in value-free research in these areas.
Weber's contribution was to point out that the investigator's own
value judgments need not (and also should not) color the conclusions that he reaches concerning the admittedly value-laden
activities and phenomena with which his research deals.

Writing in the early 1930s, Lionel Robbins pursued the Weber
doctrine still further. Under the influence of Austrian thought,
Robbins offered a definition of economics with the incidental
property of establishing that the economist's value judgments
have nothing at all to do with his concerns as a scientific investigator.[5] Robbins defined economics as the science concerned
with the implications of the insight that men are economizing
individuals who seek to allocate given scarce resources among
given competing ends. Because both the ends and the means are
given, what is being investigated is strictly the patterns of behavior generated by the particular configuration of ends and
means that happen to be given. The concrete content of the ends
does not determine these patterns of behavior. An ends-means
configuration applicable to a specific factual situation may also

be applicable to an entirely different situation in which the concrete content of both ends and means is entirely different. Economic science, therefore, is value-free in the sense that the *particular* ends being pursued are not essential to the economic analysis of a given situation. The purposes being aimed at in the economizing aspects of men's activities may be lofty or mundane. The generalizations economic science develops concerning economizing behavior are equally valid in both situations. Thus Robbins was able to show that *Wertfreiheit* emerges as an implication of this definition of economics.

In the writings of Ludwig von Mises the *Wertfreiheit* tradition was vigorously upheld. Mises was deeply concerned with insuring that the scientific truths embodied in economics be perceived as such, that they should not be disparaged as partisan propaganda. Accordingly, it was essential to guard jealously against any lapses from *Wertfreiheit* — lapses that might lay economics open to the charge of being the expression of someone's vested interests. As is well known, Mises firmly rejected all suggestions (such as those contained in Marxist literature and in the literature on the sociology of knowledge) that science is subject to a relativism in logic, that its conclusions must inevitably reflect the class consciousness or interests of the scientists.[6] Logic, Mises insisted, is universally and interpersonally valid; so is economic science. To surrender *Wertfreiheit* will unnecessarily and tragically jeopardize the acceptance of scientific conclusions by those not sharing the values revealed by the non-*wertfrei* scientist.

THE CRITICS OF WERTFREIHEIT

The *Wertfreiheit* doctrine had come under attack in a number of different ways. One episode of particular interest involves the evolution of Gunnar Myrdal's attitude toward the doctrine. In *The Political Element in the Development of Economic Theory,* published in 1929 when he was still a young man and not translated into English until 1954, he charged that economists have consistently violated the *Wertfreiheit* ideal. From the beginning of

economic science until our own times, economists have consciously or unconsciously—possibly quite innocently—
permitted their value judgments and ethical positions to color
their analyses and help determine their normative conclusions.
He saw his task as being to complete Weber's work by criticizing,
from the perspective of the *Wertfreiheit* doctrine, "the political
speculation in classical and neoclassical economic theory."[7] This
task required him to expose the errors introduced into economic
doctrines by "the insertion of valuations."[8] Both from his 1929
preface and from the 1953 preface to the English translation, it is
clear that what stimulated his research was his wish to protest the
"uncompromising laissez-faire doctrine" that "dominated the
teaching of economics in Sweden" in the late 1920s. By exposing
the valuations that must be smuggled into economic analysis
before such a normative doctrine as laissez-faire can be extracted, he hoped to discredit the dominant "economic
liberalism" of his time.[9]

Thus, in this early work, Myrdal had no quarrel with Weberian *Wertfreiheit* as a scientific ideal. He was merely pointing out
how seriously, in his view, this ideal has been trampled on in the
course of the history of economics. But in his later writings he
drastically shifted his point of view. As he himself put it,
"Throughout [this early work] there lurks the idea that when all
metaphysical elements are radically cut away, a healthy body of
positive economic theory will remain, which is altogether independent of valuations."[10] This idea he later emphatically rejected. Such an idea, as a

belief in the existence of a body of scientific knowledge acquired
independently of all valuations is . . . naive empiricism. Facts do not
organize themselves into concepts and theories just by being looked at;
indeed, except within the framework of concepts and theories, there
are no scientific facts but only chaos. . . . Questions must be asked
before answers can be given. The questions are an expression of our
interest in the world, they are at bottom valuations.[11]

Nor does Myrdal shy away from the rejection of the *Wertfreiheit*
doctrine that his later views entail. "I have therefore arrived at

the belief in the necessity of working always, from the beginning to the end, with explicit value premises."[12] This position—emphasizing the *impossibility* of·*wertfrei* social science—Myrdal vigorously pursued in a series of writings, the most important of which have been collected under the title *Value in Social Theory* (London: Routledge and Kegan Paul, 1958),

Myrdal was not, of course, alone in this rejection of *Wertfreiheit.* It will perhaps suffice, for my purpose in this article, merely to refer to the excellent history of the debate concerning *Wertfreiheit* contained in T.W. Hutchison's *"Positive" Economics and Policy Objectives* (Cambridge: Harvard University Press, 1964). We should, however, also note that after the publication of Hutchison's book Myrdal's skepticism concerning the possibility of *Wertfreiheit* in the social sciences came to characterize the position often taken by scholars on the New Left. Throughout the various branches of the social sciences, these writers denounced all claims of *Wertfreiheit* to be either examples of downright fraud or else evidence of naiveté.

It is against this Myrdal tradition, which denies the possibility and/or desirability of *Wertfreiheit* in economics, that we must contrast the mainstream perspective of Austrian economics from Menger down to Mises as outlined earlier. Furthermore, this Austrian perspective forces us to confront certain apparent inconsistencies in the Austrian (and particularly the Misesian) position.

MISES, WERTFREIHEIT, *AND POLICY PRESCRIPTIONS*

In his 1929 book Myrdal gave Austrian economics relatively good marks for disinterested objectivity:

In Austria, economics has never had direct political aims in spite of the close connection of the Austrian marginal utility theory with utilitarian philosophy. The Austrians were preoccupied with value theory and never elaborated a detailed theory of welfare economics.[13]

It is interesting to note that Fritz Machlup, in his review of the

English translation of Myrdal's book, asked with amazement whether Myrdal was not familiar with Mises's strongly anti-interventionist writings.[14] Misesian economics, it is implied in Machlup's question, can hardly qualify as being free of "direct political aims." Again, we find Hutchison in a footnote rather clearly implying that Mises was guilty of this inconsistency.[15] He juxtaposed two positions taken by Mises, which, it appears, Hutchison considered to be mutually incompatible. On the one hand, Mises vigorously defended the *Wertfreiheit* doctrine; on the other hand, he made strong normative statements concerning the desirability of the free market. Here then is the apparent difficulty that we must confront: can we reconcile Mises's strong normative position in economics with his declared insistence on *Wertfreiheit*? I believe that we can. I believe moreover that such a reconciliation bears a definite relationship to the specifically Austrian character of Misesian economics.

In arguing that a reconciliation is possible in this way, it is necessary for me to modify to some extent a position I defended a short while ago. In an eloquent article in *Intercollegiate Review*, John Davenport advocated a closer relationship between economics and philosophy.[16] Davenport deplored the gap in communication between the economists, concerned only with pure (i.e., abstract) efficiency, and those scholars in philosophy and ethics, concerned with the concrete nature of the goals and ends of efficient action. If we are to achieve a good society, Davenport argued, discussions of efficiency cannot remain divorced from philosophical concepts of the good and the bad, the beautiful and the ugly, the true and the untrue. In pursuing his critique of economics from this point of view, Davenport referred approvingly to Robbins and to Mises as having to some extent "humanized" economics. The emphasis that both Robbins and Mises placed on human choice and purpose made it inevitable, Davenport explained, that attention be paid to the *nature* of choice and purpose. To this extent, therefore, Davenport credited Robbins and Mises with having "made a beginning at least of rebuilding the bridge that connects [economics] with philosophy."[17]

Commenting recently on Davenport's paper, I took issue with this last point and argued that the subjectivism of Robbins and Mises in no way requires or implies the possibility of a synthesis between ethical values and the value-free propositions of economic science.[18] The tradition of *Wertfreiheit,* so stoutly upheld by both Robbins and Mises, was not at all inconsistent—even by implication—with their emphasis on purposeful decision making. It would, it seemed to me, be a distortion of both the Robbinsian and the Misesian points of view to perceive either of them as uniquely capable of initiating the kind of bridge building between economics and ethics that Davenport advocated.[19]

It now appears necessary for me to modify this position. While I would still insist that Misesian purposefulness in no way implies the need to surrender the ideal of *Wertfreiheit,* Davenport's observation regarding Mises may embody an insight I previously missed. Furthermore, it is by means of this insight that I hope to reconcile the apparent inconsistency between Mises's pronouncements concerning the economic advantages of the free market and his insistence on *Wertfreiheit* in economics.

The Misesian emphasis on purposeful choice enables us to avoid discussions of efficiency that depend on such notions as utility and welfare. Efficiency, in the Misesian framework, does not mean welfare maximization (not individual welfare maximization nor social welfare); it means instead the fulfillment of the purposes deemed most important rather than the fulfillment of less important purposes. It is impossible therefore to speak of efficiency in terms other than those of the purposes of specific individuals under discussion. Nothing in the concept of Misesian efficiency is consistent with the belief that an economist's approval of, say, a specific policy reflects his own approval of the ends of that policy, or even his belief that the ends will command general approval. For Mises, professional approval by an economist of a specific policy proposal merely means that the economist believes the policy will enhance the fulfillment of the purposes of those interested in the economist's professional opinion. (By contrast, other approaches to economic welfare that do not place this emphasis on individual purposes—even though it is acknowledged that welfare depends on individual tastes—tend to jeopardize their *Wertfreiheit* when making policy pronouncements. It is now a well-established conclusion of welfare economics that such policy pronouncements, insofar as they imply a maximization of social welfare, cannot escape arbitrary, and thus value-laden, assignments of weights to individuals.)

And, indeed, when one examines Mises's many statements about economic policy, whether they be about price controls, tariffs, antitrust policy, or anything else, one invariably discovers that his conclusions do not at all reflect his own personal valuations. They reflect only his opinions concerning the degree of success with which others are pursuing *their* purposes. Sometimes Mises made clear whose purposes he had in mind. Sometimes it is taken for granted that the reader will be aware of whose purposes are being used as a frame of reference, and that the general nature of the preferences expressed in these purposes is also well known. One may on occasion question such an assumption; one may on occasion find language superficially implying that a certain policy is simply wrong or bad. But a careful reading of Mises will support the interpretation we are placing here on his policy pronouncements. This was made very clear indeed in Mises's oral presentations. He would emphasize again and again that interventionist policies are "wrong," not from the point of view of the economist himself, but from the point of view of those initiating these policies (or at least from the point of view of those whose well-being the policies are supposed to enhance).

SOME FURTHER REMARKS ON VALUE-FREE ECONOMICS

In discussions concerning *Wertfreiheit* in economics, analogies have often been drawn with medical research. Almost a century and a half ago Archbishop Whately used such an analogy in responding to criticism directed against the study of economics. The critics felt that the "science of wealth" was too mundane a discipline, concerned with too sinful a subject matter, to be the proper concern of moral persons. Whately's defense was to point to medical research as a model. The critics, identifying wealth as sinful, saw the economist as promoting sin. Not so, argued Whately. The researcher investigating the causes of disease surely cannot be accused of promoting disease. If wealth be sinful, then it behooves us to encourage the study of political economy in order most effectively to eliminate the offensive immoral affluence.[20]

To put Whately's defense in other words, we may say that pure research itself is *wertfrei*. If a scientist searches for and identifies the factors that foster a specific phenomenon, we are unable without additional information to determine whether his motivation has been fueled by pure curiosity, by a desire to promote the phenomenon in question, or by a desire to eliminate it. In Misesian context the phenomenon in question turns out to be the fulfillment of individual purposes. Economic analysis is able to provide insight into the circumstances and policies that foster or frustrate the fulfillment of individual purposes. Without further information one is unable to identify any specific valuations as being implied in an economist's policy conclusions; he may be in favor of these purposes, he may abhor them, or he may be indifferent about them. Value judgments are simply not prerequisites for policy conclusions.

It has sometimes been argued that, in providing a client with policy advice, the economist is after all making a moral judgment to the effect that the client's purposes are worthy of support. Surely, it is pointed out, an economist should not as a moral being offer a prospective mass murderer *wertfrei* advice on how to achieve his purposes most effectively.[21] Apparently, economic policy advice turns out inevitably to reflect and endorse the values of those to whom advice is being proffered. This reasoning does not, it should be clear, invalidate our claim that the policy conclusions of economics can be entirely consistent with the ideals of *wertfrei* science. Here again Whately's analogy is helpful.

Research into the causes of a dread disease can, we have seen, be entirely *wertfrei*. Nonetheless, we recognize that what motivates a scientist to dedicate his life to such research may be his wish to free mankind from the scourge. Or, again, a malevolent individual intent on harming his enemies may be interested in the results of this research for sinister reasons. The *Wertfreiheit* of the research itself and the objectivity of its conclusions are not affected in the least by our recognition that the researcher should not as a moral being divulge these conclusions to the man of malevolence. The choice of his clients must indeed be governed by the scientist's moral values; policy advice can indeed be given only to those whose purposes are not repugnant to the professional; but the objectivity and *Wertfreiheit* of the analysis that led to these policy conclusions are not one whit compromised by these considerations.

To pursue this argument one step further, in many cases the economist discovers policy conclusions that are applicable to situations in which a wide variety of quite different purposes may be involved. A policy statement pointing out that voluntary exchange benefits both participants (in their own prospective estimation) may after all be made without regard to what is being exchanged or the purposes to which the exchanged items will be put. In publishing such a general policy conclusion the economist can, therefore, hardly be accused of seeking personally out of his own sense of moral worth to promote any *specific* purposes that may in fact turn out to be served by free exchange.

POLICY STATEMENTS, INTERPERSONAL COMPARISONS, AND COORDINATION

Implicit in our discussion of Mises's *wertfrei* approach to economic policy and in our argument that it is the peculiarly Austrian aspect of the Misesian approach that makes it possible is an insight to which we have briefly referred. This insight is important and deserves to be spelled out more fully.

Statements by non-Austrian economists on economic policy are made against the background of the theory of welfare economics. Crucial to this theory is the attempt to aggregate, in some sense, the tastes, the purposes, or the satisfactions of individuals into an entity that it is the ideal of economic policy to maximize. The principal conceptual difficulties involved in this procedure are two. The first is well known: the problem of interpersonal comparisons of welfare inevitably stands in the way of any kind of aggregation. The second difficulty, less well known but no less serious, was pointed out by Hayek many years ago: welfare economics, in discussing efficiency at the aggregate level, is compelled to make the illegitimate assumption that the bits of information scattered throughout society concerning individual tastes (and everything else) can somehow be spontaneously integrated and fed into a single mind in order for the notion of aggregate welfare maximization to be meaningful.[22] These difficulties make it clear that, for policy statements to be made without these embarrassments, an analytical framework is needed *that preserves the individuality of individual purposes.* If policies or institutions can be judged on the extent to which they permit individual purposes—seen simply as the unaggregated preference structures of individuals—to be fulfilled, then both of the aforementioned difficulties can be avoided. Such an approach has been found, on Austrian lines, in the notion of *coordination.*[23]

   In the coordination approach to normative economics it is made clear that the ideal is not the maximization of aggregate social welfare or any such entity. Instead, the far more modest, but meaningful, criterion of success in social economic arrangements is the degree to which the purposes of separate individuals can be harmonized through coordination of decision making and action. The obvious example of coordinated action is voluntary interpersonal exchange in which each participant acts to improve his position, with such improvement possible only because each participant's action is coordinated precisely with that of his trading partner. In using the coordination criterion as the theoretical basis for evaluating social efficiency, the individuality of purposes is not lost sight of; on the contrary, the very notion of coordination prohibits submersion of these purposes into any social aggregate.

The thesis advanced in this paper, that Misesian policy pronouncements are entirely consistent with *Wertfreiheit,* depends
crucially on the nonaggregation of individual purposes. What
we have been at pains to emphasize is that this Austrian feature
of Misesian economics may be exploited—through the cognate
notion of coordination—to escape those pitfalls that other approaches have characteristically been unable to avoid.

WERTFREIHEIT: *A CONCLUDING REMARK*

Mises the defender of the free market and Mises the economic
scientist were indeed one and the same individual. It was not
necessary for Mises, in order to extol the market and condemn
intervention, to remove his value-free scientist's cap and don a
political one. To extol and to condemn were for Mises so cir-
cumscribed as to be strictly within the limits of *Wertfreiheit.* It
remains for his followers to subject themselves to similar self-
imposed restraints, not only because of Weberian ideals of scientific propriety, but also because explicitly value-laden perspectives are frequently found consorting with Austrian economics.

There is, of course, nothing improper about the proponent of
a value-laden political position seeking support in the *wertfrei*
conclusions of science. One who values the preservation of life
and crusades against cigarette smoking is acting quite properly
in citing the conclusions of medical research to the effect that
smoking is dangerous to health. Similarly, one who wishes to
promote a free society with unhampered markets may legitimately cite the conclusions of economic science with respect to
the coordinative-allocative properties of competitive markets.
What is essential, however, if such scientific support is to be
persuasive, is that the scientific research not only be conducted
with strict objectivity but also be widely recognized as having
been so conducted. Any suspicion that the conclusions of the
economic theorist depend upon the perception of particular
goals as being more valid than others will only jeopardize the
acceptance of those conclusions as objectively determined

truths. At every stage of the process of economic reasoning, *Wertfreiheit* thus becomes a crucially important element in scientific procedure. Until the stage where scientific conclusions come to be marshalled as fuel for explicitly political-persuasive positions, any surrender of *Wertfreiheit* carries with it, therefore and in fact, the altogether unwholesome prospect that such positions will necessarily be taken without the benefit of scientific information at all. Surely, if one is imbued with the value judgment that scientific truth is worth pursuing and disseminating, one can be expected to be prepared to exercise the restraint necessary to prevent that truth from being dismissed in the eyes of the public as mere propaganda.

NOTES

1. Carl Menger, *Problems of Economics and Sociology*, trans. F. J. Nock, ed. L. Schneider (Urbana: University of Illinois Press, 1963), pp. 235-37; see above p. 51, note 5.
2. Joseph A. Schumpeter, *History of Economic Analysis* (New York: Oxford University Press, 1954), p. 802.
3. See T. W. Hutchison, *"Positive" Economics and Policy Objectives* (Cambridge: Harvard University Press, 1964), p. 43.
4. Schumpeter, *History*, p. 805.
5. See Lionel Robbins, *An Essay on the Nature and Significance of Economic Science*, 2d ed. (London: Macmillan & Co., 1935), pp. xv-xvi.
6. Ludwig von Mises, *Human Action: A Treatise on Economics* (New Haven: Yale University Press, 1949), pp. 72-91.
7. Gunnar Myrdal, *The Political Element in the Development of Economic Theory* (Cambridge: Harvard University Press, 1954), p. 12.
8. Ibid., p. 18.
9. Ibid., pp. 56-76.
10. Ibid., p. vii.
11. Ibid.
12. Ibid., p. viii.
13. Ibid., p. 128.
14. Fritz Machlup, "Review of G. Myrdal, *The Political Element in the Development of Economic Theory*," *American Economic Review* 45(December 1955):950.
15. Hutchison, *"Positive" Economics*, p. 42.

16.   John Davenport, "From a Western Window: Economics and Philosphy Have Need of Each Other," *Intercollegiate Review* 8(Spring 1973):147-58.

17.   Ibid., p. 151.

18.   Israel M. Kirzner, "Letter to the Editor," *Intercollegiate Review* 9(Winter 1973-74): pp. 59-60.

19.   This disagreement with Davenport does not imply that I am unwilling to endorse his principal theme, that is, the need for economists to speak out not merely as *wertfrei* professionals but also as concerned citizens. Professionals must be concerned with moral as well as scientific truth.

20.   See Richard Whately, *Introductory Lectures on Political Economy, Delivered at Oxford in Easter Term,* 1831, 4th ed. (London: John W. Parker, 1855), p. 25.

21.   See Murray N. Rothbard, "Value Implications of Economic Theory," *American Economist* 17(Spring 1973):35-39; see also Clarence E. Philbrook, " 'Realism' in Policy Espousal," *American Economic Review* 43(December 1953):379-82.

22.   See Israel M. Kirzner, *Competition and Entrepreneurship* (Chicago: University of Chicago Press, 1973), pp. 213-22. Hayek's critique of welfare economics was presented in "The Use of Knowledge in Society," *American Economic Review* 35(September 1945):519-30.

23.   Kirzner, *Competition and Entrepreneurship,* pp. 212-42.

Praxeology,
Value Judgments,
and Public Policy

Murray N. Rothbard

Ethics is the discipline, or what is called in classical philosophy the "science," of what goals men should or should not pursue. All men have values and place positive or negative value judgments on goods, people, and events. Ethics is the discipline that provides standards for a moral critique of these value judgments. In the final analysis, either such a discipline exists and a rational or objective system of ethics is possible, or else each individual's value judgments are ultimately arbitrary and solely a creature of individual whim. It is not my province to try to settle one of the great questions of philosophy here. But even if we believe, as I do, that an objective science of ethics exists, and even if we believe still further that ethical judgments are within the province of the historian or social scientist, one thing is certain: praxeology, economic theory, cannot itself establish ethical judgments. How could it when it deals with the formal fact that men act rather than with the content of such actions? Furthermore, praxeology is not grounded on any value judgments of the praxeologist, since what he is doing is analyzing the fact that people in general have values rather than inserting any value judgments of his own.

What, then, is the proper relationship of praxeology to values or ethics? Like other sciences, praxeology provides laws about reality, laws that those who frame ethical judgments disregard only at their peril. In brief, the citizen, or the "ethicist," may have framed, in ways which we cannot deal with here, general ethical rules or goals. But in order to decide how to arrive at such goals, he must employ all the relevant conclusions of the various sciences, all of which are *in themselves* value-free. For example, let us suppose that a person's goal is to improve his health. Having arrived at this value—which I would consider to be rational and others would consider purely emotive and arbitrary—the person tries to discover how to reach his goal. To do so, he must employ the laws and findings, value-free in themselves, of the relevant sciences. He then extends the judgment of "good," as applied to his health, on to the means he believes will further that health. His end, the improvement of his health, he pronounces to be "good"; he then, let us say, adopts the findings of medical science that x grams of vitamin C per day will improve his health; he therefore extends the ethical pronouncement of "good"—or, more technically, of "right"—to taking vitamin C as well. Similarly, if a person decides that it is "good" for him to build a house and adopts this as his goal, he must try to use the laws of engineering—in themselves value-free—to figure out the best way of constructing that house. Felix Adler put the relationship clearly, though we may question his use of the term *social* before science in this context:

The . . . end being given, the ethical formula being supplied from elsewhere, social science has its most important function to discharge in filling in the formula with a richer content, and, by a more comprehensive survey and study of the means that lead to the end, to give to the ethical imperatives a concreteness and definiteness of meaning which otherwise they could not possess. Thus ethical rule may enjoin upon us to promote . . . health, . . . but so long as the laws of hygiene remain unknown or ignored, the practical rules which we are to adopt in reference to health will be scanty and ineffectual. The new knowledge of hygiene which social science supplies will enrich our moral code in this particular. Certain things which we freely did before, we now know we may not do; certain things which we omitted to do, we now know we ought to do.[1]

Praxeology has the same methodological status as the other sciences and the same relation to ethics. Thus, to take a deliberately simple example: if our end is to be able to find gasoline when we pull up to the service station, and value-free praxeological law tells us—as it does—that, if the government fixes a maximum price for any product below the free-market price, a shortage of that product will develop, then (unless other goals supervene) we will make the ethical pronouncement that it is "bad" or "wrong" for the government to impose such a measure. Praxeology, like the other sciences, is the value-free handmaiden of values and ethics.

To our contention that the sciences, including praxeology, are in themselves value-free, it might be objected that it is values or ethics that directs the *interest* of the scientist in discovering the specific laws of his discipline. There is no question about the fact that medical science is currently far more interested in discovering a cure for cancer than in searching for a cure for some disease that might only have existed in parts of the Ukraine in the eighteenth century. But the unquestioned fact that values and ethics are important in guiding the attention of scientists to specific problems is irrelevant to the fact that the laws and disciplines of the science itself are value-free. Similarly, Crusoe on his desert island may not be particularly interested in investigating the science of bridge building, but the laws of that science itself are value-free.

Ethical questions, of course, play a far smaller role in applied medicine than they do in politics or political economy. A basic reason for this is that generally the physician and his patient agree—or are supposed to agree—on the end in view: the advancement of the patient's health. The physician can advise the patient without engaging in an intense discussion of their mutual values and goals. Of course, even here, the situation is not always that clear-cut. Two examples will reveal how ethical conflicts may arise: first, the patient needs a new kidney to continue to live; is it ethical for the physician and/or the patient to murder a third party and extract his kidney? Second, is it ethical for the physician to pursue medical research for the possible good of humanity while treating his patient as an unwitting guinea pig?

These are both cases where valuational and ethical conflicts enter the picture.

In economic and political questions, in contrast, ethical and value conflicts abound and permeate the society. It is therefore impermissible for the economist or other social scientist to act as if he were a physician, who can generally assume complete agreement on values and goals with his patient and who can therefore prescribe accordingly and with no compunction. Since, then, praxeology provides no ethics whatsoever but only the data for people to pursue their various values and goals, it follows that it is impermissible for the economist qua economist to make any ethical or value pronouncements or to advocate any social or political policy whatsoever.

The trouble is that most economists burn to make ethical pronouncements and to advocate political policies—to say, in effect, that policy X is "good" and policy Y "bad." Properly, an economist may only make such pronouncements in one of two ways: either (1) to insert his own arbitrary, ad hoc personal value judgments and advocate policy clearly on that basis; or (2) to develop and defend a coherent ethical system and make his pronouncement, not as an economist, but as an ethicist, who also uses the data of economic science. But to do the latter, he must have thought deeply about ethical problems and also believe in ethics as an objective or rational discipline—and precious few economists have done either. That leaves him with the first choice: to make crystal clear that he is speaking not as an economist but as a private citizen who is making his own confessedly arbitrary and ad hoc value pronouncements.

Most economists pay lip service to the impermissibility of making ethical pronouncements qua economist, but in practice they either ignore their own criteria or engage in elaborate procedures to evade them. Why? We can think of two possible reasons. One is the disreputable reason that, if Professor Doakes advocates policy X and basically does so *as* an economics professor, he will be listened to and followed with awe and respect; whereas if he advocates policy X as plain Joe Doakes, the mass of the citizenry may come to the perfectly valid conclusion that their *own* arbitrary and ad hoc value judgments are just as good as his, and that therefore there is no particular reason to listen to him at all. A second and more reponsible reason might be that the economist, despite his professed disbelief in a science of ethics, realizes deep down that there is something unfortunate—we might even say *bad*—about unscientific and arbitrary value judgments in public policy, and so he tries desperately to square the circle, in order to be able to advocate policy in some sort of scientific manner.

While squaring this circle is impossible, as we shall consider further, I believe that this putative uneasiness at making arbitrary value judgments is correct. While it is surely admirable (ethical?) for an economist to distinguish clearly and carefully between the value-free science and his own value judgments, I contend further that it is the responsibility of any scientist, indeed any intellectual, to refrain from any value judgment whatever *unless* he can support it on the basis of a coherent and defensible ethical system. This means, of course, that those economists who, on whatever grounds, are not prepared to think about and advance an ethical system should strictly refrain from any value pronouncements or policy conclusions at all. This position is of course itself an ethical one. But it relates to the ethical system that is the precondition of all science; for, even though particular scientific laws are themselves value-free, the very procedures of science rest on the ethical norm of honesty and the search for truth; that norm, I believe, includes the responsibility to lend coherence and system to all one's pronouncements including valuational ones. I might add in passing that anyone conceding the necessity of honesty in science ipso facto becomes willy-nilly a believer in objective ethics, but I will leave that point to the ethical subjectivists to grapple with.[2]

Let me clarify with an example. Henry C. Simons, after trenchantly criticizing various allegedly scientific arguments for progressive taxation, came out flatly in favor of progression as follows:

The case for drastic progression in taxation must be rested on the case against inequality—on the ethical or aesthetic judgment that the prevailing distribution of wealth and income reveals a degree (and/or kind) of inequality which is distinctly evil or unlovely.[3]

My point is that, while it was surely admirable for Simons to make the distinction between his scientific and his personal value judgments crystal clear, that is not enough for him to escape censure. He had, at the very least, the responsibility of analyzing the nature and implications of egalitarianism and then attempting to defend it as an ethical norm. Flat declarations of unsupported value judgments should be impermissible in intellectual, let alone scientific, discourse. In the intellectual quest for truth it is scarcely sufficient to proclaim one's value judgments as if they must be accepted as tablets from on high and not be themselves subject to intellectual criticism and evaluation.

Suppose, for example, that Simons's ethical or esthetic judgment was not on behalf of equality but of a very different social ideal. Suppose that instead he had come out in favor of the murder of all short people, of all adults under five feet six inches in height. And suppose that his sole defense of this proposal were the following:

The case for the liquidation of all short people must be rested on the case against the existence of short people—on the ethical or aesthetic judgment that the prevailing number of short adults is distinctly evil or unlovely.

One wonders if the reception accorded to Simons's remarks by his fellow economists or social scientists would have been quite the same.[4] Yet, of course, the logic of his stance would have been precisely the same.

More usual is an attempt by the economist to place himself in the status of the physician of our foregoing example, that is, as someone who is merely agreeing to or ratifying the values either of a majority in society or of every person in it. But even in these cases, it must be remembered that the physician is in no sense value-free, though he is simply sharing the value of his patient, and that the value of health is so deeply shared that there is no occasion for making it explicit. Nevertheless, the physician *does* make a value judgment, and, even if every person in society shares the same value and goal, the economist who goes along with such a value is still making a value judgment, even if indeed universally shared. He is still illegitimately going beyond the bounds of the economist per se, and his value judgments must still be supported by rational argument.

The weakest path to an economist's adoption of social values is to appeal to the majority. Thus, John F. Due commented on the progressive income tax in his text on public finance:

The strongest argument for progression is the fact that the consensus of opinion in society today regards progression as necessary for equity. This is, in turn, based on the principle that the pattern of income distribution, before taxes, involves excessive inequality (which) can be condemned on the basis of inherent unfairness in terms of the standards accepted by society.

But once again the fact that the majority of society might hold market inequality to be "unfair" does not absolve Due of the fact that, in ratifying that judgment, he himself made that value judgment and went beyond the province of the economist. Furthermore, on scientific standards, the ad hoc and arbitrary value judgments of the majority are no better than those of one person, and Due, like Simons, failed to support that judgment with any sort of argumentation. Furthermore, when we ratify the majority, what of the rights or the utilities of the minority? Felix Adler's strictures against the utilitarian ethic clearly apply here:

Other sociologists frankly express their ideals in terms of quantity and, in the fashion of Bentham, pronounce the greatest happiness of the greatest number to be the social end, although they fail to make it intelligible why the happiness of the greater number should be cogent as an end upon those who happen to belong to the lesser number.[6]

Again, with Due as with Simons, one wonders about the treatment of such a position by the American intellectual community if his imprimatur on the "consensus of opinion in society today" had been applied instead to the treatment of the Jews in Germany in the 1930s.

Just as the physician who advises his client commits himself to the ethic of good health, so the economist who advises a client is *not*, much as he would like to think so, a mere technician who is not commiting himself to the value judgment of his client and his client's goals. By advising a steel company on how to increase its profits, the economist is thereby committed to share in the steel entrepreneur's value judgment that his greater profit is a desirable goal. It is even more important to make this point about the economist who advises the State. In so doing, he commits himself to the value judgments, not simply of the majority of the society as in the case of Due, but to the value judgments of the rulers of the State apparatus. To take a deliberately dramatic example, let us suppose that an economist is hired by the Nazis to advise the government on the most efficient method of setting up concentration camps. By agreeing to help make more efficient concentration camps, he is agreeing to make them "better," in short, he is committing himself willy-nilly to concentration camps as a desirable goal. And he would, again, still be doing so even if this goal were heartily endorsed by the great majority of the German public. To underscore this point, it should be clear that an economist whose value system leads him to oppose concentration camps might well give such advice to the German government as to make the concentration camps as *inefficient* as possible, that is to sabotage their operations. In short, whatever advice he gives to his clients, a value commitment by the economist, either for or against his clients' goals, is inescapable.[7]

A more interesting variant of the economist's attempt to make value-free value judgments is the "unanimity principle," recently emphasized by James M. Buchanan. Here the idea is that the economist can safely advocate a policy if *everyone* in the society also advocates it. But, in the first place, the unanimity principle is still subject to the aforementioned strictures: that, even if the economist simply shares in everyone else's value judgment, he is still making a value judgment. Furthermore, the superficial attractiveness of the unanimity principle fades away

under more stringent analysis; for unanimity is scarcely sufficient to establish an ethical principle. For one thing, the requirement of unanimity for any action or change begins with
and freezes the status quo. For an action to be adopted, the
justice and ethical propriety of the status quo must first be
established, and of course economics can scarcely be prepared to
do that. The economist who advocates the unanimity principle as
a seemingly value-free pronouncement is thereby making a massive and totally unsupported value judgment on behalf of the
status quo. A stark but not untypical example was the debate in
the British Parliament during the early nineteenth century on
the abolition of slavery, when early adherents of the "compensation principle" variant of the unanimity principle (which has its
own additional and grave problems) maintained that the masters
must be compensated for the loss of their investment in slaves. At
that point, Benjamin Pearson, a member of the Manchester
school, declared that "he had thought it was the slaves who
should have been compensated."[8] Here is a striking example of
the need in advocating public policy of some ethical system, of a
concept of justice. Those ethicists among us who hold that slavery is unjust would always oppose the idea of compensating the
masters and would rather think in terms of reparations to compensate the slaves for their years of oppression. But what is there
for the value-free economist qua economist to say?

There are other grave problems with the compensation principle as a salvaging attempt to make it possible for value-free
economists to advocate public policy. For the compensation
principle assumes that it is conceptually possible to measure
losses and thereby to compensate losers. But since praxeology
informs us that "utility" and "cost" are purely subjective (psychic)
concepts and therefore cannot be measured or even estimated
by outside observers, it become impossible for such observers to
weigh "social costs" and "social benefits" and to decide that the
latter outweigh the former for any public policy, much less to
make the compensations involved so that the losers are no longer
losers. The usual attempt is to measure psychic losses in utility by
the monetary price of an asset; thus, if a railroad damages the

land of a farmer by smoke, it is assumed that the farmer's loss can
be measured by the market price of the land. But this ignores the
facts that the farmer may have a psychic attachment to the land
that puts its value far above the market price and that—
especially in this kind of situation that does not involve direct
action and exchange by the individuals—it is impossible to find
out what the farmer's psychic attachment to the land may be
worth. He may *say*, for example, that his attachment to the land
requires the compensation of $10 million, even though the mar-
ket price is $100,000, but of course he may be lying. However,
the government or other outside observer has no scientific way
of finding out one way or another.[9] Furthermore, the existence
in the society of just one militant anarchist, whose psychic griev-
ance against government is such that he cannot be compensated
for his psychic disutility from the existence of government, is
enough by itself to destroy the social-utility and compensation-
principle case for any government action whatever. And surely
at least one such anarchist exists.

Can praxeological economics, then, say nothing about social
utility? Not quite. If we define an "increase in social utility" in the
Paretian manner as a situation where one or more persons gain
in utility while nobody loses, then praxeology finds a definite,
but restricted, role for the concept. But it is a role where social
utilities remain unmeasurable and incomparable between persons. Briefly, praxeology maintains that when a person acts, his
utility, or at least his ex ante utility, increases; he expects to enjoy
a psychic benefit from the act, otherwise he would not have done
it. When, in a voluntary free-market exchange, for example, I
buy a newspaper from a newsdealer for 15 cents, I demonstrate
by my action that I prefer (at least ex ante) the newspaper to the
15 cents, while the newsdealer demonstrates by his action the
reverse order of preference. Since each of us is better off by the
exchange, both the newsdealer and I have demonstrably gained
in utility, while *nothing* has demonstrably happened to anyone
else. Elsewhere I have called this praxeological concept "demonstrated preference," in which action demonstrates preference, in contrast to various forms of psychologizing, which tries

to measure other person's value scales apart from action, and to behaviorism, which assumes that such values or preferences do not exist.[10] The compensation principle that I have been criticizing rests on the illegitimate psychologizing notion that a scientific economist-observer can know *anything* about someone else's value scale except as it is demonstrated through such action as the purchase or sale of a newspaper. And since the compensation principle is necessarily divorced from demonstrated preference, it cannot be employed by the scientific economist. Incidentally, I might note here that "demonstrated preference" is very different from Samuelson's famous concept of "revealed preference," for Samuelson, in illegitimate psychologizing fashion, assumed the existence of an underlying preference scale that forms the basis of a person's action and that remains constant in the course of his actions over time. There is, however, no warrant for the scientific economist to make any such assumption. All we can say is that an action, at a specific point of time, reveals some of a person's preferences *at that time*. There is no warrant for assuming that such preference orderings remain constant over time.[11]

Now since praxeology shows, by the concept of demonstrated preference, that both the newsdealer and I gain in utility from the exchange, and nothing has demonstrably happened to anyone else, we can conclude scientifically, as praxeological economists, that social utility has increased from the sale and purchase of the newspaper—since we have defined social utility in the Paretian manner. It is true, of course, that third parties may well be grinding their teeth in hatred at the exchange. There may be people, for example, who through envy suffer a psychic loss because the newspaper dealer and/or I have gained. Therefore, if we employ the Paretian definition of "social utility" in the usual psychologizing sense, we can say nothing about social utility one way or the other. But if we confine the concept to its strict scientific compass in demonstrated preference, then we can state that social utility increases from the exchange. Still further, we may know as historians, from interpretive understanding of the hearts and minds of envious neighbors, that they do lose in utility. But we are trying to determine in this paper precisely what scientific economists can say about social utility or can advocate for public policy, and since they must confine themselves to demonstrated preference, they must affirm that social utility has increased.

Conversely, since every act of the State involves coercion, at least the coercion of taxation, and since in its every act there is at least one demonstrable loser in utility, we must also conclude that no act whatever of the State can increase social utility. Here, of course, is another good reason why the economic scientist cannot use the concept of "social utility" to establish any sort of unanimity principle or any other case for government action. It has been pointed out that, similarly, we cannot say that any action of the State *decreases* social utility, at least in the short run, and that too is correct.

We must emphasize, however, that the praxeological conclusion that the free market maximizes social utility is not sufficient to enable the praxeological economist to advocate the free market while abstaining from value judgments or from an ethical system. In the first place, why *should* an economist favor increasing social utility? This in itself requires an ethical or value judgment. And, secondly, the social-utility concept has many other failings, including the fact that while the envious and the egalitarian or the admirer of coercion per se may not be included in the social-utility concept, the contemporary historian knows that he is there, lurking in the wings; it therefore requires an ethical judgment, which cannot be supplied by praxeology, to overrule him. Furthermore, many of the strictures against the unanimity principle apply here too; for example, should we really be eager to preserve the utility of the slaveholder against loss? And if so, why?

Let us now turn to the position of Ludwig von Mises on the entire matter of praxeology, value judgments, and the advocacy of public policy. The case of Mises is particularly interesting, not only because he was a leader in the modern Austrian school and in praxeology, but also because he was, of all the economists in the twentieth century, the most uncompromising and passionate adherent of laissez-faire and at the same time the most rigorous and uncompromising advocate of value-free economics and opponent of any sort of objective ethics. How then did he attempt to reconcile these two positions?[12]

Essentially, Mises offered two very different solutions to this problem. The first is a variant of the unanimity principle. Essentially this variant affirms that an economist per se cannot say that a given governmental policy is "good" or "bad." However, if a given policy will lead to consequences, as explained by praxeology, that *every one* of the supporters of the policy will agree is bad, then the value-free economist is justified in calling the policy a "bad" one. Thus, Mises wrote:

An economist investigates whether a measure *a* can bring about the result *p* for the attainment of which it is recommended, and finds that *a* does not result in *p* but in *g*, an effect which even the supporters of the measure *a* consider undesirable. If the economist states the outcome of his investigation by saying that *a* is a bad measure, he does not pronounce a judgment of value. He merely says that from the point of view of those aiming at the goal *p*, the measure *a* is inappropriate.[13]

And again:

Economics does not say that . . . government interference with the prices of only one commodity . . . is unfair, bad, or unfeasible. It says, that it makes conditions worse, not better, *from the point of view of the government and those backing its interference.*[14]

Now this is surely an ingenious attempt to allow pronouncements of "good" or "bad" by the economist without making a value judgment; for the economist is supposed to be only a praxeologist, a technician, pointing out to his readers or listeners that they will all consider a policy "bad" once he reveals its full consequences. But ingenious as it is, the attempt completely fails. For how could Mises *know* what the advocates of the particular policy consider desirable? How could he know what their value scales are now or what they will be when the consequences of the measure appear? One of the great contributions of praxeology, as I have pointed out above, is that the praxeologist, the economist, doesn't know what anyone's value scales are except as those value preferences are demonstrated by a person's concrete action. In the case of my purchase of the newspaper, historians or psychologists may make more or less informed estimates of the newsdealer's or my value scales through the process of interpretive understanding, but all that the economist can know scientifically and with certainty is the preferences relative to 15 cents or the newspaper as demonstrated through concrete action. Mises himself emphasized that

one must not forget that the scale of values or wants manifests itself only in the reality of action. These scales have no independent existence apart from the actual behavior of individuals. The only source from which our knowledge concerning these scales is derived is the observation of a man's actions. Every action is always in perfect agreement with the scale of values or wants because these scales are nothing but an instrument for the interpretation of a man's acting.[15]

Given Mises's own analysis, then, how can the economist know what the motives for advocating various policies really are or how people will regard the consequences of these policies?

Thus, Mises, qua praxeologist, might show that price control (to use his example) will lead to unforeseen shortages of a good to the consumers. But how could Mises know that some advocates of price control do not *want* shortages? They may, for example, be socialists, anxious to use the controls as a step toward full collectivism. Some may be egalitarians who prefer shortages because the rich will not be able to use their money to buy more of the product than poorer people. Some may be nihilists, eager to see shortages of goods. Others may be one of the legion of contemporary intellectuals who are eternally complaining about the excessive affluence of our society or about the great waste of energy; they may all delight in the shortages of goods. Still others may favor price control, even after learning of the shortages, because they or their political allies will enjoy well-paying jobs or power in a price-control bureaucracy. All sorts of such possibilities exist, and *none* of them are compatible with the assertion of Mises, as a value-free economist, that all supporters of price control—or of any other government intervention—must concede, after learning economics, that the measure is "bad." In fact, once Mises conceded that even a single advocate of price control or any other interventionist measure may acknowledge the economic consequences and still favor it, for whatever reason, then, as a praxeologist and economist, he could no longer call any of these measures "bad" or "good" or even "appropriate" or "inappropriate" without inserting into his economic policy pronouncements the very value judgments that he himself held to be inadmissible in a scientist of human action.[16] He would no longer be a technical reporter to all advocates of a certain policy but an advocate participating on one side of a value conflict.

Moreover, there is another fundamental reason for advocates of "inappropriate" policies to refuse to change their minds even after hearing and acknowledging the praxeological chain of consequences. For praxeology may indeed show that all types of government policies will have consequences that most people, at least, will tend to abhor. But, and this is a vital qualification, most of these consequences take *time,* some a great deal of time. No economist has done more than Ludwig von Mises to elucidate the universality of time preference in human affairs—the praxeologic law that everyone prefers to attain a given satisfaction sooner than later. And certainly Mises, as a value-free scientist, could never presume to criticize anyone's rate of time preference, to say that A's was "too high" and B's "too low." But, in that case, what about the high-time-preference people in society who retort to the praxeologist: "Perhaps this high tax and subsidy policy will lead to a decline of capital; perhaps even the price control will lead to shortages, but I don't care. Having a high time preference, I value more highly the short-run subsidies, or the short-run enjoyment of buying the current good at cheaper prices, than the prospect of suffering the future consequences." And Mises, as a value-free scientist and opponent of any concept of objective ethics, *could not* call them wrong. There is no way that he could assert the superiority of the long run over the short run without overriding the values of the high-time-preference people; and that could not be cogently done without abandoning his own subjectivist ethics.

In this connection, one of Mises's basic arguments for the free market is that, on the market, there is a "harmony of the rightly understood interests of all members of the market society." It is clear from his discussion that he could not merely mean "interests" after learning the praxeological consequences of market activity or of government intervention. He also, and in particular, meant people's long-run interests. As he stated, "For 'rightly understood' interests we may as well say interests 'in the long run.'"[17] But what about the high-time-preference folk, who prefer to consult their short- run interests? How can the long run be called "better" than the short run? Why is "right understanding" necessarily the long run?

We see, therefore, that Mises's attempt to advocate laissez-faire while remaining value-free, by assuming that all of the advocates of government intervention will abandon their position once they learn of its consequences, falls completely to the ground. There is another and very different way, however, that Mises attempted to reconcile his passionate advocacy of laissez-faire with the absolute value-freedom of the scientist. This was to take a position much more compatible with praxeology, by recognizing that the economist qua economist can only trace chains of cause and effect and may not engage in value judgments or advocate public policy. In so doing, Mises conceded that the economic scientist cannot advocate laissez-faire but then added that as a *citizen* he can do so. Mises, as a citizen, proposed a value system but it is a curiously scanty one. For he was here caught in a dilemma. As a praxeologist he knew that he could not as an economic scientist pronounce value judgments or advocate policy. Yet he could not bring himself simply to assert and inject arbitrary value judgments. And so, as a utilitarian (for Mises, along with most economists, was indeed a utilitarian in ethics, although a Kantian in epistemology), he made only one narrow value judgment: that he desired to fulfill the goals of the majority of the public (happily, in this formulation, Mises did not presume to know the goals of *everyone*).

As Mises explained in his second variant:

> Liberalism (i.e., *laissez-faire* liberalism) is a political doctrine. . . . As a political doctrine liberalism (in contrast to economic science) is not neutral with regard to values and ultimate ends sought by action. It assumes that all men or at least the majority of people are intent upon attaining certain goals. It gives them information about the means suitable to the realization of their plans. The champions of liberal doctrines are fully aware of the fact that their teachings are valid only for people who are committed to their valuational principles. While praxeology, and therefore economics too, uses the terms happiness and removal of uneasiness in a purely formal sense, liberalism attaches to them a concrete meaning. It presupposes that people prefer life to death, health to sickness . . . abundance to poverty. It teaches men how to act in accordance with these valuations.[18]

In this second variant, Mises successfully escaped the self-contradiction of being a value-free praxeologist advocating laissez-faire. Granting in this variant that the economist may not make such advocacy, he took his stand as a citizen willing to make value judgments. But he was not willing, as Simons was, to simply assert an ad hoc value judgment; presumably he felt that a valuing intellectual must present some sort of system to justify such value judgments. But for Mises the utilitarian, his system is a curiously bloodless one; even as a valuing laissez-faire liberal, he was only willing to make *the one* value judgment that he joined the majority of the people in favoring their common peace, prosperity, and abundance. In this way, as an opponent of objective ethics, and uncomfortable as he must have been with making any value judgments even as a citizen, he made the minimal possible degree of such judgments; true to his utilitarian position his value judgment is the desirability of fulfilling the subjectively desired goals of the bulk of the populace.

A full critique of this position must involve a critique of utilitarian ethics itself, and this cannot be done here. But a few points may be made. In the first place, while praxeology can indeed demonstrate that laissez-faire will lead to harmony, prosperity, and abundance, while government intervention leads to conflict and impoverishment,[19] and while it is probably true that most people value the former highly, it is not true that these are their *only* goals or values. The great analyst of ranked value scales and diminishing marginal utility should have been more aware of such competing values and goals. For example, many people, whether through envy or a misplaced theory of justice, may prefer far more equality of income than will be attained on the free market. Many people, *pace* the aforementioned intellectuals, may want less abundance in order to whittle down our allegedly excessive affluence. Others, as I have mentioned, may prefer to loot the capital of the rich or the businessman in the short run, while acknowledging but dismissing the long-run ill effects, because they have a high time preference. Probably very few of these people will want to push statist measures to the point of total impoverishment and destruction—although this may happen, as in the case of Communist China. But a majority coalition of the foregoing might well opt for *some* reduction in wealth and prosperity on behalf of these other values. They may well decide that it is worth sacrificing a modicum of wealth and efficient production because of the high opportunity cost of not being able to enjoy an alleviation of envy, or a lust for power, or a submission to power, or, for example, the thrill of "national unity," which they might enjoy from a (short-lived) economic crisis.

What could Mises reply to a majority of the public who have indeed considered all the praxeological consequences and still prefer a modicum—or, for that matter, even a drastic amount—of statism in order to achieve some of their competing goals? As a utilitarian, he could not quarrel with the ethical nature of their chosen goals: for he had to confine himself to the *one* value judgment that he favored the majority's achieving their chosen goals. The only reply that Mises could make within his own framework was to point out that government intervention has a cumulative effect, that eventually the economy must move either toward the free market or toward full socialism, which praxeology shows will bring chaos and drastic impoverishment, at least to an industrial society. But this, too, is not a fully satisfactory answer. While many programs of statist intervention—especially price controls—are indeed cumulative, others are not. Furthermore, the cumulative impact takes such a long time that the time preferences of the majority would probably lead them, in full acknowledgment of the consequences, to ignore the effect. And then what?

Mises attempted to use the cumulative argument to answer the contention that the majority of the public prefer egalitarian measures even knowingly at the expense of a portion of their own wealth. Mises's comment was that the "reserve fund" was on the point of being exhausted in Europe, and therefore that any further egalitarian measures would have to come directly out of the pockets of the masses through increased taxation. Mises assumed that once this became clear, the masses would no longer support interventionist measures.[20] In the first place, this is no argument against the *previous* egalitarian measures or in favor of their repeal. But secondly, while the masses *might* be convinced, there is certainly no apodictic certainty involved; the masses have in the past and presumably will in the future continue knowingly to support egalitarian and other statist measures on behalf of others of their goals, despite the knowledge that their income and wealth would be reduced. Thus, as William E. Rappard pointed out in his thoughtful critique of Mises's position:

Does the British voter, for instance, favor confiscatory taxation of large incomes primarily in the hope that it will redound to his material advantage, or in the certainty that it tends to reduce unwelcome and irritating social inequalities? In general, is the urge towards equality in our modern democracies not often stronger than the desire to improve one's material lot?[21]

Rappard also noted that in his own country, Switzerland, the urban industrial and commercial majority of the country have repeatedly, and often at popular referendums, endorsed measures to subsidize the minority of farmers in a deliberate effort to retard industrialization and the growth of their own incomes. The urban majority did not do so in the "absurd belief that they were thereby increasing their real income." Instead, "quite deliberately and expressly, political parties have sacrificed the immediate material welfare of their members in order to prevent, or at least somewhat to retard, the complete industrialization of the country. A more agricultural Switzerland, though poorer, such is the dominant wish of the Swiss people today."[22] The point here is that Mises, not only as a praxeologist but also as a utilitarian liberal, could have no word of criticism against these statist measures *once* the majority of the public take their praxeological consequences into account and choose them anyway on behalf of goals other than wealth and prosperity.

Furthermore, there are other types of statist intervention that clearly have little or no cumulative effect and that may even have very little effect in diminishing production or prosperity. Let us, for example, assume—and this assumption is not very far-fetched in view of the record of human history—that the great majority of a society hate and revile redheads, perhaps, to cite Simons again, because they find redheads "evil or unlovely." Let us further assume that there are very few redheads in the society. This large majority then decide that they would like very much to murder all redheads. Here they are; the murder of redheads is high on the value scales of the great majority of the public; there are few redheads so that there will be little loss in production on the market. How could Mises rebut this proposed policy either as a praxeologist or as a utilitarian liberal? I submit that he could not do so.

Mises made one further attempt to establish his position, but it was even less successful. Criticizing the arguments for state intervention on behalf of equality or other moral concerns, he dismissed them as "emotional talk." After reaffirming that "praxeology and economics . . . are neutral with regard to any moral precepts," and asserting that "the fact that the immense majority of men prefer a richer supply of material goods to a less ample supply is a datum of history; it does not have any place in economic theory," he concluded by insisting that "he who disagrees with the teachings of economics ought to refute them by discursive reasoning, not by . . . the appeal to arbitrary, allegedly ethical standards."[23]

But I submit that this will not do; for Mises would have to concede that no one can decide upon *any* policy whatever unless he makes an ultimate ethical or value judgment. But since this is so, and since according to Mises all ultimate value judgments or ethical standards are arbitrary, how then could he denounce these *particular* ethical judgments as "arbitrary"? Furthermore, it was hardly correct for Mises to dismiss these judgments as "emotional," since for him as a utilitarian, reason cannot establish ultimate ethical principles, which can therefore only be established by subjective emotions. It was pointless for Mises to call for his critics to use "discursive reasoning" since he himself denied that discursive reasoning can be used to establish ultimate ethical values. Furthermore, the man whose ultimate ethical principles would lead him to support the free market could also be dismissed by Mises as equally "arbitrary" and "emotional," even if he takes the laws of praxeology into account before making his ultimately ethical decision. And we have seen above that the majority of the public very often have other goals which they hold, at least to a certain extent, higher than their own material well-being.

The burden of this paper has been to show that, while praxeological economic theory is extremely useful for providing data and knowledge for framing economic policy, it cannot be sufficient by itself to enable the economist to make any value pronouncements or to advocate any public policy whatsoever. More specifically, Ludwig von Mises to the contrary notwithstanding, neither praxeological economics nor Mises's utilitarian liberalism is sufficient to make the case for laissez-faire and the free-market economy. To make such a case, one must go beyond economics and utilitarianism to establish an objective ethics that affirms the overriding value of liberty and morally condemns all forms of statism, from egalitarianism to the murder of redheads, as well as such goals as the lust for power and the satisfaction of envy. To make the full case for liberty, one cannot be a methodological slave to every goal that the majority of the public might happen to cherish.

NOTES

1. Felix Adler, "The Relation of Ethics to Social Science," in *Congress of Arts and Science*, ed. H. J. Rogers (Boston: Houghton Mifflin Co., 1906), 7:678.
2. See the critique of the inconsistency of the championing of intellectual honesty by the great opponent of objective ethics, Max Weber, in Leo Strauss, *Natural Right and History* (Chicago: University of Chicago Press, 1953), pp. 47-48.
3. Henry C. Simons, *Personal Income Taxation* (1938), pp. 18-19, cited by Walter J. Blum and Harry Kalven, Jr., *The Uneasy Case for Progressive Taxation* (Chicago: University of Chicago Press, 1953), p. 72.
4. Murray N. Rothbard, *Egalitarianism as a Revolt against Nature, and Other Essays* (Washington, D. C.: Libertarian Review Press, 1974), pp. 2-3.; also see idem, *Power and Market* (Menlo Park, Calif.: Institute for Humane Studies, 1970), pp. 157-160.
5. John F. Due, *Government Finance* (Homewood, Ill.: Richard D. Irwin, 1954), pp. 128-29.
6. Adler, "Relation of Ethics," p. 673.
7. Murray N. Rothbard, "Value Implications of Economic Theory," *The American Economist* 17(Spring 1973), pp. 38-39.
8. William D. Grampp, *The Manchester School of Economics* (Stanford: Stanford University Press, 1960), p. 59; also see Rothbard, "Value Implications," pp. 36-37.
9. For a further analysis of this question, see Walter Block, "Coase and Demsetz on Private Property Rights: A Comment" (unpublished manuscript, privately distributed).
10. Murray N. Rothbard, "Toward a Reconstruction of Utility and Welfare Economics," in *On Freedom and Free Enterprise: Essays in Honor of Ludwig von Mises*, ed. Mary Sennholz (Princeton: D. Van Nostrand, 1956), pp. 224-32, 243-62.
11. Rothbard, "Toward a Reconstruction," pp. 228-30; also see Ludwig von Mises, *Human Action: A Treatise on Economics* (New Haven: Yale University Press, 1949), pp. 102-4. Samuelson's views may be found, among other places, in Paul A. Samuelson, "The Empirical Implications of Utility Analysis," *Econometrica* 6(October 1938):344-56; and idem, *Foundations of Economics* (Cambridge: Harvard University Press, 1947), pp. 146-63.
12. For a posing of this question, see William E. Rappard, "On Reading von Mises," in *On Freedom and Free Enterprise*, ed. Sennholz, pp. 17-33.
13. Mises, *Human Action*, p. 879.
14. Ibid., p. 758 (Mises's italics).

15. Ibid., p. 95.

16. Mises himself conceded at one point that a government or a political party may advocate policies for "demagogic," i.e., for hidden and unannounced, reasons (ibid., p. 104 n.).

17. Ibid., pp. 670, 670 n.

18. Ibid., pp. 153-54.

19. Rothbard, *Power and Market*, pp. 194-96.

20. Mises, *Human Action*, pp. 851-55.

21. Rappard, "On Reading von Mises," pp. 32-33.

22. Ibid., p. 33.

23. Ludwig von Mises, "Epistemological Relativism in the Sciences of Human Action," in *Relativism and the Study of Man*, ed. Helmut Schoeck and J. W. Wiggins (Princeton: D. Van Nostrand, 1961), p. 133.

PART 3
APPLICATIONS

Equilibrium versus Market Process

Israel M. Kirzner

A characteristic feature of the Austrian approach to economic theory is its emphasis on the market as a *process*, rather than as a configuration of prices, qualities, and quantities that are consistent with each other in that they produce a market *equilibrium* situation.[1] This feature of Austrian economics is closely bound up with dissatisfaction with the general use made of the concept of perfect competition. It is interesting to note that economists of sharply differing persuasions within the Austrian tradition all display a characteristic dissenchantment with the orthodox emphasis on both equilibrium and perfect competition. Thus Joseph A. Schumpeter's well-known position on these matters is remarkably close to that of Ludwig von Mises.[2] Oskar Morgenstern, in a notable paper on contemporary economic theory, expressed these same Austrian criticisms of modern economic theory.[3]

EQUILIBRIUM AND PROCESS

Ludwig M. Lachmann indicated that his own unhappiness with the notion of equilibrium primarily concerns the usefulness of the Walrasian general-equilibrium construction rather than that of the simple Marshallian partial-equilibrium construction.[4] But it is precisely in the context of the simple short-run one-good market that I shall point out some of the shortcomings of the equilibrium approach.

115

In our classrooms we draw the Marshallian cross to depict competitive supply and demand, and then go on to explain how the market is cleared only at the price corresponding to the intersection of the curves. Often the explanation of market price determination proceeds no further — almost implying that the only possible price is the market-clearing price. Sometimes we address the question of how we can be confident that there is any tendency at all for the intersection price to be attained. The discussion is then usually carried on in terms of the Walrasian version of the equilibration process. Suppose, we say, the price happens to be above the intersection level. If so, the amount of the good people are prepared to supply is in the aggregate larger than the total amount people are prepared to buy. There will be unsold inventories, thereby depressing price. On the other hand, if price is below the intersection level, there will be excess demand, "forcing" price up. Thus, we explain, there will be a tendency for price to gravitate toward the equilibrium level at which quantity demanded equals quantity supplied.

Now this explanation has a certain rough-and-ready appeal. However, when price is described as being above or below equilibrium, it is understood that a single price prevails in the market. One uncomfortable question, then, is whether we may assume that a single price emerges before equilibrium is attained. Surely a single price can be postulated only as the result of the process of equilibration itself. At least to this extent, the Walrasian explanation of equilibrium price determination appears to beg the question.

Again, the Walrasian explanation usually assumes perfect competition, where all market participants are price takers. But with only price takers participating, it is not clear how unsold inventories or unmet demand effect price changes. If no one raises or lowers price bids, *how* do prices rise or fall?

The Marshallian explanation of the equilibrating process—not usually introduced into classroom discussion—is similar to the Walrasian but uses quantity rather than price as the principal decision variable.[5] Instead of drawing horizontal price lines on the demand-supply diagram to show excess supply or unmet demand, the Marshallian procedure uses vertical lines to mark off the demand prices and the supply prices for given quantities. With this procedure the ordinate of a point on the demand curve indicates the maximum price at which a quantity (represented by the abscissa of the point) will be sold. If this price is greater than the corresponding supply price (the minimum price at which the same quantity will be offered for sale), larger quantities will be offered for sale. The reverse takes place when supply price exceeds demand price. In this way a tendency toward equilibrium is allegedly demonstrated to exist.

This procedure also assumes too much. It takes for granted that the market already knows when the demand price of the quantity now available exceeds the supply price. But disequilibrium occurs precisely because market participants do not know what the market-clearing price is. In disequilibrium "the" quantity is not generally known nor is the highest (lowest) price at which this quantity can be sold (coaxed from suppliers). Thus it is not clear how the fact that the quantity on the market is less than the equilibrium quantity assures the decisions of market participants to be so modified as to increase it.

Clearly neither of these explanations for the attainment of equilibrium is satisfactory. From the Austrian perspective, which emphasizes the role of knowledge and expectations, these explanations take too much for granted. What is needed is a theory of the market process that takes explicit notice of the way in which systematic changes in the information and expectations upon which market participants act lead them in the direction of the postulated equilibrium "solution." The Austrian point of view does, in fact, help us arrive at such a theory.

ROBBINSIAN ALLOCATION AND MISESIAN ACTION

In developing a viable theory of market process it is helpful to call attention to the much-neglected role of *entrepreneurship*. The neglect of entrepreneurship in modern analysis is a direct consequence of the general preoccupation with final equilibrium positions. In order to understand the distinction between a process-conscious market theory, which makes reference to entrepreneurship, and an equilibrium market theory, which ignores entrepreneurship, it will help to compare the Misesian concept of human action with the Robbinsian concept of economizing, that is, allocative decision making.

It may be recalled that Lord Robbins defined economics as dealing with the allocative aspect of human affairs, that is, with the consequences of the circumstance that men economize by engaging in the allocation of limited resources among multiple competing ends.[6] Mises, on the other hand, emphasized the much broader notion of purposeful human action, embracing the deliberate efforts of men to improve their positions.[7] Both concepts, it should be noticed, are consistent with methodological individualism and embody the insight that market phenomena are generated by the interaction of individual decision makers.[8] But the two constructions do differ significantly.

Robbinsian economizing consists in using *known* available resources in the most efficient manner to achieve given purposes. It entails the implementation of the equimarginal principle, that is, the setting up of an allocative arrangement in which it is impossible to transfer a unit of resource from one use to another and receive a net benefit. For Robbins, economizing simply means shuffling around available resources in order to secure the most efficient utilization of *known* inputs in terms of a *given* hierarchy of ends. It is the interaction in the market of the allocative efforts of numerous economizing individuals that generates all the phenomena that modern economics seeks to explain.

The difficulty with a theory of the market couched in exclusively Robbinsian terms is that in disequilibrium many of the plans of Robbinsian economizers are bound to be unrealized. Disequilibrium is a situation in which not all plans can be carried out together; it reflects mistakes in the price information on which individual plans were made. Market experience by way of shortages and surplus reveals the incorrectness of the original price expectations. Now the Robbinsian framework suggests that the unsuccessful plans will be discarded or revised, but we are unable to say much more than this. The notion of a Robbinsian plan assumes that information is both given and known to the acting individuals. Lacking this information market participants are blocked from Robbinsian activity altogether. Without some clue as to what *new* expectations will follow disappointments in the market, we are unable to postulate any sequence of decisions. All we can say is: if all the Robbinsian decisions dovetail, we have equilibrium; if they do not dovetail, we have disequilibrium. We lack justification within this framework for stating, for example, that unsold inventories will depress price; we may only say that with excessive price expectations Robbinsian decision makers will generate unsold inventories. As decision makers they do not raise or lower price; they are strictly price takers, allocating against a background of given prices. If all participants are price takers, how then can the market price rise or fall? By what process does this happen, if it happens at all?

In order for unsold inventories to depress price, market participants with unsold goods need to realize that the previously prevailing price was too high. Participants must modify their expectations concerning the eagerness of other participants to buy. But in order to make these assertions we must transcend the narrow confines of the Robbinsian framework. We need a concept of decision making wide enough to encompass the element of *entrepreneurship* to account for the way in which market participants *change* their plans. It is here that the Misesian notion of human action comes to our assistance.

Mises's concept of human action embodies an insight about man that is entirely lacking in a world of Robbinsian economizers. This insight recognizes that men are not only calculating agents but are also *alert to opportunities.* Robbinsian theory only applies after a person is confronted with opportunities; for it does not explain how that person learns about opportunities in the first place. Misesian theory of human action conceives of the individual as having his eyes and ears open to opportunities that are "just around the corner." He is alert, waiting, continually receptive to something that may turn up. And when the prevailing price does not clear the market, market participants realize they should revise their estimates of prices bid or asked in order to avoid repeated disappointment. This alertness is the entrepreneurial element in human action, a concept lacking in analysis carried out in exclusively Robbinsian terms. At the same time that it transforms allocative decision making into a realistic view of human action, entrepreneurship converts the theory of market equilibrium into a theory of market process.

THE ROLE OF ENTREPRENEURSHIP

There have, it is true, been other definitions of the entrepreneurial role. The principal views on the question have been those of Schumpeter, Frank H. Knight, and Mises. I have argued, however, that these alternative definitions upon analysis all have in common the element of alertness to opportunities.[9] Alertness should be carefully distinguished from the mere possession of knowledge. And it is the distinction between being alert and possessing knowledge that helps us understand how the entrepreneurial market process systematically detects and helps eliminate error.

A person who possesses knowledge is not by that criterion alone an entrepreneur. Even though an employer hires an expert for his knowledge, it is the employer rather than the employee who is the entrepreneur. The employer may not have all the information the hired expert possesses, yet the employer is better "informed" than anyone else—he knows where knowledge is to be obtained and how it can be usefully employed. The hired expert does not, apparently, see how his knowledge can be usefully employed, since he is not prepared to act as his own employer. The hired expert does not perceive the opportunity presented by the possession of his information. The employer does perceive it. Entrepreneurial knowledge is a rarefied, abstract type of knowledge — the knowledge of where to obtain information (or other resources) and how to deploy it.

This entrepreneurial alertness is crucial to the market process.

Disequilibrium represents a situation of widespread market ignorance. This ignorance is responsible for the emergence of profitable opportunities. Entrepreneurial alertness exploits these opportunities when others pass them by. G. L. S. Shackle and Lachmann emphasized the unpredictability of human knowledge, and indeed we do not clearly understand how entrepreneurs get their flashes of superior foresight. We cannot explain how some men discover what is around the corner before others do. We may certainly explain — on entirely Robbinsian lines — how men explore for oil by carefully weighing alternative ways of spending a limited amount of search resources, but we cannot explain how a prescient entrepreneur realizes before others do that a search for oil may be rewarding. As an empirical matter, however, opportunities do tend to be perceived and exploited. And it is on this observed tendency that our belief in a determinate market process is founded.

ADVERTISING AS AN ASPECT OF THE COMPETITIVE PROCESS

Characterization of the market process as one involving entrepreneurial discovery clarifies a number of ambiguities about the market and dispels several misunderstandings about how it functions. Advertising provides an excellent example on which to base our discussion.

Advertising, a pervasive feature of the market economy, is widely misunderstood and often condemned as wasteful, inefficient, inimical to competition, and generally destructive of consumer sovereignty. In recent years there has been somewhat of a rehabilitation of advertising in economic literature, along the lines of the economics of information. According to this view advertising messages beamed at prospective consumers are quantities of needed knowledge, for which they are prepared to pay a price. The right quantity of information is produced and delivered by the advertising industry in response to consumer desires. For reasons having to do with cost economy, it is most efficient for this information to be produced by those for whom such production is easiest, namely, by the producers of the products about which information is needed. There is much of value in this approach to an understanding of the economics of advertising, but it does not explain everything. The economics-of-information approach tries to account for the phenomena of advertising entirely in terms of the demand for and supply of nonentrepreneurial knowledge, information that can be bought and sold and even packaged. But such an approach does not go beyond a world of Robbinsian maximizers and fails to comprehend the true role of advertising in the market process.

Let us consider the producer of the advertised product. In his entrepreneurial role, the producer anticipates the wishes of consumers and notes the availability of the resources needed for a product to satisfy consumer desires. This function might appear to be fulfilled when the producer produces the product and makes it available for purchase. In other words, it might seem that the entrepreneur's function is fulfilled when he transforms an opportunity to produce a potential product into an opportunity for the consumer to buy the finished product. Consumers themselves were not aware of the opportunities this production process represents; it is the superior alertness of the entrepreneur that has enabled him to fulfill his task. It is not sufficient, however, to make the product available; consumers must be aware of its availability. If the opportunity to buy is not perceived by the consumer, it is as if the opportunity to produce has not been perceived by the entrepreneur. It is not enough to grow food consumers do not know how to obtain; consumers must know that the food has in fact been grown! Providing consumers with information is not enough. It is essential that the opportunities available to the consumer attract his attention, whatever the degree of his alertness may be. Not only must the entrepreneur-producer marshal resources to cater to consumer desires, but also he must insure that the consumer does not miss what has been wrought. For this purpose advertising is clearly an indispensable instrument.

By viewing advertising as an entrepreneurial device, we are

able to understand why Chamberlin's distinction between fabrication costs and selling costs is invalid.[10] Fabrication (or production) costs are supposedly incurred for producing a product, as distinguished from selling costs incurred to get buyers to buy the product. Selling costs allegedly shift the demand curve for the product, while the costs of fabrication (production) affect the supply curve only. The distinction has been criticized on the grounds that most selling costs turn out to be disguised fabrication costs of one type or another.[11] Our perspective permits us to view the issue from a more general framework, which embodies the insight that all fabrication costs are at once selling costs as well. If the producer had a guaranteed market in which he could sell all he wanted of his product at a certain price, then his fabrication costs might be only fabrication costs and include no sum for coaxing consumers to buy it. But there never is a guaranteed market. The producer's decisions about what product to produce and of what quality are invariably a reflection of what he believes he will be able to sell at a worthwhile price. It is invariably an entrepreneurial choice. The costs he incurs are those that in his estimation he must, in order to sell what he produces, at the anticipated price. Every improvement in the product is introduced to make it more attractive to consumers, and certainly the product itself is produced for precisely the same reasons. All costs are in the last analysis selling costs.

PROFITS AND THE COMPETITIVE PROCESS

The Austrian concept of the entrepreneurial role emphasizes profit as being the prime objective of the market process. As such it has important implications for the analysis of entrepreneurship in nonmarket contexts (such as within firms or under socialism or in bureaucracies in general). I have already remarked that we do not know precisely how entrepreneurs experience superior foresight, but we do know, at least in a general way, that entrepreneurial alertness is stimulated by the lure of profits. Alertness to an opportunity rests on the attractiveness of that opportunity and on its ability to be grasped once it has been perceived. This incentive is different from the incentives present in a Robbinsian world. In the nonentrepreneurial context, the incentive is constituted by the satisfactions obtainable at the expense of the relevant sacrifices. Robbinsian incentives are communicated to others by simply arranging that the satisfactions offered to them are more significant (from their point of view) than the sacrifices demanded from them. Incentive is thereby provided by the comparison of known alternatives. In the entrepreneurial context, however, the incentive to be alert to a future opportunity is quite different from the incentive to trade off already known opportunities; in fact it has nothing to do with the comparison of alternatives. No prior choice is involved in perceiving an opportunity waiting to be noticed. The incentive is to try to get something for nothing, if only one can see what it is that can be done.

Robbinsian incentives can be offered in nonmarket contexts. The bureaucrat, employer, or official offers a bonus for greater effort. For entrepreneurial incentives to operate, on the other hand, it is necessary for those who perceive opportunities to gain from noticing them. An outstanding feature of the market system is that it provides these kinds of incentives. Only by analysis of the market process does this very important entrepreneurial aspect of the market economy come into view. The real economic problems in any society arise from the phenomenon of unperceived opportunities. The manner in which a market society grapples with this phenomenon cannot be understood within an exclusively equilibrium theory of the market. The Austrian approach to the theory of the market therefore holds considerable promise. Much work still needs to be done. It would be good to know more about the institutional settings that are most conducive to opportunity discovery. It would be good to apply basic Austrian theory to the theory of speculation and of the formation of expectations with regard to future prices. All this would enrich our understanding of the economics of bureaucracy and of socialism. It can be convincingly argued that Mises's famous proposition concerning economic calculation under socialism flows naturally from his "Austrianism." Here, too, there is room for further elucidation. In all this agenda, the Austrian emphasis on process analysis should stand up very well.

NOTES

1. For an elaboration of a number of issues raised in this paper, see Israel M. Kirzner, *Competition and Entrepreneurship* (Chicago: University of Chicago Press, 1973).

2. Joseph A. Schumpeter, *Capitalism, Socialism, and Democracy* (New York: Harper & Row, 1942), pp. 81-106.

3. Oscar Morgenstern, "Thirteen Critical Points in Contemporary Economic Theory: An Interpretation," *Journal of Economic Literature* 10(December 1972):1163-89.

4. Ludwig M. Lachmann, "Methodological Individualism and the Market Economy," in *Roads to Freedom: Essays in Honour of Friedrich A. von Hayek*, ed. Erich Streissler et al. (London: Routledge & Kegan Paul, 1969), p. 89.

5. Alfred Marshall, *Principles of Economics*, ed. C. W. Guillebaud, 2 vols. (London: Macmillan & Co., 1961), 1:345-48; Marshall sometimes used the Walrasian approach (ibid., pp. 333-36).

6. Lionel Robbins, *An Essay on the Nature and Significance of Economic Science* (London: Macmillan & Co., 1962), pp. 1-23.

7. Ludwig von Mises, *Human Action: A Treatise on Economics* (New Haven: Yale University Press, 1949), pp. 11-142; on the comparison of Misesian and Robbinsian notions, see Israel M. Kirzner, *The Economic Point of View* (Princeton: D. Van Nostrand, 1960), pp. 108-85.

8. In the preface to the first edition of his book, Robbins acknowledged his debt to Mises (*On the Nature*, pp. xv-xvi).

9. Kirzner, *Competition*, pp. 75-87.

10. Edward Hastings Chamberlin, *The Theory of Monopolistic Competition*, 7th ed. (Cambridge: Harvard University Press, 1962), pp. 123-29.

11. See the literature cited in Kirzner, *Competition*, pp. 141-69.

On the Central Concept of Austrian Economics: Market Process

Ludwig M. Lachmann

In setting up the market process as the central concept of Austrian economics, as opposed to the general-equilibrium approach of the neoclassical school, Austrian economists have a choice of strategies: They might, on the one hand, attempt to show the absurdity of the notion of general equilibrium, the arid formalism of the style of thought that gave rise to it, and its "irrelevance" to many urgent problems. They might, without denying the significance of equilibrating forces, stress the time aspect and show that the equilibrating forces can never do their work in time, that long before general equilibrium is established some change will supervene to render the data obsolete. They would, however, face the objection that the notion of market process requires equilibrating forces to make it work, an objection that, because it is a half-truth, might be hard to refute without drawing a distinction between "equilibrium of the individual" and "equilibrium of the economic system."

In my view, however, Austrian economists should present their case for the market process by offering a fairly comprehensive account of the human forces governing it rather than by engaging in piecemeal discussions of its various interconnected aspects, which must, in the absence of the total picture, remain obscure. The defects of the neoclassical style become obvious if the Austrian economists simply point to facts the neoclassical conceptual tools are unable to explain.

126

What keeps the market process in perpetual motion? Why does it never end, denoting the final state of equilibrium of our system? If Austrian economists answered by saying, "Something unexpected always happens," they would be accused of vagueness and reminded that only perpetual "changes in data" could have this effect. An attempt to show that continuous autonomous changes in demand or supply do account for the permanent character of the market process would involve a drawn-out discussion of the effects of ever-changing patterns of knowledge on the conduct of consumers and producers, a discussion in which Austrian economists would be at a serious disadvantage without prior elucidation of the term *knowledge*.

The market process is the outward manifestation of an unending stream of knowledge. This insight is fundamental to Austrian economics. The pattern of knowledge is continuously changing in society, a process hard to describe. Knowledge defies all attempts to treat it as a "datum" or an object identifiable in time and space.

Knowledge may be acquired at a cost, but is not always, as when we witness an accident or "learn by doing" for other than cognitive reasons. Sometimes, knowledge is jealously and expensively guarded; sometimes, it may be broadcast to reach a maximum number of listeners, as in advertising. Now knowledge, whether costly or free, may prove valuable to one and useless to another, owing to the complementarity of new and old knowledge and the diversity of human interests. Hence it is impossible to gauge the range of application of some bit of knowledge until it is obsolete. But we can never be certain that knowledge is obsolete since the future is unknown. All useful knowledge probably tends to be diffused, but in being applied for various purposes it also may change character, hence the difficulty of *identifying* it.

Knowledge then is an elusive concept wholly refractory to neoclassical methods. It cannot be quantified, has no location in space, and defies insertion into any complex of functional relationships. Though it varies in time, it is no variable, either dependent or independent. *As soon as we permit time to elapse, we must permit knowledge to change, and knowledge cannot be regarded as a function of anything else.* The state of knowledge of a society cannot be the same at two successive points of time, and time cannot elapse without demand and supply shifting. The stream of knowledge produces ever new disequilibrium situations, and entrepreneurs continually manage to find new price-cost differences to exploit. When one is eliminated by strenuous competition, the stream of knowledge throws up another. Profit is a permanent income from ever-changing sources.

Certain consequences of what has been said seem to concern the modus operandi of the market, but one appears to be significant for the methodology of all social sciences.

In the first place, how do we determine the true origin of any particular bit of knowledge? When and how do ill-founded surmises and half-baked ideas acquire the status of respectable knowledge? We can neither answer nor ignore these questions. Two things we may assert with reasonable confidence. As Karl Popper showed, we cannot have future knowledge in the present.[1] Also, men sometimes act on the basis of what cannot really be called knowledge. Here we encounter the problem of expectations.

Although old knowledge is continually being superseded by new knowledge, though nobody knows which piece will be obsolete tomorrow, men have to act with regard to the future and make plans based on expectations. Experience teaches us that in an uncertain world different men hold different expectations about the same future event. This fact has certain implications for growth theory — in my view important implications — with which I deal in my paper "Toward a Critique of Macroeconomics" (included in this volume). Here we are concerned with the fact that divergent expectations entail incoherent plans. At another place I argued that "what keeps this process in continuous motion is the occurrence of unexpected change as well as the inconsistency of human plans. Both are necessary conditions."[2] Are we entitled, then, to be confident that the market process will in the end eliminate incoherence of plans which would thus prove to be only transient? What is being asked here is a fairly fundamental question about the nature of the market process.

The subject of expectations, a subjective element in human action, is eminently "Austrian." Expectations must be regarded as autonomous, as autonomous as human preferences are. To be sure, they are modified by experience, but we are unable to postulate any particular mode of change. To say that the market gradually produces a consistency among plans is to say that the divergence of expectations, on which the initial incoherence of plans rests, will gradually be turned into convergence. But to reach this conclusion we must deny the autonomous character of expectations. We have to make the (diminishing) degree of divergence of expectations a function of the time sequence of the stages of the market process. If the stream of knowledge is not a function of anything, how can the degree of divergence of expectations, which are but rudimentary forms of incomplete knowledge, be made a function of time?

Unsuccessful plans have to be revised. No doubt planners learn from experience. But what they learn is not known; also different men learn different lessons. We might say that unsuccessful planners make capital losses and thus gradually lose their control over resources and their ability to engage in new enterprises; the successful are able to plan with more confidence and on a much larger scale. Mises used such an argument. But how can we be sure? History shows many examples of men who were "ahead of their times," whose expectations were vindicated when it was too late, who had to give up the struggle for lack of resources when a few more would have brought them triumph instead of defeat. There is no reason why a man who fails three times should not succeed the fourth. Expectations are autonomous. We cannot predict their mode of change as prompted by failure or success.

What we have here is a difference of opinion on the nature of the market process. For one view the market process is propelled by a mechanism of given and known forces of demand and supply. The outcome of the interaction of these forces, namely, equilibrium, is in principle predictable. But outside forces in the form of autonomous changes in demand and supply continually impinge on the system and prevent equilibrium from being reached. The system is ever moving in the direction of *an* equilibrium, but it never gets there. The competitive action of entrepreneurs tending to wipe out price-cost differences is regarded as "equilibrating"; for in equilibrium no such differences could exist.

The other view, which I happen to hold, regards the distinction between external forces and the internal market mechanism as essentially misleading. Successive stages in the flow of knowledge must be manifest in both. Market action is not independent of expectations, and every expectation is an attempt "to catch a glimpse of future knowledge now." To say that each market moves toward a price that "clears" it has little meaning where speculators are busy piling up and unloading stocks. The relationship between different markets in disequilibrium is infinitely complex. I shall say nothing more about it here, though I deal with some aspects of this complex problem in "Toward a Critique of Macroeconomics" (included in this volume).

Having set out to replace the paradigm of general equilibrium by that of the market process, why should we concentrate on the equilibrating nature of the latter — on showing that but for the perennial impact of external forces general equilibrium would be reached after all? It might be held, however, that every process must have a *direction*, and unless we are able to show that every stage of the market process "points" in the direction of equilibrium, no satisfactory theory of the market process is possible.

But this is not a convincing view. In the first place, though a process may have a direction at each point of time, it may change direction over time. The direction the process follows need not be the same throughout. Second and more important, two kinds of process have to be distinguished here. The first is a limited process, in the course of which we witness the successive modes of interaction of a set of forces, given initially and limited in number. Such a process may terminate or go on forever; whatever happens depends entirely on the nature of the (given) set of forces. The system may be subjected to random shocks from external sources, which it may take some time to absorb, such absorption interfering with the interaction of the forces. The second variety of process is the very opposite of the first. No initial set of forces delimits the boundaries of events. Any force from anywhere may at any time affect our process, and forces that impinged on it yesterday may suddenly vanish from the scene. There is no end or final point of rest in sight. Need I assert that history is a process of the second, not of the first, variety?

While our market process is not of the first kind, it is not completely unlimited. Two things may be said about it. The notion of general equilibrium is to be abandoned, but that of *individual equilibrium* is to be retained at all costs. It is simply tantamount to *rational action*. Without it we should lose our "sense of direction." The market process consists of a sequence of individual interactions, each denoting the encounter (and sometimes collision) of a number of plans, which, while coherent individually and reflecting the individual equilibrium of the actor, are incoherent as a group. The process would not go on otherwise.

Walrasians, in using the same notion of equilibrium on the three levels of analysis — the individual, the market, and the entire system — succumbed to the fallacy of unwarranted generalization: they erroneously believed that the key that unlocks one door will also unlock a number of others. Action controlled by one mind is, as Mises showed, necessarily consistent. The actions of a number of minds in the same market lack such consistency, as the simultaneous presence of bulls and bears shows. Consistency of actions in a number of markets within a system constitutes an even greater presumption.

Finally, the divergence of expectations, apart from being an obstacle to equilibrium, has an important positive function in a market economy. *It is an anticipatory device.* The more extended the range of expectations, the greater the likelihood that somebody will catch a glimpse of things to come and be "right." Those who take their orientation from the future rather than the present, the "speculators," permit the future to make its impact on the market process earlier than otherwise. They contrive to inject a glimpse of future knowledge into the emergent market pattern. Of course they may make mistakes for which they will pay. Without divergent expectations and incoherent plans, however, it could not happen at all.

NOTES

1.   Karl R. Popper, *The Poverty of Historicism* (London: Routledge & Kegan Paul, 1957).
2.   Ludwig M. Lachmann, "Methodological Individualism and the Market Economy," in *Roads to Freedom: Essays in Honour of Friedrich A. von Hayek,* ed. Erich Streissler et al. (London: Routledge & Kegan Paul, 1969), p.91.

The Theory of Capital

Israel M. Kirzner

It is not my purpose here to offer a concise Austrian theory of capital. Rather I shall present an Austrian perspective on several concepts fundamental to modern capital theory. I shall show how this perspective enables us to fit certain characteristically Austrian ideas about capital into the more comprehensive Austrian view of the way in which the market system operates. To clarify what constitutes the uniquely Austrian way of thinking about capital, I shall begin with a critical interpretation of a 1974 paper by Sir John Hicks. My use of Hicks's work as a springboard also helps to explain why Hicks considered his book on capital theory to be "neo-Austrian" in character.[1]

HICKS, MATERIALISTS, AND FUNDISTS

Hicks grouped the numerous views on capital that have been expounded throughout the history of economic thought under two broad headings.[2] By means of this classification Hicks called attention to the two basic ways economists conceptualize the notion of a stock of capital goods existing in the economy at a given moment in time. One is to see the stock as a collection of physical goods; by this approach aggregation into a stock provides us with a measure of the "volume of capital." An important implication of this view is that "as between two economies which have capital stocks that are physically identical [the] Volume of Capital must be the same."[3] Those who share this view of the aggregate stock of capital, Hicks called "materialists." The alternative view conceives of the aggregate stock of capital goods, not

133

as a volume of physical capital, but as a "sum of values which may conveniently be described as a Fund" — something evidently quite different from the physical goods themselves — with the values derived from the expected future output flows. Those holding this view, Hicks called "fundists."[4]

This fundist-materialist dichotomy is an elaboration (and partial revision) of a comment that Hicks made in the 1963 edition of his *Theory of Wages*.[5] In that discussion Hicks identified "the two basic ways in which economists have regarded the capital stock of an economy" as involving, first, a "physical concept," which treats capital "as consisting of actual capital goods," and, second, a "fund concept," which reduces capital to the "consumption goods that are foregone to get it."[6] These are the same two concepts Hicks identified in his 1974 paper, except that there he preferred an interpretation of the fund view in terms of future outputs rather than in terms of opportunity cost.

FUNDISTS: A TERMINOLOGICAL PUZZLE

Now Hicks's use of the label *fund* to identify that notion of capital *not* viewed as physical goods is puzzling and could cause much confusion about the meaning of his discussion. Hicks declared that he "of course" borrowed the term *fund* from the history of economic thought; it is here that the confusion begins. The notion of capital as a fund is well known in the history of capital theory. It was carefully developed by John Bates Clark[7] and repeatedly expounded by Frank H. Knight.[8] Those who objected most vigorously to this view of capital were Eugen von Böhm-Bawerk in the first decade of the century and Friedrich A. Hayek in the fourth decade. Böhm-Bawerk declared that Clark's concept of capital was mystical, and he insisted that to measure a stock of capital in value units in no way implies that what is being measured is an abstract quantity apart from the physical goods themselves.[9] Hayek, in his debate with Knight, argued against the notion of capital as a fund of value, that is, a quantity apart from the particular goods making up the capital stock.[10] Thus

Hicks's list of fundists must include Clark and Knight, and Böhm-Bawerk and Hayek must be on his list of materialists (certainly not on the list of fundists).

However, this was not the way Hicks classified these economists. J. B. Clark was "clearly" a materialist, and Hayek "of course, was a fundist."[11] Also, Böhm-Bawerk "kept the fundist flag flying!"[12] A basic familiarity with the history of capital theory leaves one puzzled, if not startled, by Hicks's choice of terminology. Let us look more closely at how he employs his definitions.

HICKSIAN FUNDISM

To Hicks, the term *fund* apparently denotes a concept entirely different from that Clark and Knight had in mind when they used it. Knight's capital-as-a-fund notion refers to a special way of viewing capital goods — as the temporary embodiment of a permanent store, or "fund," of value. Hicks's declaration that the Austrians are fundists has to do with their treatment of capital goods as essentially forward-looking components of multiperiod plans.[13] The Clark-Knight view of capital as something other than the capital goods themselves is quite different from Hicks's fundists' view. Hicks himself — now a "neo-Austrian" — is on the side of his brand of fundists — the forward-looking kind. Without denying the propriety of a materialist, or backward-looking, perspective on capital, Hicks endorsed a "sophisticated" fundism in which the forward-looking character of capital goods is repeatedly emphasized. This made it easier for Hicks to recognize the importance of expectations in capital theory—a characteristically Austrian point of view.

Hicks apparently was inspired in his novel use of the term *fund* by Böhm-Bawerk's notion of a subsistence fund.[14] Despite my criticism of Hicks's usage of the term *fund*, I must agree that Böhm-Bawerk did set a precedent for using it in this way. Moreover, by insisting that the notion of a subsistence fund is characteristic of Böhm-Bawerk's approach, Hicks preserved what we must consider to be the essentially pure Austrian element in Böhm-Bawerk's theory. Some effort has been made in recent work to ignore the forward-looking, multiperiod-planning aspect of Böhm-Bawerk's theory. The productivity side of his system has been emphasized, and the time-preference aspect has been either suppressed altogether or treated as an inessential encumbrance.[15] However, as Hicks recognized, the notion of a subsistence fund is an essential element of Böhm-Bawerk's thinking about capital. This notion embodies the insight that, in choosing between processes of production of different durations, men appraise the prospective sacrifices these processes call for in terms of abstaining from more immediate consumption. Crucial to such appraisals is the size of the available capital stock, because it influences the prospective disutility associated with each of the alternatively required periods of waiting. Not only is this notion of a subsistence fund central to Böhm-Bawerk's theory of capital, but it also is — in spite of his disconcerting concessions to the productivity-interest theorists[16] — the essentially "Austrian" element in his thought. In the subsistence-fund concept is encapsulated Böhm-Bawerk's concern for forward-looking, multiperiod human decision making; here the influence of subjective comparative evaluation of alternative future streams of income makes itself felt; and here there is room for a discussion of expectations and uncertainty. Hicks recognized all this when he identified the Austrians as fundists. Not only does the notion of the subsistence fund qualify Böhm-Bawerk as a Hicksian fundist, but it also, as Hicks implied, epitomizes what is "Austrian" in Böhm-Bawerk's theory. I heartily agree with all this. At the same time, to emphasize the differences between the fund notion as used by Hicks and as usually associated with Clark and Knight, we may recall Hayek's powerful criticisms of the subsistence-fund idea.[17] Hayek's extreme opposition to the Clark-Knight notion of a fund led him to point out some difficulties in Böhm-Bawerk's original presentation of the subsistence-fund idea. While we can understand why Hicks labeled Böhm-Bawerk a fundist, we must still decide whether

Hicks was correct in naming Hayek and modern-day Austrians fundists as well.

AUSTRIANS, MATERIALISTS, AND FUNDISTS

Where indeed does modern Austrianism stand in relation to the Hicksian materialist-fundist dichotomy? I contend that — whatever validity Hicks's view of the Austrians has in terms of the older Austrian writers — Austrianism today does not at all fit this classification. Austrian economists occupy a position that is neither fundist nor materialist; they dismiss the basic question to which the fundists and materialists have traditionally addressed themselves as being unhelpful and completely irrevelant.

Austrians reject the fundist-materialist dichotomy because of their special understanding of the role individual plans play in the market process. A capital good is *not* merely a produced factor of production. Rather it is a good produced as part of a multiperiod plan in which it has been assigned a specific function in a projected process of production. A capital good is thus a physical good with an assigned productive purpose. To treat the stock of capital goods as a Hicksian materialist would is out of the question, for as Hicks recognized, this approach ignores the future streams of output that these capital goods are designed to help produce. But to treat the stock of capital goods as a Hicksian fundist might is also unacceptable, for it submerges the individualities of the various capital goods into a stock and replaces them with the sum of values supposed to represent the aggregate expected future value of the output imputed to these goods. To treat the stock of capital goods this way ignores the problem of the degree of consistency that prevails among the purposes assigned to each of the goods composing the capital stock. It also ignores questions of complementarity among goods, as well as the possibility that the productive purpose assigned by one producer to a particular capital good is unrealizable in the light of the plans of other producers or potential users of other capital goods. But all this is precisely what, to an Austrian economist, cannot be ignored.

In somewhat different terms, the Hicksian materialist-fundist classification is objectionable not so much for these alternative formulations as for the incompatibility of the task they attempt to carry out with the Austrian approach. That task is to arrive at a single value aggregate to represent the *size* of the stock of capital goods in an economy. It is this very attempt to collapse the multidimensional collection of capital goods into a single number that Austrian economists find unacceptable. If one wishes to talk about the total stock of all capital goods in an economy at a particular moment in time, one must not overlook the roles assigned to the various goods by individuals; in other words, one must treat the stock as consisting at all times of essentially heterogeneous items that defy aggregation. They defy aggregation not only because of physical heterogeneity but also, more important, because of the diversity of the purposes to which these goods have been assigned. Mises emphatically dismissed the very notion of an aggregate of physical capital goods as empty and useless. The "totality of the produced factors of production," Mises wrote, "is merely an enumeration of physical quantities of thousands and thousands of various goods. Such an inventory is of no use to acting. It is a description of a part of the universe in terms of technology and topography and has no reference whatever to the problems raised by the endeavors to improve human well-being."[18]

ON MEASURING CAPITAL: THE INDIVIDUAL

Other economists as well as the Austrians see the serious theoretical difficulties that face all attempts to measure real capital. It seems useful to review briefly where these difficulties lie, both in the attempt to measure a single individual's stock of capital goods and the attempt to measure society's stock of capital goods.[19]

Consider a list of all the physical items that make up a single individual's stock of capital goods. Their physical heterogeneity prohibits "adding them up" — there is no natural unit of measurement. Instead one may try to devise an index number that will permit the heterogeneous items to be treated as one dimensional. But if the measure thus obtained is to be interpreted as representing the quantity of physical goods in the stock, the attempt hardly seems worthwhile. Not only is the advantage in replacing a list by a number unclear, but such a replacement obviously hides an important aspect of economic reality. A man's future plans depend not only on the aggregate size of his capital stock but also very crucially upon the particular properties of the various goods making up the stock. Goods that can be used in a complementary relationship permit certain plans that a purely physical measure necessarily suppresses.

Instead of seeking to measure the quantity of physical goods as physical goods, one may seek to measure one's capital stock in terms of the amount of past sacrifice undertaken to achieve the present stock. This would be a backward-looking measure. For such a measure, the heterogeneity of the goods making up the capital stock would present no difficulty. While one may question the usefulness of measuring past sacrifice, it is at least a task that does not lack meaning. On the other hand, measuring the size of the capital stock in terms of past sacrifice raises heterogeneity problems of a different kind. Past sacrifices are unlikely to have been homogeneous in character. And even if market values, say, are employed to express past sacrifices, there remains a very special "heterogeneity" difficulty arising from the circumstance that past sacrifices were undertaken at different dates in the past. These difficulties must necessarily render the search for a backward-looking measure unsuccessful.

A far more popular alternative is to measure the size of stocks of capital goods in terms of expected contribution to future streams of output. Attempts to arrive at so-called forward-looking measures of capital are, of course, the essence of Hicksian fundism. It is misleading to talk of a particular resource as being unambiguously associated with a definite stream of forthcoming output, in the sense that such an output stream flows automatically from the resource itself. Decisions must be made as to how a resource is to be deployed before one can talk of its future contribution to output. Because there are alternative uses for a resource and alternative clusters of complementary inputs with which a resource may be used, it is confusing to see a resource as representing a definite future output flow before the necessary decisions on its behalf have been made.

Nonetheless, recognizing all these difficulties, it cannot be denied, in the last analysis, that forward-looking measures of the size of capital stocks are being made all the time. Individuals do measure the potential contributions of particular capital goods to future output. They do so whenever these goods are bought and sold, and whenever owners of such goods refrain from selling them at going market prices. What cannot be "objectively" measured by the outsider turns out to be evaluated subjectively by the relevant decision maker.

MEASURING CAPITAL: THE ECONOMY

The difficulties involved in measuring the size of an individual's stock of capital goods become exaggerated when it is the size of an entire nations's stock of capital goods that one is measuring. The theoretical difficulties involved in aggregating physical items present formidable obstacles to thoroughgoing, "aggregative," Hicksian materialism. As Hicks correctly pointed out, Austrian economists have little sympathy with such an approach. But measuring the size of the capital stock in economic rather than in physical terms is hardly more promising. We may dismiss backward-looking measures as having failed, even at the individual level. Forward-looking measures of an individual's capital stock are impossible to achieve in an objective way but are being made all the time in the private dealings of individual agents. In considering forward-looking measures of a nation's stock of capital goods — that is, Hicks's fundism in the 1973 version — the possibility of subjective evaluation loses virtually all meaning (except in a sense to be discussed in the subsequent section); the problems that prevent objective measurement at the level of the individual are intensely reinforced by additional problems. One difficulty is relating a given item (in the inventory of the social stock of capital goods) to its prospective output before the preliminary decisions, necessary for the identification of that output, have been made; another is that the prospective output associated with a capital good owned by Jones may be inconsistent with a capital good owned by Smith. A forward-looking measure of Jones's capital stock and also of Smith's must presume plans on the part of Jones and of Smith, but Jones's plan and Smith's plan may be, in whole or in part, mutually exclusive. Perhaps Jones expects rain and builds a factory to produce umbrellas, whereas Smith expects fine weather and builds a factory to produce tennis racquets. That one of the two has overestimated the possible output of his factory (and thus will, in the future, be seen to have incorrectly measured the size of his capital stock) is not significant. What is significant is that it is already *now* meaningless to add a valuation of Jones's factory to a valuation of Smith's factory when each valuation depends on the expectation of one that the expectation of the other will prove erroneous. We are, therefore, forced as Austrian economists to decline Hicks's invitation to join the fundist club. To view the aggregate capital stock as a fund requires us in the end to give up our concern with individual plans upon which forward-looking measures ultimately depend for their very meaning! By refusing to surrender our Austrian interest in individual plans, however, we face another difficulty.

ON THE NOTION OF THE QUANTITY OF CAPITAL PER HEAD

We have seen that attempts to measure the quantity of capital goods in an economy must fail on theoretical grounds. Yet it is virtually impossible to avoid making statements in which such measurement is implied. In the writing of Mises, for example, we find frequent reference to the consequences of the fact that one country possesses a greater quantity of capital (or a greater quantity of capital per worker) than a second country.[20] Such statements imply the possibility that aggregate capital measurement has a rough meaningfulness. Yet how do we reconcile our theoretical rejection of aggregative capital measurement with a willingness to make statements of this kind?

The answer to this difficulty lies in the possibility, mentioned above, of subjective evaluation by an *individual* of the aggregate worth of his own stock of capital goods. Individual forward-looking measurement is both possible and feasible, because the problem of possibly inconsistent plans does not arise. An individual evaluates each component of his capital stock in terms of the plans he has in mind; *he* may have to take care to avoid possible inconsistencies, but in appraising his measurement of his capital we may assume that he *has* successfully integrated his own plans. What cannot, except in the state of general equilibrium, be assumed for an economy as a whole is assumed as a matter of course for the individual.

Underlying statements that compare the quantity of capital in one country with that in another is a convenient and relatively harmless fiction. One imagines that one has complete control over all the items in a nation's capital stock — that one is, in effect, the economic czar of a socialist economy. One is then in exactly the same position in relation to the nation's stock of capital as an individual is in relation to his own stock. By the use of this fiction, problems of inconsistent plans have been simply imagined away.

In sidestepping in this way the theoretical difficulties that frustrate attempts to arrive at aggregate measures of capital, we have, it may be argued, endorsed Hicksian fundism after all. But this is by no means the case. In the context of a market economy the fiction that all inconsistencies among plans may be ignored is, for most purposes, highly hazardous and misleading. Although there are instances in which needed reference to the aggregate quantity of capital can be supported in the way described, to use this fiction to construct a general treatment of aggregated capital is entirely unacceptable to Austrian economists. It is the market process that has the property of discovering inconsistencies among plans and of offering incentives for their elimination. To introduce capital into the analysis of the market process in a way that assumes that plan inconsistencies do not exist is to espouse decidedly non-Austrian assumptions and to become enmeshed in those insoluble contradictions characterizing orthodox microeconomic theory, the escape from which provides the strongest case for a return (or an advance) to the Austrian position.

NOTES

1. John R. Hicks, *Capital and Time: A Neo-Austrian Theory* (Oxford: Clarendon Press, 1973).

2. John R. Hicks, "Capital Controversies: Ancient and Modern," *American Economic Review* 64(May 1974):307-16.

3. Ibid., p. 308.

4. Ibid., p. 309.

5. John R. Hicks, *The Theory of Wages*, 2d ed. (London: Macmillan & Co., 1963), pp. 342-48.

6. Ibid.

7. John Bates Clark, *The Distribution of Wealth* (1899; reprint ed., New York: Kelley & Millman, Inc., 1956), p. 117; Friedrich A. Hayek, *The Pure Theory of Capital* (London: Routledge & Kegan Paul, 1941), p. 93; George J. Stigler, *Production and Distribution Theories: The Formative Period* (New York: Macmillan Co., 1941), pp. 308-10.

8. See Frank H. Knight, "Capital, Time, and the Interest Rate," *Economica* 1(August 1934):259; idem, "The Theory of Investment Once More: Mr. Boulding and the Austrians," *Quarterly Journal of Economics* 50 (November 1935):57; and idem, "The Ricardian Theory of Production and Distribution," in *On the History and Method of Economics*, ed. Frank H. Knight (Chicago: University of Chicago Press, 1956), p. 47; see also Hayek, *Pure Theory*, pp. 93-94.

9. Eugen von Böhm-Bawerk, *Positive Theory of Capital*, vol. 2, *Capital and Interest*, trans. George D. Huncke and Hans F. Sennholz (South Holland, Ill.: Libertarian Press, 1959), pp. 60-66, 282; see also Israel M. Kirzner, *An Essay on Capital* (New York: Augustus M. Kelley, 1966), p. 123.

10. See particularly Friedrich A. Hayek, "The Mythology of Capital," *Quarterly Journal of Economics* 50(February 1936): 199-228.

144 *The Foundations of Modern Austrian Economics*

11. Hicks, "Capital Controversies," p. 309.
12. Ibid., p. 315.
13. This refers to the 1973 rather than the 1963 classification that Hicks presented.
14. Hicks, *Theory of Wages*, p. 343.
15. See, for example, Robert Dorfman, "A Graphical Exposition of Böhm-Bawerk's Interest Theory," *Review of Economic Studies* 26(February 1959):153-58; Kirzner, *Essay on Capital*, pp. 84-86.
16. See Frank A. Fetter's remarks in "The 'Roundabout Process' in the Interest Theory," *Quarterly Journal of Economics* 17(November 1902):177.
17. Hayek, "Mythology," pp. 204-10; idem, *Pure Theory*, pp. 93, 146-53, 189-92.
18. Ludwig von Mises, *Human Action: A Treatise on Economics* (New Haven: Yale University Press, 1949), p. 264; for Mises's views on capital and interest, see Israel M. Kirzner, "Ludwig von Mises and the Theory of Capital and Interest," in *The Economics of Ludwig von Mises: Toward a Critical Reappraisal*, ed. Laurence S. Moss (Kansas City: Sheed & Ward, 1976).
19. See Kirzner, *Essay on Capital*, pp. 103-41.
20. Mises, *Human Action*, pp. 495-99, 611.

On Austrian Capital Theory

Ludwig M. Lachmann

To most economists today the words *Austrian capital theory* denote work in the line of succession of Eugen von Böhm-Bawerk. Sir John Hicks noted that the tradition originated before the last quarter of the nineteenth century and can even be traced to the Renaissance, yet described his book *Capital and Time* as *A Neo-Austrian Theory* inasmuch as it deals with production processes that take time to complete.[1] How many know that Carl Menger regarded Böhm-Bawerk's theory as "one of the greatest errors ever committed"?[2]

I wish to argue, however, that Böhm-Bawerk's model, being essentially macroeconomic, does not provide an adequate basis for a capital theory that could properly be called Austrian. Work in constructing such a theory must start at the foundation, and this means at the level of individual action. Böhm-Bawerk never meant to be a capital theorist. He was essentially a Ricardian who asked a Ricardian question: "Why are the owners of impermanent resources able to enjoy a permanent income and what determines its magnitude?" The notion of a temporal capital structure consisting of a sequence of stages of production was a mere by-product of an inquiry into the causes and the magnitude of the rate of return on capital and not the main subject. In pursuit of this Ricardian inquiry Böhm-Bawerk battled on and failed like a Ricardian. In his model there are one factor of production, labor, and one final consumption good. Ricardo failed when trying to apply conclusions holding in a simple corn economy to a multicommodity world, in which the real wage rate depends on the workers' expenditure pattern and relative prices of wage goods (hence on choice!). Böhm-Bawerk's argument foundered on the same rock.

With a number of consumption goods, we need a price system which must be invariant to changes in the rate of interest that accompany the accumulation of capital. But such a price system cannot exist. Moreover, with the subsistence fund consisting of a number of goods, some of the capital invested will be malinvested if the composition of the fund does not correspond to the workers' expenditure pattern. In the absence of perfect foresight on the part of the capital owners, some malinvestment is inevitable, and some of the capital accumulated vanishes from the scene.

There are other reasons for abandoning Böhm-Bawerk's theory. As Samuelson pointed out[3] and Hicks noted,[4] the possibility of "reswitching" affects the "average length of the period of production" just as much as the "quantity of capital." Moreover, to reduce the whole complex of relationships among capital resources—within firms as well as between firms in different industries and stages of processing, often with relations of complementarity in time but just as often not—to the single dimension of time is a bold idea (originating with Ricardo), but not a very good one. From an Austrian point of view, too much violence is done to the diversity of the world.

I suggest that we reverse the Ricardian approach to the problem of capital and make the capital structure the primary object of study by starting at the ground level, that is, at the microlevel where production plans are made and carried out.

On the other hand, can the rate of return on capital, Ricardo's and Böhm-Bawerk's primary object, have any place in a market economy if, in an Austrian mood, the variety of goods and services and its corollary, the heterogeneity of capital, are recognized? This rate of return is of central concern to the neoclassical theorists, from Irving Fisher to Robert Solow, and constitutes the main issue of controversy. For the neoclassical economist it is a dependant variable of the general-equilibrium system. To the contrary, the neo-Ricardians hold that it has to be determined outside this system since there can be no quantity of capital and hence no marginal product of it. In my view this controversy about a fictitious macroeconomic magnitude is a symptom of the arid macroeconomic formalism that afflicts both schools. For in a market economy a uniform rate of return on all capital invested does not exist.

If we follow Menger instead of Böhm-Bawerk, a distinction may be made between the rate of interest on loans and the rate of profit on capital invested. The former does exist, that is, there is a structure of interest rates determined daily in the loan market as its equilibrium price. The latter does not.[5] There is also in a market economy a uniform rate of (dividend and earnings) yield on capital assets that the market assigns to the same class. But this uniform rate of yield has nothing to do with either Ricardo's rate of profits or Fisher's rate of return over cost. It reflects all capital gains and losses made since the inception of the company in question. It is precisely the diversity of such gains and losses recorded on the stock of different companies that permits the market to make the present rate of yield on all assets uniform. This Mengerian criticism of Böhm-Bawerk is confirmed by Hicks, the leading neoclassical thinker, who, having proclaimed the "'Austrian' affiliation of my ideas" and paid a tribute to Böhm-Bawerk,[6] nevertheless concluded on the last page of his book that "only in the steady state can we unambiguously determine the size of profits. Out of the steady state the profit that is allocated to a particular period depends on expectations . . . there is no such convention that is unambiguously right."[7] But the "steady state," like all equilibria, is a fiction, and the real Austrian view has been Hicks's final view all the time!

Our main task is to lay the foundation for a theory of the capital structure. Our capital theory, unlike Böhm-Bawerk's, is not devised to serve as a basis for an interest theory. Its purpose is to make the shape, order, and coherence of the capital structure intelligible in terms of human action.

Starting with the facts of the heterogeneity of capital and following its logic, we find in every firm a capital combination—a combination of land, buildings, equipment, machines, and stocks of various goods. There are constraints on the possible modes of complementarity of these resources, some of them technological, some the results of the market situation. Relevant here are both the market for the products of the firm and those for labor and materials. Within these boundaries the manager-entrepreneur chooses a mode for the use of the capital under his control to maximize his profits. And since his decision involves the future as well as the present, he bases his plan on his expectations.

Since his capital combination could produce a number of different output streams of various composition, he has to choose among them. But his capital combination is not immutable; he can reshuffle it, discarding some capital goods and buying others. Entrepreneurial action with regard to capital, then, requires continuous "alertness" to change and a willingness to make frequent changes, the switching "on" or "off" of various output streams as well as the reshuffling of capital combinations. The firm and its resources are immersed in the stream of knowledge. Technical progress in the form of "learning by doing" probably takes place within the firm's walls. But new knowledge usually reaches it by way of the markets for its products, factor services and alternative capital goods that might be added to, or used as substitutes in, the existing capital combinations.

A comparison may be made between the just described heterogeneity of capital and that in other models. Neoclassical writers like Samuelson and Solow apparently admit the heterogeneity of capital as a matter of fact and in principle, but eschew the consequences, whenever a problem germane to it arises, by means of such devices as the surrogate production function or the assumption of a one-commodity world. Neo-Ricardian criticism emphasizes the need for a price system invariant to interest changes but can carry the matter no farther since the dynamics of the market process is beyond its reach.

In commodity markets prices are fixed directly and incomes indirectly. Each firm with its capital combination is always in disequilibrium and by its action in this state contributes to the continuous reshaping of the capital structure.

The individuality of each firm rests on the varying interpretations it places on the ceaseless stream of knowledge, different
segments in the minds of different manager-entrepreneurs
finding expression in the specific composition of their capital
combinations. In time, output streams are switched on and off,
and the composition of capital combinations is modified. New
investment is but a by-product of the regrouping of existing
capital resources. Hence the futility of all attempts to "measure"
capital.

In dealing with the capital structure of society and its complex
relationships with the capital combinations of the firms, we
should be aware of the prototypical relationship it reflects between an aggregate and its particles, between the macrostruc·
ture and its microelements. If we criticize the inadequacy of
macromodels, we should be able to show that we can do better.
We must be able to deal with them without losing sight of their
microbasis.

The capital structure of society is an aggregate of capital
combinations, but only in a state of general equilibrium can the
capital goods belonging to different firms be regarded as addi-
tive, when they stand to each other in a relationship of complementarity. It is, however, a type of complementarity different
from that governing capital goods within the same capital combination. We have to distinguish between the planned complementarity of the latter, the result of entrepreneurial choice
and decision, and the unplanned complementarity of capital
resources at various stages of production, which is an outcome of
the operation of the market process

The capital structure of society is never completely integrated.
The competitive nature of the market process entails incoherence of plans and limits the coherence of the resulting order. A
tendency toward the integration of the structure does exist.
Capital goods that do not fit into any existing comoination are
useless to their owners, are "not really capital," and will soon be
scrapped. "Holes" in the existing complementarity pattern, on
the other hand, must cause price-cost differences and thus call
for their elimination. But expectations of early change in the

present situation may impede the process of adjustment, and even when this does not happen, the forces of adjustment themselves may be overtaken by other forces.

One result of the recent discussion on "reswitching" is to the advantage of the Austrian school. As long as all capital is regarded as homogeneous, managers may respond to a marginal fall in the rate of interest by a marginal act of substitution of capital for labor. But heterogeneity of capital entails a regrouping of the existing capital combination; some capital goods may have to be discarded, others acquired. It is no longer a marginal adjustment that is called for but entrepreneurial choice and decision. As Pasinetti pointed out, "Two techniques may well be as near as one likes on the scale of variation of the rate of profit and yet the physical capital goods they require may be completely different."[8]

In a world of disequilibrium, entrepreneurs continually have to regroup their capital combinations in response to changes of all kinds, present and expected, on the cost side as well as on the market side. A change in the mode of income distribution is merely one special case of a very large class of cases to which the entrepreneur has to give constant attention. No matter whether switching or reswitching is to be undertaken, or any other response to market change, expectations play a part, and the individuality of each firm finds its expression in its own way. Yet only "reswitching" has of late attracted the interest of theoreticians. There is more in the world of capital and markets than is dreamt of in their philosophy.

NOTES

1. John Hicks, *Capital and Time; A Neo-Austrian Theory* (Oxford: Clarendon Press, 1973), p. 12.
2. Joseph A. Schumpeter, *A History of Economic Analysis* (New York: Oxford University Press, 1954), p. 847.

3.   Paul A. Samuelson, "A Summing Up," *Quarterly Journal of Economics* 80(November 1966):568-83.

4.   Hicks, *Capital and Time,* p. 45.

5.   Carl Menger, "Zur Theorie des Kapitals," in *The Collected Works of Carl Menger,* ed. Friedrich A. Hayek, 4 vols.(London: London School of Economics, 1936)3:135-83.

6.   Hicks, *Capital and Time,* p. 12.

7.   Ibid., p. 184.

8.   L. L. Pasinetti, "Switches of Technique and the 'Rate of Return,'" *Economic Journal* 79(September 1969):523.

Toward a Critique
of Macroeconomics

Ludwig M. Lachmann

In reconstructing Austrian economics, I have recommended the concept of market process as the foundation of all economic life (see my paper "On the Central Concept," included in this volume). In other words, we must start at the microlevel. How, then, shall we deal with such aggregates as income, consumption, and wages, which, according to the same terminology, must be regarded as macroeconomic magnitudes?

In my paper "On Austrian Capital Theory" (also included in this volume) I said that we may regard the relationship between the capital structure of society and its capital combinations as the prototype of the relationship between a macroeconomic magnitude and its microelements. In other words, the former must never be brought into an argument without giving a careful account of the latter; for changes in the constellation of the microelements will affect the macromagnitude itself.

However, in modern macroeconomic literature, whether neoclassical or neo-Ricardian, there is little awareness of this fundamental postulate. From the moment of inception, the macroeconomic aggregates in these writings seem to lead a life of their own, to be endowed with qualities sufficient to allow their adjustment to change in their environment, but change within them is ignored.

Among the macroeconomic aggregates, we have to distinguish between stocks and flows. While it is generally agreed that the former cannot in a world of uncertainty be measured, the reasons given are not satisfactory. Why, then, cannot capital be measured?

In stationary equilibrium capital *can* be measured; for here, but only here, the discounted present value of the highest income stream obtainable from a given capital resource must be exactly equal to its cost of reproduction if the same interest rate is used for both calculations. Otherwise there would be investment or disinvestment, neither of which is compatible with a stationary state.

Outside the equilibrium of the stationary state, replacement cost and present value of a discounted future income stream will diverge. If we regard the latter as the economically significant value—and few economists doubt that (bygones are bygones)—we still have no yardstick by which to measure the assets of different firms. The neo-Ricardians stress the role of the interest rate as a discount factor; every time it changes, so does capital value. True as this may be, the real reason for our inability to measure capital lies in the subjective nature of expectations concerning future income streams. If we tried to measure capital by asking each owner for his valuation of his capital stock (for example, fire insurance value), we would get a set of consistent answers, but every change in ownership would invalidate at least one answer. Such an attempt to extract measurable objective value from subjective valuation must fail. This does not mean, however, that in a more limited context and for more limited purposes similar attempts may not be more sucessful.

The second part of the argument is that, while stocks cannot be measured, flows can. All of modern macroeconomics—the theories about investment, income, exports, and wages, as well as the social accounting systems that are widely regarded as one of its triumphs—rests on the assumption that output and income streams can be measured. Can they? As we shall see, the main support for this assumption is superficial as well as highly misleading.

Here we have one of the most intricate problems of measurement we encounter in a multicommodity world. In a classical corn economy all stocks and flows have their physical measures, but in a multicommodity world gallons of brandy and of whiskey, surgical instruments and musical instruments cannot be added up. Like David Ricardo and Eugen von Böhm-Bawerk, we need a price system invariant to the very effects of the variations of the variables we wish to measure. Can such a system exist?

The market prices on which national income measurement is ostensibly based are presumably equilibrium prices. But what kind of equilibrium prices are they? Is consistent aggregation, which macroeconomic thought requires to make sense, possible on the basis of prices that may not be consistent? Walrasian-Paretian long-run equilibrium does provide a consistent price system, but the market prices at which output flows are evaluated in the national income statistics are no such long-run equilibrium prices. They are market-day-equilibrium prices at best. There is no reason why they should be consistent with each other. The whole argument for using average market prices over a year as a basis for the valuation of output flows appears to rest on a confusion between long-run, short-run, and market-day equilibrium. Only prices belonging to the first category are elements of a coherent price system and might be used for the purpose of consistent aggregation. All the others are not. An average of market-day-equilibrium prices over a long period is not the same thing as a Walrasian long-run equilibrium price. Yet the computation of the macroeconomic aggregates that are released daily by the media and are so prominent in the products of the textbook industry rests on such elementary confusion.

Even if such a coherent long-run equilibrium price system did exist and could be known, it would not last. Its data would not remain the same for long. The steady flow of knowledge will tomorrow produce a pattern of knowledge different from today's, and apparent changes in demand and supply will entail a new set of equilibrium prices. Not without reason are we compelled to look for a paradigm to replace the general-equilibrium model.

In a market economy, on the other hand, we have in the stock exchange a center for the consistent daily evaluation of all the more important capital combinations. This, to be sure, is not objective measurement. The measurement of capital is forever beyond our reach. But it is something more than mere subjective evaluation. Stock exchange prices of capital assets reflect a balance of expectations. There are two classes of traders in the market, and in an asset market the *fundamentum divisionis* is the optimism or pessimism of expectations. Hence, market prices of securities (and the capital assets they represent) have social significance, we might say a "social objectivity," which transcends the mere subjective expectations of buyers and sellers on which they are based. The objects of valuation are not individual capital goods but fractions of capital combinations that are the substrate of multiperiod plans. It is expectations about the success of multiperiod plans that bulls and bears are continuously expressing.

Stock exchange equilibrium is market-day equilibrium. Tomorrow's set of equilibrium prices will be different from today's. But as we are dealing with an exchange economy, not a production economy, the fact of change does not impair the consistency and significance of market valuation. Free access to all parts of the market, together with the speed at which brokers carry out their clients' instructions, makes it possible to be at once a buyer of one kind of security and a seller of another. Arbitrage does the rest to produce a valuation of all company-owned assets that is consistent in that it reflects a balance of expectations between bulls and bears. The fact that tomorrow's balance will be different from today's faithfully reflects the flow of knowledge.

The difference between the commodity market and the securities market is instructive. Today's potato price may not be consistent with today's prices for other vegetables. If so, equilibrating forces that require time will come into operation. But today's market equilibrium price may also be inconsistent with the long-run supply and demand for potatoes. The equilibrating forces released by the second disparity may impede or reinforce those released by the first. Certainly they require a different time dimension to be fully deployed. And the longer the time required by any force, the greater the probability that it will be affected by unexpected change. To opt for the market process against general equilibrium means to accept the implication that a fully coherent price system providing a basis for consistent aggregation can never exist.

We find here another reason why steady growth—uniform motion of that supermacroaggregate, the economic system—has to be regarded as absurd. Equilibrating forces in different markets, even if none is affected by unexpected change, require different time periods to do their work. This is obvious if we contrast agricultural produce markets with those for industrial goods. Steady growth, however, requires all equilibrating forces to operate within the same time period.

But the main argument against steady growth is a necessary consequence of the divergence of expectations. Equilibrium in a production economy requires an equilibrium composition of the capital stock.[1] With at least some capital goods durable and specific, can we conceive of such a state? A growing economy is a changing economy. It exists in an uncertain world in which men have to formulate expectations on which to base their plans. Different men will characteristically have different expectations about the same future event, and they cannot all be right. Some expectations will be disappointed, and the plans based upon them will have to be revised. The capital invested will turn out to have been malinvested. But the existence of malinvested capital is incompatible with the equilibrium composition of the capital stock. Hence steady growth is impossible. "Macroequilibrium in motion" is not an acceptable paradigm and has to be replaced by the market process.

As has been noted, the stock exchange, a fundamental institution of the market economy, imparts an element of social objectivity to individual stock valuations. This is by no means its only, or even its only significant, function. It facilitates the take-over bid by means of which capital resources get into the hands of those who can promise their owners a higher return. Without a stock exchange such bids would of course still be possible. Shareholders could be notified that, if their capital resources were used in a different way (by producing a different output stream), better results could be obtained. But in the absence of market prices shareholders would be without a yardstick to measure the advantage offered them. For the optimal use of existing resources in a socialist economy, an elaborate bureaucratic organization would be needed to shift resources from points of lower to points of higher usefulness.

Perhaps the most important economic function of the stock exchange is the redistribution of wealth by means of the capital gains and losses it engenders in accordance with the market view about the probable success or failure of present multiperiod plans. In certain neoclassical writings the present distribution of resources is a datum of the set of equilibrium prices and quantities at each point of time. Over time, however, the mode of distribution of wealth changes as reflected in capital gains and losses. In fact, the present mode of distribution of wealth is nothing less than the cumulative result of the capital gains and losses of the past. Devotees of a redistribution of wealth in the name of social justice should be aware that, even if the state by the use of coercion were able to produce a supposedly socially desirable mode of distribution today, the market, if permitted to exist, via capital gains and losses would produce a different mode tomorrow.

I have tried to show that—in contrast to an opinion apparently widely held—flows in a multicommodity world are all too often inconsistent aggregates, whereas stocks, while unmeasurable in an uncertain world, may in favorable circumstances be subjected to consistent evaluation. The former is particularly true of the Keynesian I=S, current investment, the "net addition to the capital stock." If the stock is unmeasurable, how can we tell what is an addition to it? Gross investment is in principle measurable and would be in practice if we had a consistent price system for capital goods. But to divide this flow into net investment and replacement, we need an objective criterion.

Individual decisions by capital owners on such division may be consistent in the sense that the decisions of individual owners do not conflict, but not in the sense that the word *measurement* implies, that is, that different individuals measuring the same object get identical results. Each owner's judgment of his investment expenditure for maintenance and replacement of his existing wealth on the one hand and for a "net addition" on the other rests on a subjective expectation about the future, as nobody explained more forcefully than Keynes in his unjustly neglected "Appendix on User Cost."[2] It follows that a macroeconomic magnitude investment as an objectively measurable, that is, consistently ascertainable, entity does not exist. What does exist is an aggregate of subjective valuations dependent on owners' expectations and the distribution of ownership. An important part of what appears as investment in the official reports of government and business rests on subjective estimates of those who compile the statistics or of those who release the returns.

This imperfection in macroeconomics, like many others in an imperfect world, could be regarded as inherent in any application of abstract theory to a concrete situation. This defense, however, is not valid. We have to distinguish between defects due to the unsatisfactory nature of our material, that is, the state of our statistical sources, and defects due to muddled thinking. A cure for the former is no cure for the latter. Piero Sraffa on a famous occasion made this point with vigor and clarity. His position has been summarized as follows:

Mr. Sraffa thought one should emphasize the distinction between two types of measurement. First, there was the one in which the statisticians were mainly interested. Second, there was measurement in theory. The statisticians' measures were only approximate and provided a suitable field for work in solving index number problems. The theoretical measures required absolute precision. Any imperfections in these theoretical measures were not merely upsetting, but knocked down the whole theoretical basis. ...*Mr. Sraffa* took the view that if one could not get the measures required by the theorists' definitions, this was a criticism of theory, which the theorists could not escape by saying that they hoped their theories would not often fail. If a theory failed to explain a situation, it was unsatisfactory.[3]

NOTES

1. "An equilibrium path, let us remember, is a path that will (and can) be followed if expectations are appropriate to it, and if the initial capital stock is appropriate to it; both conditions are necessary" (John Hicks, *Capital and Growth* [Oxford: Oxford University Press, 1965], p. 116).

2. John Maynard Keynes, *The General Theory of Employment, Interest, and Money* (New York: Harcourt, Brace & World, 1936), pp. 66-73.

3. Douglas C. Hague, "Summary Record of the Debate," in *The Theory of Capital*, ed. F. A. Lutz and D. C. Hague (London: Macmillan & Co., 1961), pp. 305-6.

The Austrian
Theory of Money

Murray N. Rothbard

The Austrian theory of money virtually begins and ends with
Ludwig von Mises's monumental *Theory of Money and Credit*,
published in 1912.[1] Mises's fundamental accomplishment was to
take the theory of marginal utility, built up by Austrian
economists and other marginalists as the explanation for consumer demand and market price, and apply it to the demand for
and the value, or the price, of money. No longer did the theory
of money need to be separated from the general economic
theory of individual action and utility, of supply, demand, and
price; no longer did monetary theory have to suffer isolation in a
context of "velocities of circulation," "price levels," and "equations of exchange."

In applying the analysis of supply and demand to money,
Mises used the Wicksteedian concept: supply is the total stock of
a commodity at any given time; and demand is the total market
demand to gain and hold cash balances, built up out of the
marginal-utility rankings of units of money on the value scales of
individuals on the market. The Wicksteedian concept is particularly appropriate to money for several reasons: first, because the
supply of money is either extremely durable in relation to current production, as under the gold standard, or is determined
exogenously to the market by government authority; and, second and most important, because money, uniquely among
commodities desired and demanded on the market, is acquired
not to be consumed, but to be held for later exchange. Demand-
to-hold thereby becomes the appropriate concept for analyzing

160

the uniquely broad monetary function of being held as stock for later sale. Mises was also able to explain the demand for cash balances as the resultant of marginal utilities on value scales that are strictly ordinal for each individual. In the course of his analysis Mises built on the insight of his fellow Austrian Franz Cuhel to develop a marginal utility that was strictly ordinal, lexicographic, and purged of all traces of the error of assuming the measurability of utilities.

The relative utilities of money units as against other goods determine each person's demand for cash balances, that is, how much of his income or wealth he will keep in cash balance as against how much he will spend. Applying the law of diminishing (ordinal) marginal utility to money and bearing in mind that money's "use" is to be held for future exchange, Mises arrived implicitly at a falling demand curve for money in relation to the purchasing power of the currency unit. The purchasing power of the money unit, which Mises also termed the "objective exchange-value" of money, was then determined, as in the usual supply-and-demand analysis, by the intersection of the money stock and the demand for cash balance schedule. We can see this visually by putting the purchasing power of the money unit on the y-axis and the quantity of money on the x-axis of the conventional two-dimensional diagram corresponding to the price of any good and its quantity. Mises wrapped up the analysis by pointing out that the total supply of money at any given time is no more or less than the sum of the individual cash balances at that time. No money in a society remains unowned by someone and is therefore outside some individual's cash balance.

While, for purposes of convenience, Mises's analysis may be expressed in the usual supply-and-demand diagram with the purchasing power of the money unit serving as the price of money, relying solely on such a simplified diagram falsifies the theory. For, as Mises pointed out in a brilliant analysis whose lessons have still not been absorbed in the mainstream of economic theory, the purchasing power of the money unit is not simply the inverse of the so-called price level of goods and services. In describing the advantages of money as a general medium of exchange and how such a general medium arose on the market, Mises pointed out that the currency unit serves as unit of account and as a common denominator of all other prices, but that the money commodity itself is still in a state of barter with all other goods and services. Thus, in the premoney state of barter, there is no unitary "price of eggs"; a unit of eggs (say, one dozen) will have many different "prices": the "butter" price in terms of pounds of butter, the "hat" price in terms of hats, the "horse" price in terms of horses, and so on. Every good and service will have an almost infinite array of prices in terms of every other good and service. After one commodity, say gold, is chosen to be the medium for all exchanges, every other good except gold will enjoy a unitary price, so that we know that the price of eggs is one dollar a dozen; the price of a hat is ten dollars, and so on. But while every good and service except gold now has a single price in terms of money, money itself has a virtually infinite array of individual prices in terms of every other good and service. To put it another way, the price of any good is the same thing as its purchasing power in terms of other goods and services. Under barter, if the price of a dozen eggs is two pounds of butter, the purchasing power of a dozen eggs is, inter alia, two pounds of butter. The purchasing power of a dozen eggs will also be one-tenth of a hat, and so on. Conversely, the purchasing power of butter is its price in terms of eggs; in this case the purchasing power of a pound of butter is a half dozen eggs. After the arrival of money, the purchasing power of a dozen eggs is the same as its money price, in our example, one dollar. The purchasing power of a pound of butter will be fifty cents, of a hat ten dollars, and so forth.

What, then, is the purchasing power, or the price, of a dollar? It will be a vast array of all the goods and services that can be purchased for a dollar, that is, of all the goods and services in the economy. In our example, we would say that the purchasing power of a dollar equals one dozen eggs, or two pounds of butter, or one-tenth of a hat, and so on, for the entire economy. In short, the price, or purchasing power, of the money unit will be an array of the quantities of alternative goods and services that can be purchased for a dollar. Since the array is heterogeneous and specific, it cannot be summed up in some unitary price-level figure.

The fallacy of the price-level concept is further shown by Mises's analysis of precisely how prices rise (that is, the purchasing power of money falls) in response to an increase in the quantity of money (assuming, of course, that the individual demand schedules for cash balances or, more generally, individual value scales remain constant). In contrast to the hermetic neoclassical separation of money and price levels from the relative prices of individual goods and services, Mises showed that an increased supply of money impinges differently upon different spheres of the market and thereby ineluctably changes relative prices.

Suppose, for example, that the supply of money increases by 20 percent. The result will not be, as neoclassical economics assumes, a simple across-the-board increase of 20 percent in all prices. Let us assume the most favorable case — what we might call the Angel Gabriel model, that the Angel Gabriel descends and overnight increases everyone's cash balance by precisely 20 percent. Now all prices will not simply rise by 20 percent; for each individual has a different value scale, a different ordinal ranking of utilities, including the relative marginal utilities of dollars and of all the other goods on his value scale. As each person's stock of dollars increases, his purchases of goods and services will change in accordance with their new position on his value scale in relation to dollars. The structure of demand will therefore change, as will relative prices and relative incomes in production. The composition of the array constituting the purchasing power of the dollar will change.

If relative demands and prices change in the Angel Gabriel model, they will change much more in the course of real-world increases in the supply of money. For, as Mises showed, in the real world an inflation of money is alluring to the inflators precisely because the injection of new money does not follow the Angel Gabriel model. Instead, the government or the banks create new money to be spent on specific goods and services. The demand for these goods thereby rises, raising these specific prices. Gradually, the new money ripples through the economy, raising demand and prices as it goes. Income and wealth are redistributed to those who receive the new money early in the process, at the expense of those who receive the new money late in the day and of those on fixed incomes who receive no new money at all. Two types of shifts in relative prices occur as the result of this increase in money: (1) the redistribution from late receivers to early receivers that occurs during the inflation process and (2) the permanent shifts in wealth and income that continue even after the effects of the increase in the money supply have worked themselves out. For the new equilibrium will reflect a changed pattern of wealth, income, and demand resulting from the changes during the intervening inflationary process. For example, the fixed income groups permanently lose in relative wealth and income.[2]

If the concept of a unitary price level is a fallacious one, still more fallacious is any attempt to measure changes in that level. To use our previous example, suppose that at one point in time the dollar can buy one dozen eggs, or one-tenth of a hat, or two pounds of butter. If, for the sake of simplicity, we restrict the available goods and services to just these three, we are describing the purchasing power of the dollar at that time. But suppose that, at the next point in time, perhaps because of an increase in the supply of dollars, prices rise, so that butter costs one dollar a pound, a hat twelve dollars, and eggs three dollars a dozen. Prices rise but not uniformly, and all that we can now say quantitatively about the purchasing power of the dollar is that it is four eggs, or one-twelfth of a hat, or one pound of butter. It is impermissible to try to group the changes in the purchasing power of the dollar into a single average index number. Any such index conjures up some sort of totality of goods whose relative prices remain unchanged, so that a general averaging can arrive at a measure of changes in the purchasing power of money itself. But we have seen that relative prices cannot remain unchanged, much less the valuations that individuals place upon these goods and services.[3]

Just as the price of any good tends to be uniform, so the price, or purchasing power of money as Mises demonstrated, will tend to be uniform throughout its trading area. The purchasing power of the dollar will tend to be uniform throughout the United States. Similarly, in the era of the gold standard, the purchasing power of a unit of gold tended to be uniform throughout those areas where gold was in use. Critics who point to persistent tendencies for differences in the price of money between one location and another fail to understand the Austrian concept of what a good or a service actually is. A good is not defined by its technological properties but by its homogeneity in relation to the demands and wishes of the consumers. It is easy to explain, for example, why the price of wheat in Kansas will not be the same as the price of wheat in New York. From the point of view of the consumer in New York, the wheat, while technologically identical in the two places, is in reality two different commodities: one being "wheat in Kansas" and the other "wheat in New York." Wheat in New York, being closer to his use, is a more valuable commodity than wheat in Kansas and will have a higher price on the market. Similarly, the fact that a technologically similar apartment will not have the same rental price in New York City as in rural Ohio does not mean that the price of the same apartment commodity differs persistently; for the apartment in New York enjoys a more valuable and more desirable location and hence will be more highly priced on the market. The "apartment in New York" is a different and more valuable good than the "apartment in rural Ohio," since the respective locations are part and parcel of the good itself. At all times, a homogeneous good must be defined in terms of its usefulness to the consumer rather than by its technological properties.

To extend the analysis, the fact that the cost of living may be persistently higher in New York than in rural Ohio does not negate the tendency for a uniform purchasing power of the dollar throughout the country. For the two locations constitute a different set of goods and services, New York providing a vastly wider range of goods and services to the consumer. The higher costs of living in New York are the reflection of the greater locational advantages, of the more abundant range of goods and services available.[4]

In his valuable history of the theory of international prices, C. Y. Wu emphasized the Mises contribution and pointed out that Mises's explanation was in the tradition of Ricardo and Nassau Senior, who "was the first economist to give a clear explanation of the meaning of the classical doctrine that the value of money was everywhere the same and to demonstrate that differences in the prices of goods of similar composition in different places were perfectly reconcilable with the assumption of an equality of the value of money."[5] Pointing out that Mises arrived at this concept independently of Senior, Wu then developed Mises's application to the alleged locational differences in the cost of living. As Wu stated, "To him [Mises] those who believe in national differences in the value of money have left out of account the positional factor in the nature of economic goods; otherwise they should have understood that the alleged differences are explicable by differences in the quality of the commodities offered and demanded." Wu concluded with a quote from Mises's *Theory of Money and Credit:* "The exchange-ratio between commodities and money is everywhere the same. But men and their wants are not everywhere the same, and neither are commodities."[6]

If the tendency of the purchasing power of money is to be everywhere the same, what happens if one or more moneys coexist in the world? By way of explanation, Mises developed the Ricardian analysis into what was to be called the purchasing-power-parity theory of exchange rates, namely, that the market exchange rate between two independent moneys will tend to equal the ratio of their purchasing powers. Mises showed that this analysis applies both to the exchange rate between gold and silver — whether or not the two circulate side by side within the same country — and to independent fiat currencies issued by two nations. Wu explained the difference between Mises's theory and the unfortunately better known version of the purchasing-power-parity theory set forth a bit later by Gustav Cassel. The Cassel version ignores the Austrian emphasis on locational differences in accounting for differences in value of technologically similar goods, and this in turn complements the broader Austrian and classical position that the purchasing power of money is an array of specific goods. This contrasts with Cassel and the neoclassicists, who think of the purchasing power money as the inverse of a unitary price level. Thus Wu stated:

> The purchasing power parity theory is that the rate of exchange would be in equilibrium when the "purchasing power of the moneys" is equal in all trading countries. If the term *purchasing power* refers to the power of purchasing commodities, which are not only similar in technological composition, but also in the *same* geographical situation, the theory becomes the classical doctrine of comparative values of moneys in different countries and is a sound doctrine. But unfortunately the term purchasing power in connection with the theory sometimes implies the reciprocal of the general price level in a country. While so interpreted the theory becomes that the equilibrium point for the foreign exchanges is to be found at the quotient between the price levels of the different countries. That is . . . an erroneous version of the purchasing power parity theory.[7]

Unfortunately, Cassel, instead of correcting the error in his concept of purchasing power, soon abandoned the full-parity doctrine in favor of a different and highly attenuated contention that only changes in exchange rates reflect changes in respective purchasing power — perhaps because of his desire to use measurement and index numbers in applying the theory.[8]

When he set out to apply the theory of marginal utility to the price of money, Mises confronted the problem that was later to be called "the Austrian circle." In short, when someone ranks eggs or beef or shoes on his value scale, he values these goods for their direct use in consumption. Such valuations are, of course, independent of and prior to pricing on the market. But people demand money to hold in their cash balances, not for eventual direct use in consumption, but precisely in order to exchange those balances for other goods that will be used directly. Thus, money is not useful in itself but because it has a prior exchange value, because it has been and therefore presumably will be exchangeable in terms of other goods. In short, money is demanded because it has a preexisting purchasing power; its demand not only is not independent of its existing price on the market but is precisely due to its already having a price in terms of other goods and services. But if the demand for, and hence the utility of, money depends on its preexisting price or purchasing power, how then can that price be explained by the demand? It seems that any Austrian attempt to apply marginal utility theory to money is inextricably caught in a circular trap. For that reason mainstream economics has not been able to apply marginal utility theory to the value of money and has therefore gone off in multicausal (or *non*causal) Walrasian directions.

Mises, however, succeeded in solving this problem in 1912 in developing his so-called regression theorem. Briefly, Mises held that the demand for money, or cash balances, at the present time — say day X — rests on the fact that money on the previous day, day X-1, had a purchasing power. The purchasing power of money on day X is determined by the interaction on day X of the supply of money on that day and that day's demand for cash balances, which in turn is determined by the marginal utility of money for individuals on day X. But this marginal utility, and hence this demand, has an inevitable historical component: the fact that money had prior purchasing power on day X-1, and that therefore individuals know that this commodity has a monetary function and will be exchangeable on future days for other goods and services. But what then determined the purchasing power of money on day X-1? Again, that purchasing power was determined by the supply of, and demand for, money on day X-1, and that in turn depended on the fact that the money had had purchasing power on day X-2. But are we not caught in an infinite regression, with no escape from the circular trap and no ultimate explanation? No. What we must do is to push the temporal regression to that point when the money commodity was not used as a medium of indirect exchange but was demanded purely for its own direct consumption use. Let us go back logically to the second day that a commodity, say gold, was used as a medium of exchange. On that day, gold was demanded partly because it had a preexisting purchasing power as a money, or rather as a medium of exchange, on the first day. But what of that first day? On that day, the demand for gold again depended on the fact that gold had had a previous purchasing power, and so we push the analysis back to the last day of barter. The demand for gold on the last day of barter was purely a consumption use and had no historical component referring to any previous day; for under barter, every commodity was demanded purely for its current consumption use, and gold was no different. On the first day of its use as a medium of exchange, gold began to have two components in its demand, or utility: first, a consumption use as had existed in barter and, second, a monetary use, or use as a medium of exchange, which had a historical component in its utility. In short, the demand for money can be pushed back to the last day of barter, at which point the temporal element in the demand for the money commodity disappears, and the causal forces in the current demand and purchasing power of money are fully and completely explained.

Not only does the Mises regression theorem fully explain the current demand for money and integrate the theory of money with the theory of marginal utility, but it also shows that money must have originated in this fashion — on the market — with individuals on the market gradually beginning to use some previously valuable commodity as a medium of exchange. No money could have originated either by a social compact to consider some previously valueless thing as a "money" or by sudden governmental fiat. For in those cases, the money commodity could not have a previous purchasing power, which could be taken into account in the individual's demands for money. In this way, Mises demonstrated that Carl Menger's historical insight into the way in which money arose on the market was not simply a historical summary but a theoretical necessity. On the other hand, while money had to originate as a directly useful commodity, for example, gold, there is no reason, in the light of the regression theorem, why such direct uses must continue afterward for the commodity to be used as money. Once established as a money, gold or gold substitutes can lose or be deprived of their direct use function and still continue as money;

for the historical reference to a previous day's purchasing power will already have been established.[9]

In his comprehensive 1949 treatise, *Human Action*, Mises successfully refuted earlier criticisms of the regression theorem by Anderson and Ellis.[10] Subsequently criticisms were leveled at the theory by J. C. Gilbert and Don Patinkin. Gilbert asserted that the theory fails to explain how a new paper money can be introduced when the previous monetary system breaks down. Presumably he was referring to such examples as the German *Rentenmark* after the runaway inflation of 1923. But the point is that the new paper was not introduced de novo; gold and foreign currencies had existed previously, and the *Rentenmark* could and did undergo exchange in terms of these previously existing moneys; furthermore, it was introduced at a fixed relation to the previous, extremely depreciated mark.[11] Patinkin criticized Mises for allegedly claiming that the marginal utility of money refers to the marginal utility of the goods for which money is exchanged rather than the marginal utility of holding money itself; he also charged Mises with inconsistently holding the latter view in the other parts of *The Theory of Money and Credit*. But Patinkin was mistaken; Mises's concept of the marginal utility of money always refers to the utility of holding money. Mises's point in the regression theorem is a different one, namely, that the marginal utility-to-hold is itself based on the prior fact that money can be exchanged for goods, that is, on the prior purchasing power of money in terms of goods. In short, that money prices of goods, the purchasing power of money, has first to exist in order for money to have a marginal utility to hold, hence the need for the regression theorem to break out of the circularity.[12.]

Modern orthodox economics has abandoned the quest for causal explanation in behalf of a Walrasian world of "mutual determination" suitable for the current fashion of mathematical economics. Patinkin himself feebly accepted the circular trap by stating that in analyzing the market ("market experiment") he began with utility while in analyzing utility he began with prices ("individual experiment"). With characteristic arrogance, Samuelson and Stigler each attacked the Austrian concern with escaping circularity in order to analyze causal relations. Samuelson fell back on Walras, who developed the idea of "general equilibrium in which all magnitudes are simultaneously determined by efficacious interdependent relations," which he contrasted to the "fears of literary writers" (that is, economists who write in English) about circular reasoning.[13] Stigler dismissed Böhm-Bawerk for his "failure to understand some of the most essential elements of modern economic theory, the concepts of mutual determination and equilibrium (developed by the use of the theory of simultaneous equations). Mutual determination . . . is spurned for the older concept of cause and effect." Stigler added the snide note that "Böhm-Bawerk was not trained in mathematics."[14] Thus, orthodox economists reflect the unfortunate influence of the mathematical method in economics. The idea of mutual functional determination — so adaptable to mathematical presentation — is appropriate in physics, which tries to explain the unmotivated motions of physical matter. But in praxeology, the study of human action, of which economics is the best elaborated part, the cause is known: individual purpose. In economics, therefore, the proper method is to proceed from the causing action to its consequent effects.

In *Human Action,* Mises advanced the Austrian theory of money by delivering a shattering blow to the very concept of Walrasian general equilibrium. To arrive at that equilibrium, the basic data of the economy — values, technology, and resources — must all be frozen and understood by every participant in the market to be frozen indefinitely. Given such a magical freeze, the economy would sooner or later settle into an endless round of constant prices and production, with each firm earning a uniform rate of interest (or, in some constructions, a zero rate of interest). The idea of certainty and fixity in what Mises called "the evenly rotating economy" is absurd, but what Mises went on to show is that in such a world of fixity and certainty no one would hold cash balances. Everyone's demand for cash balances would fall to zero. For since everyone would have perfect foresight and knowledge of his future sales and purchases, there would be no point in holding any cash balance at all. Thus, the man who knew he would be spending $5,000 on 1 January 1977 would lend out all his money to be returned at precisely that date. As Mises stated:

Every individual knows precisely what amount of money he will need at any future date. He is therefore in a position to lend all the funds he receives in such a way that the loans fall due on the date he will need them ... When the equilibrium of the evenly rotating economy is finally reached, there are no more cash holdings.[15]

But if no one holds cash and the demand for cash balances falls to zero, all prices rise to infinity, and the entire general equilibrium system of the market, which implies the continuing existence of monetary exchange, falls apart. As Mises concluded:

In the imaginary construction of an evenly rotating economy, indirect exchange and the use of money are tacitly implied .... Where there is no uncertainty concerning the future, there is no need for any cash holding. As money must necessarily be kept by people in their cash holdings, there cannot be any money. ... But the very notion of a market economy without money is self-contradictory.[16]

The very notion of a Walrasian general equilibrium is not simply totally unrealistic, it is conceptually impossible, since money and monetary exchange cannot be sustained in that kind of system. Another corollary contribution of Mises in this analysis was to demonstrate that, far from being only one of many "motives" for holding cash balances, uncertainty is crucial to the holding of any cash at all.

That such problems are now troubling mainstream economics is revealed by F. H. Hahn's demonstration that Patinkin's well-known model of general equilibrium can only establish the existence of a demand for money by appealing to such notions as an alleged uncertainty of the exact moments of future sales and purchases, and to "imperfections" in the credit market — neither of which, as Hahn pointed out, is consistent with the concept of general equilibrium.[17]

With respect to the supply of money, Mises returned to the basic Ricardian insight that an increase in the supply of money never confers any general benefit upon society. For money is fundamentally different from consumers' and producers' goods in at least one vital respect. Other things being equal, an increase in the supply of consumers' goods benefits society since one or more consumers will be better off. The same is true of an increase in the supply of producers' goods, which will be eventually transformed into an increased supply of consumers' goods; for production itself is the process of transforming natural resources into new forms and locations desired by consumers for direct use. But money is very different: money is not used directly in consumption or production but is exchanged for such directly usable goods. Yet, once any commodity or object is established as a money, it performs the maximum exchange work of which it is capable. An increase in the supply of money causes no increase whatever in the exchange service of money; all that happens is that the purchasing power of each unit of money is diluted by the increased supply of units. Hence there is never a social need for increasing the supply of money, either because of an increased supply of goods or because of an increase in population. People can acquire an increased proportion of cash balances with a fixed supply of money by spending less and thereby increasing the purchasing power of their cash balances, thus raising their real cash balances overall. As Mises wrote:

The services money renders are conditioned by the height of its purchasing power. Nobody wants to have in his cash holding a definite number of pieces of money or a definite weight of money; he wants to keep a cash holding of a definite amount of purchasing power. As the operation of the market tends to determine the final state of money's purchasing power at a height at which the supply of and the demand for money coincide, there can never be an excess or a deficiency of money. Each individual and all individuals together always enjoy fully the advantages which they can derive from indirect exchange and the use of money, no matter whether the total quantity of money is great or small. Changes in money's purchasing power generate changes in the disposition of wealth among the various members of society. From the point of view of people eager to be enriched by such changes, the supply of money may be called insufficient or excessive, and the appetite for such gains may result in policies designed to bring about cash-induced alterations in purchasing power. However, the services which money renders can be neither improved nor impaired by changing the supply of money. . . . The quantity of money available in the whole economy is always sufficient to secure for everybody all that money does and can do.[18]

A world of constant money supply would be one similar to that of much of the eighteenth and nineteenth centuries, marked by the successful flowering of the Industrial Revolution with increased capital investment increasing the supply of goods and with falling prices for these goods as well as falling costs of production.[19] As demonstrated by the notable Austrian theory of the business cycle, even an inflationary expansion of money and credit merely offsetting the secular fall in prices will create the distortions of production that bring about the business cycle.

In the face of overwhelming arguments against inflationary expansion of the money supply (including those not detailed here), what accounts for the persistence of the inflationary trend in the modern world? The answer lies in the way new money is injected into the economy, in the fact that it is most definitely not done according to the Angel Gabriel model. For example, a government does not multiply the money supply tenfold across the board by issuing a decree adding another zero to every monetary number in the economy. In any economy not on a 100 percent commodity standard, the money supply is under the control of government, the central bank, and the controlled banking system. These institutions issue new money and inject it into the economy by spending it or lending it out to favored debtors. As we have seen, an increase in the supply of money benefits the early receivers, that is, the government, the banks, and their favored debtors or contractors, at the expense of the relatively fixed income groups that receive the new money late or not at all and suffer a loss in real income and wealth. In short, monetary inflation is a method by which the government, its controlled banking system, and favored political groups are able to partially expropriate the wealth of other groups in society. Those empowered to control the money supply issue new money to their own economic advantage and at the expense of the remainder of the population. Yield to government the monopoly over the issue and supply of money, and government will inflate that supply to its own advantage and to the detriment of the politically powerless. Once we adopt the distinctively Austrian approach of "methodological individualism," once we realize that government is not a superhuman institution dedicated to the common good and the general welfare, but a group of individuals devoted to furthering their economic interests, then the reason for the inherent inflationism of government as money monopolist becomes crystal clear.

As the Austrian analysis of money shows, however, the process of generated inflation cannot last indefinitely, for the government cannot in the final analysis control the pace of monetary deterioration and the loss of purchasing power. The ultimate result of a policy of persistent inflation is runaway inflation and the total collapse of the currency. As Mises analyzed the course of runaway inflation (both before and after the first example of such a collapse in an industrialized country, in post-World-War-I Germany), such inflation generally proceeds as follows: At first the government's increase of the money supply and the subsequent rise in prices are regarded by the public as temporary. Since, as was true in Germany during World War I, the onset of inflation is often occasioned by the extraordinary expenses of a war, the public assumes that after the war conditions including prices will return to the preinflation normal. Hence, the public's demand for cash balances rises as it awaits the anticipated lowering of prices. As a result, prices rise proportionately and often substantially less than the money supply, and the monetary authorities become bolder. As in the case of the assignats during the French Revolution, here is a magical panacea for the difficulties of government: pump more money into the economy, and prices will rise only a little! Encouraged by the seeming success, the authorities apply more of what has worked so well, and the monetary inflation proceeds apace. In time, however, the public's expectations and views of the economic present and future undergo a vitally important change. They begin to see that there will be no return to the prewar norm, that the new norm is a continuing price inflation — that prices will continue to go up rather than down. Phase two of the inflationary process ensues, with a continuing fall in the demand for cash balances based on this analysis: "I'd better spend my money on X, Y, and Z now, because I know full well that next year prices will be higher." Prices begin to rise more than the increase in the supply of money. The critical turning point has arrived.

At this point, the economy is regarded as suffering from a money shortage as evidenced by the outstripping of monetary expansion by the rise in prices. What is now called a liquidity crunch occurs on a broad scale, and a clamor arises for greater increases in the supply of money. As the Austrian school economist Bresciani-Turroni wrote in his definitive study of the German hyperinflation:

The rise of prices caused an intense demand for the circulating medium to arise, because the existing quantity was not sufficient for the volume of transactions. At the same time the State's need of money increased rapidly ... the eyes of all were turned to the Reichsbank. The pressure exercised on it became more and more insistent and the increase of issues, from the central bank, appeared as a remedy . . . .

The authorities therefore had not the courage to resist the pressure of those who demanded ever greater quantities of paper money, and to face boldly the crisis which . . . would be, undeniably, the result of a stoppage of the issue of notes. They preferred to continue the convenient method of continually increasing the issues of notes, thus making the continuation of business possible, but at the same time prolonging the pathological state of the German economy. The Government increased salaries in proportion to the depreciation of the mark, and employers in their turn granted continual increases in wages, to avoid disputes, on the condition that they could raise the prices of their products. . . .

Thus was the vicious circle established; the exchange depreciated; internal prices rose; note-issues were increased; the increase of the quantity of paper money lowered once more the value of the mark in terms of gold; prices rose once more; and so on. . . .

For a long time the Reichsbank — having adopted the fatalistic idea that the increase in the note-issues was the inevitable consequence of the depreciation of the mark—considered as its principal task, not the regulation of the circulation, but the preparation for the German economy of the continually increasing quantities of paper money, which the rise in prices required. It devoted itself especially to the organization, on a large scale, of the production of paper marks.[20]

The sort of thinking that gripped the German monetary authorities at the height of the hyperinflation may be gauged from this statement by the president of the Reichsbank, Rudolf Havenstein:

The wholly extraordinary depreciation of the mark has naturally created a rapidly increasing demand for additional currency, which the Reichsbank has not always been able fully to satisfy. A simplified production of notes of large denominations enabled us to bring ever greater amounts into circulation. But these enormous sums are barely adequate to cover the vastly increased demand for the means of payment, which has just recently attained an absolutely fantastic level. . . .

The running of the Reichsbank's note-printing organization, which has become absolutely enormous, is making the most extreme demands on our personnel.[21]

The United States seems to be entering phase two of inflation (1975), and it is noteworthy that economists such as Walter Heller have already raised the cry that the supply of money must be expanded in order to restore the real cash balances of the public, in effect to alleviate the shortage of real balances. As in Germany in the early 1920s, the argument is being employed that the quantity of money cannot be the culprit for inflation since prices are rising at a greater rate than the supply of money.[22]

Phase three of the inflation is the ultimate runaway stage: the collapse of the currency. The public takes panicky flight from money into real values, into any commodity whatever. The public's psychology is not simply to buy now rather than later but to buy anything immediately. The public's demand for cash balances hurtles toward zero.

The reason for the enthusiasm of Mises and other Austrian economists for the gold standard, the purer and less diluted the better, should now be crystal clear. It is not that this "barbaric relic" has any fetishistic attraction. The reason is that a money under the control of the government and its banking system is subject to inexorable pressures toward continuing monetary inflation. In contrast, the supply of gold cannot be manufactured *ad libitum* by the monetary authorities; it must be extracted from the ground, by the same costly process as governs the supply of any other commodities on the market. Essentially the choice is: gold or government. The choice of gold rather than other market commodities is the historical experience of centuries that gold (as well as silver) is uniquely suitable as a monetary commodity — for reasons once set forth in the first chapter of every money-and-banking textbook.

The criticism might be made that gold, too, can increase in quantity, and that this rise in supply, however limited, would also confer no benefit upon society. Apart from the gold versus government choice, however, there is another important consideration: an increase in the supply of gold improves its availability for nonmonetary uses, an advantage scarcely conferred by the fiat currencies of government or the deposits of the banking system.

In contrast to the Misesian "monetary overinvestment" theory of business cycles, on which considerable work has been done by F. A. Hayek and other Austrian economists, almost nothing has been done on the theory of money proper except by Mises himself. There are three cloudy and interrelated areas that need further elaboration. One is the route by which money can be released from government control. Of primary importance would be the return to a pure gold standard. To do so would involve, first, raising the "price of gold" (actually, lowering the definition of the weight of the dollar) drastically above the current pseudoprice of $42.22 an ounce and, second, a deflationary transformation of current bank deposits into nonmonetary savings certificates or certificates of deposit. What the precise price or the precise mix should be is a matter for research. Initially, the Mises proposal for a return to gold at a market price and the proposal of such Austrian monetary theorists as Jacques Rueff and Michael Heilperin for a return at a deliberately doubled price of $70 an ounce seemed far apart. But the current (1975) market price of approximately $160 an ounce brings the routes of a deliberately higher price and the market price much closer together.[23]

A second area for research is the matter of free banking as against 100 percent reserve requirements for bank deposits in relation to gold. Mises's *Theory of Money and Credit* was one of the first works to develop systematically the way in which the banks create money through an expansion of credit. It was followed by Austrian economist C.A. Phillips's famous distinction between the expansionary powers of individual banks and those of the banking system as a whole. However, one of Mises's arguments has remained neglected: that under a regime of free banking, that is, where banks are unregulated but held strictly to account for honoring their obligations to redeem notes or deposits in standard money, the operations of the market check monetary expansion by the banks. The threat of bank runs, combined with the impossibility of one bank's expanding more than a competitor, keeps credit expansion at a minimum. Perhaps Mises underestimated the possibility of a successful bank cartel for the promotion of credit expansion; it seems clear, however, that there is less chance for bank-credit expansion in the absence of a central bank to supply reserves and to be a lender of last resort.[24]

Finally, there is the related question, which Mises did not develop fully, of the proper definition of the crucial concept of the money supply. In current mainstream economics, there are at least four competing definitions, ranging from M_1 to M_4. Of one point an Austrian is certain: the definition must rest on the inner essence of the concept itself and not on the currently fashionable but question-begging methodology of statistical correlation with national income. Leland Yeager was trenchantly critical of such an approach:

One familiar approach to the definition of money scorns any supposedly *a priori* line between money and near-moneys. Instead, it seeks the definition that works best with statistics. One strand of that approach . . . seeks the narrowly or broadly defined quantity that correlates most closely with income in equations fitted to historical data . . . . But it would be awkward if the definition of money accordingly had to change from time to time and country to country. Furthermore, even if money defined to include certain near-moneys does correlate somewhat more closely with income than money narrowly defined, that fact does not necessarily impose the broad definition. Perhaps the amount of these near-moneys depends on the level of money-income and in turn on the amount of medium of exchange. . . . More generally, it is not obvious why the magnitude with which some other magnitude correlates most closely deserves overriding attention. . . . The number of bathers at a beach may correlate more closely with the numbers of cars parked there than with either the temperature or the price of admission, yet the former correlation may be less interesting or useful than either of the latter. The correlation with national income might be closer for either consumption or investment than for the quantity of money.[25]

Money is the medium of exchange, the asset for which all other goods and services are traded on the market. If a thing functions as such a medium, as final payment for other things on the market, then it serves as part of the money supply. In his *Theory of Money and Credit*, Mises distinguished between standard money (money in the narrow sense) and money substitutes, such as bank notes and demand deposits, which function as an additional money supply. It should be noted, for example, that in Irving Fisher's non-Austrian classic, *The Purchasing Power of Money*, written at about the same time (1913), M consisted of standard money only, while M^1 consisted of money substitutes in the form of bank demand deposits redeemable in standard money at par. Today no economist would think of excluding demand deposits from the definition of money. But if we ponder the problem, we see that if a bank begins to fail, its deposits are no longer equivalent to money; they no longer serve as money on the market. They are only money until a bank's imminent collapse.

Furthermore, in the same way that M^1 (currency plus demand deposits) is broader than the narrowest definition, we can establish even broader definitions by including savings deposits of commercial banks, savings bank deposits, shares of savings and loan banks, and cash surrender values of life insurance companies, which are all redeemable on demand at par in standard money, and therefore all serve as money substitutes and as part of the money supply until the public begins to doubt that they are redeemable. Partisans of M1 argue that commercial banks are uniquely powerful in creating deposits and, further, that their deposits circulate more actively than the deposits of other banks. Let us suppose, however, that in a gold-standard country, a man has some gold coins in his bureau and others locked in a bank vault. His stock of gold coins at home will circulate actively and the ones in his vault sluggishly, but surely both are part of his stock of cash. And, if it also be objected that the deposits of savings banks and similar institutions pyramid on top of commercial bank deposits, it should also be noted that the latter in turn pyramid on top of reserves and standard money.

Another example will serve to answer the common objection that a savings bank deposit is not money because it cannot be used directly as a medium of exchange but must be redeemed in that medium. (This is apart from the fact that savings banks are increasingly being empowered to issue checks and open up checking accounts.) Suppose that, through some cultural quirk, everyone in the country decided not to use five-dollar bills in actual exchange. They would only use ten-dollar and one-dollar bills, and keep their longer-term cash balances in five-dollar bills. As a result, five-dollar bills would tend to circulate far more slowly than the other bills. If a man wanted to spend some of his cash balance, he could not spend a five-dollar bill directly; instead, he would go to a bank and exchange it for five one-dollar bills for use in trade. In this hypothetical situation, the status of the five-dollar bill would be the same as that of the savings deposit today. But while the holder of the five-dollar bill would have to go to a bank and exchange it for dollar bills before spending it, surely no one would say that his five-dollar bills were not part of his cash balance or of the money supply.

A broad definition of the money supply, however, excludes assets not redeemable on demand at par in standard money, that is, any form of genuine time liability, such as savings certificates, certificates of deposit whether negotiable or nonnegotiable, and government bonds. Savings bonds, redeemable at par, are money substitutes and hence are part of the total supply of money. Finally, just as commercial bank reserves are properly excluded from the outstanding supply of money, so those demand deposits that in turn function as reserves for the deposits of these other financial institutions would have to be excluded as well. It would be double counting to include both the base and the multiple of any of the inverted money pyramids in the economy.

NOTES

1. Ludwig von Mises, *Theorie des Geldes und der Umlaufsmittel* (1912); see the third English edition, *The Theory of Money and Credit* (New Haven: Yale University Press, 1953).

2. On the changes in relative prices attendant on an increase in the money supply, see Mises, *Theory of Money and Credit*, pp. 139-45.

3. For more on the fallacies of measurement and index numbers, see Mises, *Theory of Money and Credit*, pp. 187-94; idem, *Human Action: A Treatise on Economics* (New Haven: Yale University Press, 1949), pp. 221-24; Murray N. Rothbard, *Man, Economy, and State* (Princeton: D. Van Nostrand, 1962), 2:737-40; Bassett Jones, *Horses and Apples: A Study of Index Numbers* (New York: John Day & Co., 1934); and Oskar Morgenstern, *On the Accuracy of Economic Observations* 2d ed. rev. (Princeton: Princeton University Press, 1963).

4. See Mises, *Theory of Money and Credit*, pp. 170-78.

5. Chi-Yuen Wu, *An Outline of International Price Theories* (London: George Routledge & Sons, 1939), p. 126.

6. Wu, *Outline*, p. 234; Mises, *Theory of Money and Credit*, p. 178. Mises's development of the theory was independent of Senior's because the latter was only published in 1928 in *Industrial Efficiency and Social Economy* (New York, 1928), pp. 55-56; see Wu, *Outline*, p. 127 n.

7. Wu, *Outline*, p. 250; Mises's formulation is in *Theory of Money and Credit*, pp. 179-88.

8. See Wu, *Outline*, pp. 251-60.

9. Mises's regression theorem may be found in *Theory of Money and Credit*, pp. 97-123. For an explanation and a diagrammatic representation of the regression theorem, see Rothbard, *Man, Economy, and State*, pp. 231-37. Menger's insight into the origin of money on the market may be found in Carl Menger, *Principles of Economics* (Glencoe, Ill.: Free Press, 1950), pp. 257-62. On the relationship between Menger's ap-

proach and the regression theorem, see Mises, *Human Action*, pp. 402-4.

10. Mises, *Human Action*, pp. 405-7. The regression analysis was either adopted by or arrived at independently by William A. Scott in *Money and Banking*, 6th ed. (New York: Henry Holt & Co., 1926), pp. 54-55.

11. J. C. Gilbert, "The Demand for Money: The Development of an Economic Concept," *Journal of Political Economy* 61(April 1953):149.

12. Don Patinkin, *Money, Interest, and Prices* (Evanston, Ill.: Row, Peterson & Co., 1956), pp. 71-72, 414.

13. Paul A. Samuelson, *Foundations of Economic Analysis* (Cambridge: Harvard University Press, 1947), pp. 117-18.

14. George J. Stigler, *Production and Distribution Theories: The Formative Period* (New York: Macmillan Co., 1946), p. 181; also see the similar, if more polite, attack on Menger by Frank H. Knight, "Introduction," in Menger, *Principles*, p. 23. For a contrasting discussion by the mathematical economist son of Menger, Karl Menger, see "Austrian Marginalism and Mathematical Economics," in *Carl Menger and the Austrian School of Economics*, ed. John R. Hicks and Wilhelm Weber (Oxford: Clarendon Press, 1973), pp. 54-60.

15. Mises, *Human Action*, p. 250.

16. Ibid., pp. 249-50, 414.

17. F. H. Hahn, "On Some Problems of Proving the Existence of an Equilibrium in a Monetary Economy," in *The Theory of Interest Rates*, ed. F. H. Hahn and F. P. R. Breckling (London: Macmillan & Co., 1965), pp. 128-32.

18. Mises, *Human Action*, p. 418.

19. On the advantages of a secularly falling price "level," see C. A. Phillips, T. F. McManus, and R. W. Nelson, *Banking and the Business Cycle* (New York: Macmillan Co., 1937), pp. 186-88, 203-7.

20. Costantino Bresciani-Turroni, *The Economics of Inflation* (London: George Allen & Unwin, 1937), pp. 80-82; also see Frank D. Graham, *Exchange, Prices, and Production in Hyper-inflation: Germany 1920-23* (New York: Russell & Russell, 1930), pp. 104-7. For an analysis of hyperinflation, see Mises, *Theory of Money and Credit*, pp. 227-30; and idem, *Human Action*, pp. 423-25.

21. Rudolf Havenstein, Address to the Executive Committee of the Reichsbank, 25 August 1923, translated in Fritz K. Ringer, ed., *The German Inflation of 1923* (New York: Oxford University Press, 1969), p. 96.

22. See Denis S. Karnofsky, "Real Money Balances: A Misleading Indicator of Monetary Actions," *Federal Reserve Bank of St. Louis Review* 56(February 1974):2-10.

23.   Mises's proposal is in *Theory of Money and Credit*, pp. 448-57; also see Michael A. Heilperin, *Aspects of the Pathology of Money* (Geneva: Michael Joseph, 1968); and Jacques Rueff, *The Monetary Sin of the West* (New York: Macmillan Co., 1972).

24.   See Mises, *Human Action*, pp. 431-45.

25.   Leland B. Yeager, "Essential Properties of the Medium of Exchange," *Kyklos* (1968), reprinted in *Monetary Theory*, ed. R. W. Clower (London: Penguin Books, 1969), p. 38.

Inflation, Recession, and Stagflation

Gerald P. O'Driscoll, Jr., and Sudha R. Shenoy

Those who are sufficiently steeped in the old point of view simply cannot bring themselves to believe that I am asking them to step into a new pair of trousers, and will insist on regarding it as nothing but an embroidered version of the old pair which they have been wearing for years (John Maynard Keynes, "The Pure Theory of Money: A Reply to Dr. Hayek," *Economica* 11 [November 1931]:390).

The major macroeconomic problem facing Western economies today is that of explaining why the supposedly mild inflations of the two decades following World War II turned into the intractable "stagflation" besetting theorist and policymaker alike. The two major analytical approaches to the problem, that of the Keynesians and that of the monetarists, have a serious failing in common: they ignore the real side of the economy and hence the real maladjustments brought about by a monetary policy that interferes with the coordination of economic activities. Both views implicitly assume that the real side of the economy is always in some sort of long-term equilibrium, in which money influences only the price level or money income and not the structure of relative prices or the composition of real output. As we intend to show, such a point of view belongs to a stage in the history of economic thought before the structure of output and the influence of prices on production had been worked out.

We shall also offer an exposition of an alternative analysis derived from the Austrian school of economic thought, especially from the writings of Friedrich A. Hayek. In so doing, we shall indicate how a Hayekian analysis of the effects of monetary changes on the structure of prices and outputs enables us to delve beneath the monetary surface to the real underlying phenomena and thereby call attention to the misallocation resulting from a monetary system that discoordinates economic activity.

Not all possible alternatives to the Austrian view will be covered. For instance, we shall not examine the extensive neo-Ricardian critiques of the current orthodoxy advanced by Joan Robinson, Nicholas Kaldor, and Piero Sraffa, since we regard these criticisms as part of a more general attack on subjectivist marginalist economics. Nor shall we consider in detail the work of Robert W. Clower and Axel Leijonhufvud, which in part complements our own work here.[1] We would argue, however, that virtually all writers and all non-Austrian schools of thought have ignored the importance of Hayek's work in explaining important features of the business cycle.

I

World War II marked a great shift in the character of the macroeconomic problems developed countries had to face. In the years after World War I, policymakers had to cope with a "typical" economic crisis, which was followed by what in the 1920s had been taken to be a stable expansion and then by a second crisis, only this time one of unprecedented intensity and length. However, after 1945, the problem turned around completely and became that of gently (and later, more rapidly) rising prices. In eleven major developed countries, prices declined hardly at all, and when they did, it was only for a couple of years during the early fifties.[2] Price indices remained stable for some years in several of these countries, but these periods of relative price stability were outnumbered by years of rising prices, so that in effect prices have been rising more or less steadily ever since the end of World War II.

Generally output rose pari passu with prices. Indeed, the countries of the European Economic Community, together with the outstanding examples of Israel and Japan, were generally extolled for their economic growth record in comparison with such "slow growers" as the United Kingdom.[3]

However, two ominous symptoms of underlying structural distortions then appeared: annual rates of price increases sharply accelerated, running in most developed countries well into two-digit figures, and rates of increase in output began to slacken. Unemployment percentages, at historic lows since the late forties, started an upward climb, and every attempt to reduce the rate of price increase brought fresh upward jumps in unemployment and excess industrial capacity. Forecasts of the Organization for Economic Cooperation and Development described the price situation as "worrying" and reported that, although price inflation continued at historically high rates (in excess of 12 percent per annum in early 1974), growth continued to decelerate (that is, aggregate demand fell in relation to aggregate supply). "Over the last few years unemployment seems to have risen in relation to demand pressures," and the "unemployment rate at the peak of the boom is higher than at earlier peaks."[4]

This stagflation dilemma seemed far more serious in the United Kingdom than elsewhere. Retail prices rose every year after 1945, yet growth rates in output remained low compared to the European Economic Community. Periodic attempts to bolster the rate of growth regularly ran into balance-of-payments problems leading to the well-known "stop-go" cycle. Here, too, the interval between "go" and "stop" steadily decreased. For example, in 1974 the chancellor of the exchequer chose to introduce "reflationary" preelection measures hardly two months after a "deflationary" postelection budget.

In the United Kingdom more than in any other developed country, acceleration in the rate of price increase was combined not merely with a low rate of growth in output but with a *zero* or even a negative growth rate. The rate of increase in the retail price index exceeded 10 percent well before it did in any other developed country, and even before this happened, the retail price index began climbing well ahead of output. In late 1974 the price increase showed every sign of continuing into the 20 percent range, while output continued to slacken. For the United Kingdom an inflationary depression in the eighties seemed quite likely.[5] While inflation in the United States was not so serious as that in the United Kingdom, there was every indication that the United States was but a few years behind the United Kingdom in this respect. Unemployment rates were higher in the United States than in the United Kingdom. And some would argue that the United States was already experiencing the inflationary depression feared for the United Kingdom.

What went wrong? Why did the gently rising price level of the fifties and the sixties give way to two-digit increases, which hardly anyone expected? Why did unemployment rear its head with every slackening of the rate of price increase?

THE KEYNESIAN DIAGNOSIS

Many Keynesians view the post-1945 situation as one of "cost inflation," that is, of rising cost levels pushing up the price level, with a passive monetary system furnishing the necessary finance.[6] Costs, the active variable, determine prices, while the money supply adapts passively.[7] Attempts to control the supply of money, rather than to control costs directly, must create unemployment without reducing prices, since costs continue to rise. However, if costs can be controlled directly, for example, by some kind of incomes policy, it would be possible to achieve both full employment and a stable price level.[8] And the thirties are viewed as a warning (not only by the Keynesians but others as well), as an example of what happens when money income and expenditure are not expanded sufficiently to restore full employment.[9]

This view epitomizes the policy teachings of modern macroeconomics. The modern treatment of interest rates is a good

example of the way Keynesian analysis neglects the microeconomic significance of the structure of relative prices and
outputs that actually characterizes the real world. The interest
rate—or market spectrum of interest rates—is the closest approach in macroeconomics to anything like a price. Of course, in
the one-or-two-commodity worlds usually treated in macromodels, changes in interest rates have—by hypothesis—no
micro implications.[10] But even here the Keynesian approach
offers no long-run theory of interest rates or even bothers to
discuss in detail the real factors affecting the money rate of
interest.[11] What we have instead is an analysis of the impact on
interest rates of changes in the rate at which the money stream
enters the money market. This may give us a hypothesis for
explaining short-run changes in market interest rates, but it is
not itself a theory of interest. As D. H. Robertson pointed out, in
his classic characterization of Keynes's liquidity-preference
theory:

> Thus the rate of interest is what it is because it is expected to become
> other than it is; if it is not expected to become other than it is, there is
> nothing left to tell us why it is what it is. The organ which secretes it has
> been amputated. And yet it somehow still exists—a grin without a cat.[12]

In the Keynesian macro approach prices remain completely
rigid in both absolute and relative terms. Changes in the structure of relative prices are ignored as analysis often explicitly
assumes that prices remain always "at their historic levels."[13]

In a similar manner, the structural composition of output is
also considered irrelevant; indeed, the Keynesian concept may
be said to be that of full *un*employment, that is, the implicit
assumption that all goods and services are available in abundance, so that output and employment can be increased by all
firms simultaneously. Or, to put this point somewhat differently,
the level of unemployment and excess capacity at the bottom of
the cycle is assumed to be uniform throughout the economy.
The substantial variations, in both unemployment and excess
capacity, as among different firms, industries, and regions, are
disregarded in the Keynesian framework as having little analytical significance.

In such a scheme, then, the level of output and employment depends on the level of monetary expenditure or, in more sophisticated variants, the rate of increase of monetary expenditure. The supply side is implicitly ignored, and, as just mentioned, the concentration on levels of utilization (of labor and other factors) implies that on the real side there is a constant equilibrium being maintained in the structure of output.

It might also be pointed out that for the Keynesian, an inflationary recession (that is, a rising price level and a rising unemployment rate) is a particularly difficult problem with which to deal. Inflation should only result when aggregate demand continues to rise as full employment is reached.

THE MONETARIST POSITION[14]

At the other extreme (or so it seems) we have Milton Friedman and the monetarist school of thought. Yet Friedman also interprets the historical experience of the twenties and the thirties in purely monetary terms. For him also, as we shall see, there is no real problem of coordination to worry about at the macroeconomic level.

The monetarist approach may be represented by a quotation from John S. Mill:

In considering value, we were only concerned with causes which acted upon particular commodities apart from the rest. Causes which affect all commodities alike do not act upon values. But in considering the relation between goods and money, it is with the causes that operate upon all goods whatever that we are especially concerned. We are comparing goods of all sorts on one side, with money on the other side, as things to be exchanged against each other.[15]

For Mill, as for many of the classical economists, changes in the money supply affect aggregate spending but not relative prices. Pricing—the determination of value—is not affected by monetary disturbances. For the most part, Mill analyzed changes in the quantity of money in terms of what the modern economist would describe as a discrepancy between actual and desired cash balances. The real side of production is assumed to be largely unaffected.[16]

Monetarism has hardly advanced beyond the classical position; accordingly, it is not surprising that the classical economists can sound quite modern. In his analysis of some specific problems in microeconomics, Friedman adopted what is basically the outlook of methodological individualism. But in his monetary theory (and in that of others of the same school) we find, quite inconsistently, an aggregative analysis, utilizing holistic macro-constructs that are treated (wrongly) as if they interacted directly with one another. This procedure entirely ignores the microeconomic pricing process, which actually determines the real structure of prices and output.[17] Monetarism then does not differ in its fundamental approach from the other dominant branch of orthodox economics, that of Keynesianism. A microtheorist is distinguished by his adherence to the principle of methodological individualism when answering all questions; that is, he analyzes economic problems in terms of the effects of a given change on the expected costs and benefits facing transactors. A microeconomist is thus led to analyze (among other things) the market process and its complex interrelationships. In this respect, at least, Friedman is not a consistent methodological individualist.

Friedman argued that real factors determine real magnitudes. Real forces thus determine real income, while monetary forces determine nominal income, with the price level as the joint outcome of the two forces. (Such an approach differs little from the older views of Irving Fisher and is open to all the criticisms leveled against that approach.)[18] To the foregoing, Friedman appended a short-run adjustment process "in which the rate of adjustment in a variable is a function of the discrepancy between the measured and the anticipated value of the variable or its rate of change, as well, perhaps, as of other variables or their rates of change."[19]

Friedman hypothesized such an adjustment process because for him the key question of monetary theory is the reaction to a discrepancy between the nominal quantity of money supplied and the nominal quantity demanded. Monetary expansion, then, affects only the price level; there are no structural maladjustments, while depressions, on the other hand, are largely, if not entirely, the outcome of a decline in the rate of growth of the stock of money. True, in the transition from a rising to a stable price level, there may be some unavoidable transitional decline in output and employment, as money prices adjust themselves to the reduced rate of increase in the stock of money. But provided this reduction is gradual, there need not be any significant impact on employment and certainly not a fall in aggregate output. A monetary expansion, on the other hand, simply reverses this process: initially, as the money supply expands and prices rise, wages (and other costs) fail to rise (because the information has not yet spread throughout the economy), and mostly profits increase. Hence output and employment expand—temporarily. Once nominal wages and other costs are bid up in line with the new price level, profits shrink to their "normal" level, as determined by the real elements of the situation. There are no prolonged misallocations anywhere. The pattern of output is untouched. If we wish to push unemployment below its "natural" level and expand the money supply to this end, larger and larger increases will become necessary, as the system adjusts to the rises in money prices. But a serious recession or depression need not result, since monetary expansion creates no real distortions, and the banking system is now geared to prevent any serious deflations in the stock of money.[20] Consistent with these views, Friedman attached no real significance to the monetary expansion of the twenties inasmuch as the price level remained fairly stable, while in the early thirties the substantial decline in output and employment in United States was due directly to the substantial contraction in the stock of money during the years 1929-32 but not to what had preceded it.

The monetarist position may be restated as follows: in real terms, prices are always tending to their long-term equilibrium level; monetary changes affect only their nominal height and have no lasting impact on production. Because Friedman viewed underlying economic reality as being adequately described by long-run Walrasian equations, such a position is the only reasonable one—since long-run equilibrium by definition excludes any real disequilibrium! Nor could Friedman consistently superimpose imperfect anticipations onto a system in which all expectations are by definition consistent and realized. Finally, in the ad hoc "adjustment process" Friedman postulated, he failed to distinguish between price changes that coordinate production and those that do the opposite! In other words, he assumed that price changes represent movements from one equilibrium to another. But the proposition under question is precisely whether price changes can be assumed to automatically coordinate: the Hayekian analysis, as will be shown, demonstrates that under certain monetary conditions some price changes may seriously discoordinate production. In short, in the terminology originally introduced by Hayek, money is not always "neutral." In any case, general equilibrium equations, being solely definitional, leave out of consideration the whole market process—indeed, such equations can tell us nothing about this intertemporal process.[21] But it is precisely these interrelated price changes that guide production over time and therefore cannot be overlooked.

The aggregative macro constructs, on which Friedman and the monetarists base their analyses, are in the end similar to other orthodox schools of thought (including the Keynesians, as Friedman readily acknowledges).[22] In relying on these constructs the monetarists appear to be unaware of the real effects of money on the economic system—money's effect on individual prices and price interrelationships and hence on the whole structure of outputs and employments. By ignoring the structure of production and the influences of prices on production, the monetarist analysis shares a common deficiency, not only with the Keynesians, but indeed with the entire analytic framework of the current orthodoxy. The monetarists no less than the Keynesians lay themselves open to Hayek's criticism that such thinking takes "us back to the pre-scientific stage of economics, when the whole working of the price mechanism was not yet understood, and only the problems of the impact of a varying money stream on a supply of goods and services with given prices aroused interest."[23]

II

As we have seen, the principal deficiency of both the Keynesian and the monetarist approach is the neglect of the microeconomics of business cycles. Furthermore, it is doubtful whether even the existence of money can be adequately accounted for in a Walrasian framework.[24] In any case, Keynesians and monetarists alike fail to find any place for money in the pricing process: money is given no role in determining relative prices.

The Austrian contribution to monetary theory is two-fold: First, it emphasizes the role of money in the pricing process and incorporates money—or, more precisely, changes in the stream of money payments—into the determination of relative prices. Second, it analyzes the effects of such money-induced relative price changes on the time structure of production, that is, the capital structure.

Carl Menger provided the theoretical framework for explaining why a medium of exchange was used.[25] Then, after Knut Wicksell drew attention to the failure of the classical quantity theory to explain how changes in the money supply affect prices,[26] Mises, building on Menger and Wicksell, showed more completely how money could be integrated into general economic theory. He went on to outline a theory of cyclical fluctuations in which monetary disturbances lead to misallocations.[27] Hayek built on the theories of Menger, Böhm-Bawerk, Wicksell, and Mises to amplify and expand the Austrian monetary tradition, especially in capital and business cycle theory.[28] The analysis that follows builds on this tradition.

MONETARY EXPANSION, PRICING, AND RESOURCE ALLOCATION

Monetary changes are not neutral—they do not affect all prices uniformly so as to change their nominal height but leave relative price relationships unaltered. In reality money does not enter the economy by way of a simple uniform change in all money balances, as many textbook writers like to assume. Rather, newly created money always enters the economy at a specific point and is spent on certain specific goods before gradually working through the system.

Thus some prices and expenditures are altered first, and other prices and expenditures, later. As long as the original monetary change is maintained, this monetary "pull" on price interrelationships will persist. This point is fundamental to the analysis that follows.

Hayek likened the effects of money on pricing to the process of pouring a viscous liquid (honey in his example) into a vessel:

There will, of course, be a tendency for it to spread to an even surface. But if the stream (of honey) hits the surface at one point, a little mound will form there from which the additional matter will slowly spread outward. Even after we have stopped pouring in more, it will take some time until the even surface will be fully restored. It will, of course, not reach the height which the top of the mound had reached when the inflow had stopped. But as long as we pour at a constant rate, the mound will preserve its height relative to the surrounding pool.[29]

Resource allocation will not be left unchanged as a result of these relative price changes. At the point at which the new money enters the economy, prices will rise relative to prices elsewhere. The pattern of outputs will be altered correspondingly. Monetary expansion also prevents some prices from falling that otherwise might. Thus some businesses make profits that otherwise would have losses, and workers are employed in jobs they otherwise would leave. Another result of the monetary expansion is that more new and different kinds of businesses are started. Firms are also led to embark on new and/or different lines of production. In short, the pattern of expenditures, resource allocation, and above all relative prices is changed by monetary expansion.

Typically an expansion of the money supply takes the form of an increase in bank credit. (While governments can simply print extra currency, they usually prefer less obvious methods of reaching this objective and thereby bridging the chronic gap between fiscal incomes and expenditures.) Let us consider the impact of an increase in the rate of growth of bank credit. Bank-credit expansion at first reduces interest rates below the level they otherwise would attain. The overall pattern of expenditures is necessarily altered: investment expenditures rise relative to current consumption expenditures and to savings, the increase being measured approximately by the increase in the money supply.

Monetary expansion thus leads to a discoordination between the saving and investment plans of the nongovernmental public. The Keynesian and the monetarist would find little to quarrel with in the analysis up to this point: the former would agree that if planned investment exceeds planned savings, incomes and output and possibly prices will rise; the latter would say that an increase in the stock of money will raise incomes and prices and perhaps output. The Austrian analysis, however, goes farther—to detail the changes in the pattern of expenditures and hence in the pattern of outputs, resulting from the consequent changes in relative prices.

MONETARY EXPANSION AND THE PRODUCTION STRUCTURE

As we have just seen, in crudely aggregative terms, monetary expansion leads initially to a drop in interest rates relative to what they would have been and a rise in investment expenditures relative to consumption expenditures, that is, a decline in the uniform rate of discount will raise the demand-price schedule for durable capital goods—and even more so, for the more durable goods—in relation to the demand-price schedule for current consumption services. But this is only the beginning.

There has not been a change in the supply of capital goods. Capital is not a homogeneous stock but an interconnected structure of interrelated capital goods. By disrupting price signals, the effect of monetary expansion is to throw this structure out of coordination.

In the Hayekian view, production is seen as a series of "stages," beginning with final consumption and extending through to stages systematically and successively farther removed from this final stage.[30] Factor services are applied to the unfinished products moving through these stages. In other words, production consists of a series of interrelated processes in which heterogeneous capital goods are grouped in specific combinations, together with land and labor services.

Capital goods usually and land and labor to some extent are specific to particular stages of production. Capital goods are thus in general not homogeneous and substitutable; they are heterogeneous and complementary and usable only in specific combinations: for example, a machine from a shoe factory cannot be combined at random with a machine from an automobile plant to produce some third product.[31] Generally, if capital investments (such as shoe factories and automobile plants) are to add more to final output than any other capital combination, they must fit into an integrated production structure completed to the final consumption stage, that is, they must fit into an interlinked series of complementary investments.[32]

The increased bank credit flowing into the system at temporarily depressed interest rates alters the relative profitability of capital invested in different stages; the streams of quasi-rents accruing to the various capital goods are changed; and these goods are rearranged into different capital combinations. At the lower interest rates, certain formerly unprofitable investments become profitable. Additional bank credit does not produce additional labor and land services; hence the new investments must necessarily use relatively less labor. Because more money is available and interest rates are lower, factor rental prices are bid up relative to product prices, that is, real factor costs increase.[33] Hence entrepreneurs try to adopt less labor-intensive (that is, more "capitalistic") production methods. Demand for raw materials increases also.

Conversely, certain formerly profitable investments now become unprofitable: returns decline on capital goods that are usable only in relatively more labor-intensive methods and that cannot readily be adapted to the use of less labor. Demand for the different sorts of capital goods depends on relative factor costs and on the expected returns from using the machines to produce other products. Firms producing capital goods geared to unprofitable capital combinations find that they face increased factor costs while demand for their machines is falling off. Hence these firms (or lines of production) contract, while other firms producing goods adapted to the newer, more profitable capital combinations find demand rising and increase their output.

Changing price signals reduce profits on production for current consumption and increase profits on production for future consumption, thus altering rates of return on the different capital combinations involved.[34] Returns decline in production stages nearer to consumption, while returns increase in stages farthest from final consumption. Nonspecific resources are thus shifted from the former to the latter: output of consumer goods declines, while the pattern of production of capital goods is so altered as to produce goods that fit into a production structure extending through more stages than was previously possible.

In order that these investments may all be completed down to the final consumption stage, it is necessary that the requisite resources continue to be released from consumption, that is, that a decline in consumption output be maintained until the new production structure is completed. It must be remembered that, because of intertemporal complementarity, a machine whose usefulness depends on the construction of additional capital goods will be economically useless if the requisite resources are diverted elsewhere (that is, to the production of consumption output in this case). In order to complete all the capital combinations appropriate to an extended production structure, capital goods are now required that, given the intensity of consumption demand, are not available.

THE SELF-REVERSIBILITY OF MONETARY CHANGES

Consumption demand begins to increase as a result of the increased money incomes that factor owners have been receiving as a consequence of the increase in bank money. By hypothesis there has been no change in the rate of saving out of income. As these incomes are spent, the increased consumption expenditure meets an attenuated supply of consumer goods. Prices of consumer goods now, at this later stage, begin to rise relative to the prices of unfinished products, especially those farthest away from the final consumption stage. The process described earlier is now reversed: returns rise in stages nearer consumption, while returns decline in stages farthest from consumption. Nonspecific resources are once more drawn back into the production of consumer goods. All those capital goods intended for a different production structure have now to be readapted, to fit another, less capitalistic structure, with concomitant losses and unemployment. These losses are particularly heavy on those capital goods most suited only to a more capitalistic structure. Capital goods that are profitable to produce only at the lower rates of interest have been overproduced. They have been over-produced because the price signals generated by the hypothesized monetary policy have resulted in the production of inappropriate combinations of capital goods. Capital goods appropriate to the real factors (including transactors' time preferences or propensity to consume out of income) have been underproduced. In summary, the attempted extension of the production structure cannot be completed for lack of resources.

Monetary expansion began by lowering interest rates. Entrepreneurs, misled by the uncoordinated price signals, attempted to reduce all marginal rates of return to the same level. But in attempting to do so, they actually drove up ex post returns on some goods to levels higher than these interest rates.[35] Monetary expansion thus induces disproportionalities in the production of capital goods that are revealed in the depression: there is over-production in some lines, underproduction in others. The focus on the disproportionalities that occur in a cyclical process and the emphasis placed on these discoordinating price signals are perhaps the distinguishing features of Austrian, or Hayekian, analysis. It is precisely these effects that are lost in modern aggregative macromodels.

From the foregoing analysis, it is clear that the aggregation of individual investment-demand curves into one aggregate-investment curve has no price-theoretic foundation. Demand for any capital good depends on its position in the production structure and the profitability of integrating it into different and varying capital combinations. Equally, changes in interest rates affect prices and supplies, not merely of produced goods used in further production, but also of land and labor services. In short, monetary expansion affects not merely "the" interest rate but alters an enormous complex of price-cost margins and resource allocations; "*the* interest rate" is merely an extremely clumsy and misleading shorthand phrase covering this vast and intricate web of interrelationships.

Monetary expansion thus sets in train an unsustainable change in the pattern of production, a change that must eventually be modified and reversed. Initially, as money incomes rise, the effects of the expansion may appear to be beneficial. But it is now that the unsustainable misallocations are being made, as prices of unfinished products rise relative to consumer goods prices. As the money permeates through the system, this relative price change is reversed, and consumer goods prices rise. The cluster of misallocations now stands revealed in the form of losses and unemployment, additional to those necessary for the continuous adaptation of production to changing circumstances. More specifically, resources become unemployed in stages farthest from consumption. This unemployment is reduced as consumer goods production picks up. Continuous monetary expansion can only perpetuate this cyclical discoordination in the capital structure and thus raise losses and unemployment above the level they would otherwise reach.

Such expansion cannot prevent real scarcities from manifesting themselves. Prices may be initially and temporarily influenced in a direction opposite to that of the underlying real factors. But it is not as if there were an infinite array of prices consistent with the real factors. Prices reflect not only monetary disturbances but also real influences—tastes, technology, and, above all, real scarcities.

Consequently, although monetary expansion has real *misal*-locating effects, these "purely" monetary changes are self-reversing.[36] Most contemporary economists would be chary of accepting this proposition. This reluctance stems, we feel, from the current approach, which assumes that output always has its equilibrium composition, and which treats money as determining only the nominal heights of prices that are always at their real equilibrium levels. If money has no real effect whatsoever, then there is none to reverse, and furthermore there are no misallocations to correct.[37]

A final word: a monetary disturbance differs substantially from, for example, a tax-and-subsidy scheme. Taxes and subsidies do indeed reduce outputs of the taxed commodities while stimulating production of the subsidized ones. But there is no purely economic reason why taxes and subsidies, once imposed, need ever be removed. These disturbances merely lead to a new and stable allocation of resources, which persists as long as the taxes and subsidies continue. In the tax-cum-subsidy case, economic behavior is coordinated. There is no self-reversal.

PRICE EXPECTATIONS AND RESOURCE ALLOCATION

We have seen that monetary expansion systematically transmits misinformation throughout the economic system by moving prices in a direction opposite to that required by real structural factors. However, as expansion continues, price increases come to be expected.[38] Real scarcities and changed price expectations together serve to reduce somewhat those profit margins widened by purely monetary factors. If entrepreneurs find that ex post rates of return on certain goods (that is, consumer goods in general) are persistently higher than were expected ex ante, then they will come to anticipate this. Entrepreneurs will be willing to pay more to hire factors to produce those goods whose profit margins have proved to be greatest. Thus factor costs increase and profit margins decline for the producers of these capital goods appropriate to the lower rate of interest. Demand for these capital goods declines as entrepreneurs come to demand a different set of heterogeneous capital goods. Hence even with a constant rate of monetary expansion, we have the onset of the recessionary symptoms of a corrective reallocation. In these circumstances, if policymakers wish to raise apparent profit margins on firms producing inappropriate capital combinations to their previously inflated level, they must accelerate the monetary expansion. The ultimate limit to such a monetary policy is the abandonment of that money as a medium of exchange.

But even if monetary expansion proceeds at a constant rate, price expectations and real scarcities by no means obviate all the discoordinating effects of such a continuous disturbance; for it is not a matter of transactors' coming to anticipate the average increase in a set of prices—that is, the change in a price index. The impact on individual prices is still somewhat unpredictable, and hence profit margins on particular capital goods will continue to differ from expectations, because of purely monetary influences; some capital dislocation will thus continue.[39]

THE INADEQUACIES OF A PURELY MONETARY APPROACH

We may now see the inadequacies of the Keynesian approach that argues that, when there is excess capacity and unemployed labor in both capital and consumption goods industries, credit expansion permits higher employment and output. If the excess capacity is idle because it has been malinvested and hence cannot be fitted into the capital structure, the increased credit can only add to these misallocations and thus create further potential future idleness for both capital and labor resources. As Hayek incisively noted:

It has of course never been denied that employment can be rapidly increased, and a position of 'full employment' achieved in the shortest possible time by means of monetary expansion—least of all by those economists whose outlook has been influenced by the experience of a major inflation. All that has been contended is that the kind of full employment which can be created in this way is inherently unstable, and that to create employment by these means is to perpetuate fluctuations. There may be desperate situations in which it may indeed be necessary to increase employment at all costs, even if it be only for a short period. . . . But the economist should not conceal the fact that to aim at the maximum of employment which can be achieved in the short run by means of monetary policy is essentially the policy of the desperado who has nothing to lose and everything to gain from a short breathing space.[40]

If many contemporary economists refer to recessions or depressions today, it is almost invariably to their purely monetary aspects. Thus Friedman argued that "the American economy is depression-proof": a drastic monetary decline on the lines of 1930-33 is now impossible because of deposit insurance and banking and fiscal changes.[41] Paul W. McCracken concurred that economic management "can probably avert a major and a generalized depression"—financial collapse on the 1930s scale has been so rare that it would be premature to anticipate something similar. (However, he sternly warned companies and financial institutions against the risks of unwise financing policies.)[42] Harry G. Johnson stated that it is a "virtual certainty that nations will never again allow a massive world recession to develop" since "their economists would know better than to accept disaster as inevitable or inexplicable."[43] Haberler entitled the foreword to the 1964 edition of his *Prosperity and Depression* "Why Depressions Are Extinct." He cited the strength of the United States financial structure, deposit insurance, refusal to tolerate a wholesale deflation, and the powerful built-in stabilizer of the government budget. By preventing a decline in expenditure, this policy has "proved to be a very powerful brake on deflationary spirals and has been a major factor in keeping depressions mild." Outlining the main features of business cycles, he stated:

A very significant fact is that the wholesale price level almost always rises during the upswing and falls during the downswing, and the money values—payrolls, aggregate profits etc.—always go with the cycle. This proves that changes in effective demand, rather than changes in supply, are the proximate cause of the cyclical movement in real output and employment.[44]

None of these statements deal with the real misallocations resulting from monetary expansion or with the counteracting forces then set in motion. As we have seen, such counteracting forces, that is, recessionary symptoms, may appear to be (temporarily) fended off only if monetary expansion proceeds at an accelerating rate. If an expansion proceeds at a steady rate, recessionary symptoms appear nonetheless, and their onset is more rapid if the expansion decelerates.

STAGFLATION AND MONETARY ACCELERATION

In either case, it is the investment goods industries farthest from the production of consumer goods that feel the pinch first. If the monetary expansion continues steadily with the relative increase in consumer goods prices, firms nearer consumption bid away nonspecific resources from these industries, which now find that their costs rise faster than their selling prices. If the expansion slows down, there is an unambiguous decline in monetary demand for the investment projects begun at the lower interest rates. But even while unemployment and malinvested excess capacity appear in stages farthest from consumption, the incomes generated in the expansion are still working through the system. Consumer goods industries will maintain and even increase their demand for factor services: whereas at the beginning of the expansion these industries were outbid for factor services, they now face both an increase in demand and an increasing supply of nonspecific factors, as these are released by firms farther from consumption. Consumer prices may well continue to rise, but much depends on how rapidly output can be increased in these industries and nonspecific resources shifted back into consumer goods production. Mitigation of the level of employment also depends on both these elements.

From this analysis it is clear that attempts to maintain inflated capital values and incomes in the capital goods industries most affected would perpetuate the misallocation. Undoubtedly, there will be political pressure to do this:[45] the incomes of specific factors are most strongly affected by changes in demand for their services. But reflation—accelerated expansion—will lead to further maladjustments. Moreover, given the continuous steep rise in consumer prices, there will also undoubtedly be an opposing pressure from groups whose incomes lag behind. This pressure will often take the form of controls on prices (particularly those of consumer goods). Consumer price controls can only exacerbate the situation. By reducing returns in the consumer goods industries, they intensify the shortage of consumption goods.

As we have seen, it is the rise in consumption expenditures that precipitates the market pressure for resource reallocation. Attempts to stimulate consumption would intensify these reallocative pressures. A rise in voluntary saving, on the other hand, would help salvage some of the malinvestments. But these misallocations were created by the monetary expansion; as long as expansion continues, the capital structure will be dislocated, and malinvestments will arise, only some of which are salvageable.

To summarize: Under the impact of a monetary disturbance, prices will transmit misinformation. The revelation of this misinformation and its correction constitute a recession. The abnormal rise in losses and unemployment is the counterpart to the misallocations created by the misinformation. In short, *monetary expansion and recession are inseparable!*

If the expansion is halted, the recession is precipitated rapidly. It may be extensive and deep. But once the readjustment is completed and a sustainable pattern of output and employment established, there need be no further allocative difficulties and certainly no currency depreciation.

If monetary expansion continues, recessionary symptoms of greater and greater intensity appear. But the readjustment will not be wholly completed. The pattern of output and employ-

ment is continuously dislocated. Eventually, losses and unemployment persist in rising and continue at ever higher levels
despite the continuing expansion.[46]

If the expansion is repeatedly accelerated to overcome the
recession, the outcome is obvious. Such a situation may well
come to face the developed economies of the Western world,
unintentionally, no doubt as the consequence of the cumulative
outcome of successive decisions to expand the money supply in
the face of the threatening depression. The economists quoted
here assure us that our financial system will never permit
another Great Depression. Can they also assure us that it will
never permit a hyperinflation?

Samuelson seemed to think not. He pointed out that monetary
expansion occurs in response to "populist" pressures to "avoid
policies that would worsen short-run unemployment and stagnation problems." He therefore saw the outlook as one of "creep-
ing or trotting inflation. The problem is how to keep the creep or
trot from accelerating. This includes the challenge of finding
new macroeconomic policies beyond conventional fiscal and
monetary policies that will enable a happier compromise between the evils of unemployment and of price inflation." But he
stressed that "a Draconian policy of insisting upon stable prices
at whatever cost to current unemployment and short-run
growth" would be a "costly investment in fighting inflation,"
since he saw no guarantee "that even in the longest run the
benefits to be derived from militant anti-inflationary policies
don't carry excessive costs as far as average levels of unemployment and growth are concerned." He went on to warn that
"mankind at this stage of the game can ill afford to make
irreversible academic experiments whose outcomes are necessarily doubtful" and whose implementation would exacerbate
political tensions. He was confident such an anti-inflation policy
"will assuredly never be followed."[47]

Truly, inflation does leave us holding a "tiger by the tail," as
Hayek remarked:

Now we have an inflation-borne prosperity which depends for its continuation on continued inflation. If prices rise less than expected, then a depressing effect is exerted on the economy. . . . to slow down inflation produces a recession. We now have a tiger by the tail: how long can this inflation continue? If the tiger (or inflation) is freed, he will eat us up; yet if he runs faster and faster while we desperately hold on, we are *still* finished! I'm glad I won't be here to see the final outcome.[48]

NOTES

1. John B. Egger, "Information and Unemployment in the Trade Cycle" (Paper delivered at Second Symposium on Austrian Economics, University of Hartford, June 1975), p. 16.

2. The eleven countries are: Belgium, Canada, France, Israel, Japan, Netherlands, Sweden, Switzerland, United Kingdom, United States, and West Germany. For data supporting the statements in the text, see Arthur Seldon, ed., *Inflation: Economy and Society* (London: Institute of Economic Affairs, 1972), Appendix.

3. See, for example, United Nations, Economic Commission for Europe, *Economic Survey of Europe in 1961: Some Factors in Economic Growth in Europe during the 1950's* (E/ECE/452/Add. 1) (Geneva 1954), pp. 23-32; Great Britain, Council on Prices, Productivity, and Incomes, *Fourth Report* (HMSO 1961); Great Britain, National Economic Development Council, *Conditions Favourable to Faster Growth* (HMSO April 1963); Great Britain, National Economic Development Council, *Growth in the U.K. Economy to 1966* (HMSO February 1963); Political and Economic Planning, *Growth in the British Economy* (London: Allen & Unwin, 1960), pp. 1-53, 197-219; Angus Maddison, *Economic Growth in the West: Comparative Experience in Europe and North America* (London: Allen & Unwin, 1964).

4. Organization for Economic Cooperation and Development, *OECD Economic Outlook*, 14(December 1973):32; ibid., 15(July 1974):18.

5. See tables referred to in note 2; also see Organization for Economic Cooperation and Development, *OECD Economic Outlook* 15(July 1974):73-77; and almost any issue of *The Economist*, e. g., "To Meet Slumpflation" and "Mass Unemployment Ahead?" *The Economist* 250(23 March 1974):14-16; "Before Taking to Wheelbarrows," *The Economist* 252(20 July 1974):65-66; see also the report from Peter Jay, "OECD forecasts increased inflation in Britain for first half of next

year; Reflation 'would make matters worse,' " *Times* (London), 3 October 1974, p. 1; and National Institute of Economic and Social Research, *National Institute Economic Review* 69(August 1974):4-26.

6.   J.C.R. Dow, *The Management of the British Economy, 1945-60* (Cambridge: Cambridge University Press, 1964), chap. 13; L.A. Dicks-Mireaux, *Cost or Demand Inflation?* Woolwich Economic Papers, no. 6 (London, 1965).

7.   Nicholas Kaldor, "The New Monetarism," *Lloyd's Bank Review*, no. 97 (July 1970), pp. 1-17.

8.   Ibid.; see also Joan Mitchell, "Why We Need an Incomes Policy," *Lloyd's Bank Review*, no. 92 (April 1969), pp. 1-14.

9.   This view is shared by several Austrians as well; see Ludwig M. Lachmann, *Macroeconomic Thinking and the Market Economy*, Institute of Economic Affairs, Hobart Paper no. 56 (London, 1973), p. 50.

10.   For an indirect demonstration that the existence of money makes sense only in a multicommodity world and that a multicommodity world is virtually inconceivable in the absence of a medium of exchange, see Carl Menger, *Principles of Economics* (Glencoe, Ill.: Free Press, 1950), pp. 236-85. It should be pointed out that in the more sophisticated versions of the Keynesian analysis, changes in interest rates do affect the prices of investment goods relative to the prices of consumer goods. See the extensive discussions of aggregation in Axel Leijonhufvud, *On Keynesian Economics and the Economics of Keynes* (New York: Oxford University Press, 1969), pp.20-23, 111-85.

11.   "The aspect of Keynes' theory which has created the most trouble . . . is his theory of interest—which is rather a theory of short-run interest *movements*" (Leijonhufvud, *Keynesian Economics*, pp. 12-13). We maintain that modern Keynesian writers have still not solved this problem.

12.   D. H. Robertson, "Mr. Keynes and the Rate of Interest," in *Essays in Monetary Theory*, ed. idem (London: P. S. King & Son, 1940), p. 25.

13.   See Charles W. Baird, *Macroeconomics* (Chicago: Science Research Associates, 1973), for an example of a recent attempt to introduce price-level flexibility and to adopt a micro approach in macroanalysis. Attempts like this, though praiseworthy, have not been successful. Microanalysis deals with pricing and resource allocation and hence with the time structure of output and prices. Microeconomics is far more than the analysis of single prices in isolation. Manipulation of price levels would seem to have little to do with microanalysis in this sense.

14.   The following analysis and interpretation of the monetarist position is based on Milton Friedman, "A Theoretical Framework for Monetary Analysis," *Journal of Political Economy* 78(March-April

1970):193-238; idem, "A Monetary Theory of Nominal Income," *Journal of Political Economy* 79(March-April 1971): 323-37; idem, *Dollars and Deficits* (Englewood Cliffs, N. J.; Prentice-Hall, 1969).

15.   John Stuart Mill, *Principles of Political Economy*, ed. Sir William Ashley (Clifton Heights, N. J.: Augustus M. Kelley, 1973), p. 491.

16.   See Thomas Sowell, *Classical Economics Reconsidered* (Princeton: Princeton University Press, 1974), pp. 52-66.

17.   Friedman admitted that he and Anna J. Schwartz "have little confidence in [their] knowledge of the transmission mechanism, except in such broad and vague terms as to constitute little more than an impressionistic representation rather than an engineering blueprint" (*The Optimum Quantity of Money* [Chicago: Aldine Publishing Co., 1969], p. 222).

18.   Ludwig von Mises, *The Theory of Money and Credit* (New Haven: Yale University Press, 1953), pp. 124-31.

19.   Friedman, "Theoretical Framework," p. 223.

20.   Milton Friedman, *Dollars and Deficits*, pp. 72-96.

21.   See Trygve Haavelmo, "What Can Static Equilibrium Models Tell Us?" *Economic Inquiry* 12(March 1974):27-34.

22.   See, for example, "The Rising Risk of Recession," *Time Magazine*, 19 December 1969, pp. 66-72.

23.   Friedrich A. Hayek, *The Pure Theory of Capital* (London: Routledge & Kegan Paul, 1941), pp. 409-10.

24.   F. H. Hahn, "On Some Problems of Proving the Existence of an Equilibrium in a Monetary Economy," in *The Theory of Interest Rates*, ed. F. H. Hahn and F. P. R. Beckling (London: Macmillan & Co., 1965), pp. 128-32.

25.   Menger, *Principles*, pp. 236-85.

26.   Knut Wicksell, *Lectures on Political Economy*, ed. Lionel Robbins, 2 vols. (New York: Macmillan Co., 1935) 2:141-90.

27.   For an appreciation of Mises's contributions to the development of monetary theory, see Laurence S. Moss, "The Monetary Economics of Ludwig von Mises," in *The Economics of Ludwig von Mises: Toward a Critical Reappraisal*, ed. Laurence S. Moss (Kansas City: Sheed & Ward, 1976).

28.   Hayek first presented his monetary analysis of the business cycle to the English-speaking world in four lectures at London University in 1931; see Friedrich A. Hayek, *Prices and Production* (London: Routledge & Kegan Paul, 1935). His earlier German work on monetary theory was translated and published in 1933; idem, *Monetary Theory and the Trade Cycle* (New York: Augustus M. Kelley, 1966). In 1939 Hayek developed his theory further in an essay entitled "Profits, Interest, and Investment," which he published along with some of his earlier articles under the same title; see idem, *Profits Interest and Investment* (New York:

Augustus M. Kelley, 1970); see also idem, "Three Elucidations of the Ricardo Effect," *Journal of Political Economy* 77 (March-April 1969):274-85.

29. Ibid., p. 281.

30. Hayek, *Prices and Production*.

31. Ludwig M. Lachmann, *Capital and Its Structure* (London: London School of Economics, 1956).

32. Two types of complementarity exist: "horizontal complementarity," where goods in any one stage of production must be integrated, and "vertical complementarity," where goods must be integrated between stages.

33. Hayek referred to this effect as the "Ricardo effect." For references to Hayek's writings and further explanations, see Gerald P. O'Driscoll, Jr., "The Specialization Gap and the Ricardo Effect: Comment on Ferguson," *History of Political Economy* 7(Summer 1975): 261-69.

34. The physical durability of a capital good is not the only determining factor in its demand price; also important is its position in the overall capital structure (Hayek, *Pure Theory*, pp. 46-49).

35. We are discussing changes in the real rate of interest; the nominal rate may vary owing, among other factors, to the impact of future price expectations.

36. Hayek, *Pure Theory*, pp. 33-34.

37. The view that the effects of monetary expansion are self-reversing meets with hostility; see, for example, Friedman, "Comments on the Critics," *Journal of Political Economy* 80(September-October 1972): 936-41. It is ironic that, in his 1974 address to the Southern Economics Association in Atlanta, Friedman acknowledged that less unemployment now (caused by an unanticipated increase in the growth rate of the money supply) will result in more unemployment later; that is, cyclical expansions bring about cyclical contractions. While it is true that Friedman's talk made no reference to real factors of the type discussed here, still it is an improvement over his earlier attitude where he refused to consider this form of reasoning at all.

38. See Hayek, "Three Elucidations," pp. 284-85.

39. Even with "indexation," however widespread, new money would still enter the economy at a specific point and first alter some relative prices and outputs before altering other prices and outputs. These misallocations and subsequent corrections would continue as long as the increase in the money supply persisted. Indexation of money payments would merely add yet another unpredictable relative price change to those already set in motion by the monetary disturbances. In particular, some incomes would continue to rise ahead of the consumer price index while others would rise after it. Indexation

would only allow for (known) past changes in the consumer price index resulting from those increases in the money supply that had already worked through the economy. It could do little ex ante about present increases in the money supply still working their way through the economy. The case for indexation is made by a number of economists; see especially Milton Friedman, *Monetary Correction* (London: Institute of Economic Affairs, 1974).

40. Hayek, *Profits, Interest, and Investment*, pp. 63 n, 64 n.

41. Friedman, *Dollars and Deficits*, pp. 72-96.

42. Paul W. McCracken, "Are the Latter Days Upon Us?" *Wall Street Journal*, 22 July 1974, p. 8.

43. Harry G. Johnson, "Mercantilism, Past, Present and Future," *Manchester School* 42(March 1974):15.

44. Gottfried Haberler, *Prosperity and Depression*, 5th ed. (London: Allen & Unwin, 1964), pp. viii, xi.

45. The general council of the U.K. Trades Union Congress demanded government subsidies for all firms threated with losses and therefore having to lay off workers; see the report by John Elliott, "TUC urges more government control over redundancies," *Financial Times* (London), 24 October 1974, p. 1.

46. Thus aggregate money expenditure rose by 248 percent in the United Kingdom between 1949 and 1969, but output rose only 69 percent. Similar money increases may be adduced for other developed countries. Nevertheless, Denis Healey, chancellor of the exchequer, found it necessary to issue a warning to the 1974 Conference of the International Monetary Fund not to repeat "the tragedy of the 1930's [by attempting] to deal with inflation by measures likely to produce mass unemployment"; see the report entitled "Mr. Healey warns the world on threat of 1930's tragedy being repeated," and the report from Peter Jay, "Chancellor emphasizes need to avoid mass unemployment," *The Times* (London), 2 October 1974, p. 1.

47. Paul A. Samuelson, "Worldwide Stagflation," *Morgan Guaranty Survey*, June 1974, pp. 4-9.

48. From Hayek's remarks at the Mont Pelerin Conference, Caracas, September 1969; these remarks are on record only in Friedrich A. Hayek, *A Tiger by The Tail*, ed. Sudha R. Shenoy, Institute of Economic Affairs, Hobart Paper no. 4 (London, 1972), p. 112.

Part 4
Conclusion

Austrian Economics in the Age of the Neo-Ricardian Counterrevolution

Ludwig M. Lachmann

It is widely acknowledged today that economics is passing through a period of crisis, though its exact nature is in dispute. Austrian economists must assess the present position of, and the outlook for, their body of thought as well. A school of thought cannot decide on what to do without taking its bearings. Even were one to decide to do nothing but let one's ship be swayed by the shifting winds, something might be said for a thorough study of weather charts! The student of contemporary affairs always suffers from the handicap that, unlike the historian, he does not know how far tomorrow's changes will nullify the model he makes of today's world. But this is a risk that has to be taken. It is not for nothing that we are living in a kaleidic society.

When making an assessment of the present situation of Austrian economics, our first task is, of course, to define it. What is Austrian economics? The perspective of the economic world that characteristically distinguishes Austrian thought from other (classical or neoclassical) thought can best be defined in terms of the three following postulates:

1. Economics has two tasks, one backward looking, the other forward looking. As G. L. S. Shackle pointed out:

Economic theory is about the sources of individual conduct and the

215

consequences of its interaction. It is the intimate fusing together of the two questions, concerning the mode of choice of conduct and the outcome of the combination of many men's choices, that constitutes economics as a distinct body of ideas and a discipline on its own.[1]

We cannot know whether economists in the course of time will have to shoulder tasks other than these two. However, it is characteristic of the Austrian style of thought that the backward-looking task is regarded as the more important. It is more important to make the world of action as it unfolds intelligible than it is to deduce the unintended consequences of action. This postulate entails certain limits to the degree of abstraction we may employ and to our freedom in constructing models. Abstraction is necessary, useful, even inevitable, to let our minds grasp the essentials of a situation, but we must not abstract from those acts of the mind in choice and interpretation that shape and constitute the social world. We must reject mere formal entities as elements of models. Different men finding themselves in the same situation may give it widely differing interpretations. Austrian economics is always concerned with action, never solely with reaction. It rejects as mere formalism, whether neoclassical or neo-Ricardian, all those endeavours that in a quest for "formal uniformities" are ready to assign causal roles to entities like quantities and prices, and all those models in which the economic system assumes the appearance of a "goods circus."[2]

2.   The human mind can grasp many forms and patterns, structures as well as uniformities of sequence in nature. Only individuals, however, have minds and therefore can make plans and act. Hence, if our main task is to understand the world of human action, we must reject any explanation of events other than in terms of plans and action. To be sure, individuals acting are oriented to their environment, natural and human. But this orientation is always a matter of subjective perspective and interpretation. Moreover, where the environment is human, problems arise of multiple perspectives and interpretations, hence the difficulties with any notion of equilibrium involving interaction of many minds, and hence the superiority of the market process as a model of interaction.

3. It follows from (1) and (2) that formal entities that do violence to the dazzling diversity of the social world are alien to the Austrian style of thought. This means that Austrian economists must erect several sets of limits to abstraction. The diversity that matters is diversity of tastes, interpretations, and expectations. The Ricardians ignore the first, admit (with a bad conscience) the second, and do not know what to do with the third. Their neoclassical opponents assure us with some enthusiasm that they accept the first but have to ignore the second (since their formal apparatus offers no scope for the interpretative action of the human mind), and (wrongly) think they can cope with the third by using the formal apparatus of probability theory, clear though it is that this was originally developed to deal with a quite different set of problems.

There is no need for me to deal at great length with the neo-Ricardian counterrevolution of our day. Its numerous exponents in Cambridge and elsewhere are propagating its cause with considerable enthusiasm and remarkable polemical skill. Suffice it to say that, for the first time, the neoclassical ascendancy, established by John Bates Clark, Irving Fisher, Vilfredo Pareto, and Knut Wicksell around the turn of the century, appears seriously threatened. The defensive strategy adopted by such outstanding neoclassical leaders as John Hicks and Frank H. Hahn leaves the impression that they are only too well aware of the weakness inherent in the position they have inherited.

What is the Austrian position on this battleground? Let me outline it in terms of points of Austrian agreement and disagreement with the views held by the rival schools.

Austrian economists must disagree strongly with most of the ideas flaunted by the neo-Ricardians. Any return to the classical world of economic thought would nullify Menger's work, as well as that of most of his successors. The strange dichotomy between cost of production determining price and demand determining quantity sold is quite untenable. In any circumstances other than those of constant cost, whatever the scale of output, demand must have some effect on price. The underlying methodological egalitarianism—the view of competition as a state of affairs in which all producers sell identical goods, the failure to understand that the contribution of each entrepreneur is an individual contribution—is also no more attractive. To watch neo-Ricardians handle expectations is, according to taste, a sad or an amusing spectacle: they play with them like children playing with ancient coins, the value and origin of which they fail to understand. The diversity of the world is to them a closed book. As radical subjectivists Austrians must stand in the forefront of the resistance to this counterrevolution.

We can, however, perhaps agree with them on several points: that general equilibrium is a precarious notion; that in reality it could never be attained; and that events taking place on the path to equilibrium must shape its final constellation. They, on their part, are unlikely to accept the notion of the market process.

The list of points of disagreement between Austrian and neoclassical economics is hardly shorter. A kaleidic world can offer no congenial habitat to the neoclassical mind, to which all time sequences at once appear in the familiar form of difference equations. Will they ever understand that "frequency distributions" *e tutti quanti* can have no place outside a homogeneous world, a world in which we are entitled to judge the unknown future by the standards of a known past? Or that "orthodox welfare analysis calmly assumes that the critically important social task of making all the scattered bits of information available to those making decisions has already been performed."[3] Without this assumption the vaunted Pareto optimum makes little sense. From time to time neoclassical economists are apt to flaunt consumers' tastes, one of their data, as a mark of their individualism. But on closer inspection their individualism turns out to be a pseudoindividualism. The individual interests them only in his capacity as a possessor of given tastes, not as a possessor of a mind capable of probing and digesting experience, of acquiring and diffusing knowledge. Pareto saw quite clearly that real individuals, continuously having experiences bound to modify given tastes, can have no place in the neoclassical model, and that a photograph of their tastes is all that is required.[4] It is thus only at a point in time that we can speak of utility functions of individuals.[5] Their unpredictable change over time forms the basis of the kaleidic society and provides the rationale for the market process.

At present a good deal of soul-searching appears to be going on in the higher ranks of the neoclassical establishment. My own impression is that little will change. The very language in which criticism of neoclassical orthodoxy is presented inspires little confidence. When Hahn, after having noticed that "the argument will here turn on the absence of futures markets and contingent futures markets," observed that "practical men and ill-trained theorists everywhere in the world do not understand what they are claiming to be the case when they claim a beneficent and coherent role for the invisible hand,"[6] it is painfully obvious that he has paid no attention to Austrian economics. He apparently was unable to conceive of the function of the market in terms other than those of some kind of intertemporal Pareto optimum.

Also, we hear of a "state of nature" (but no state of culture) emanating "messages" received by the individuals acting. While admittedly individuals cannot be in equilibrium while they are learning (hence no equilibrium over time?), the neo-Darwinist language in which we are told how man, as he learns about his environment, makes a better adjustment to it, sounds rather forbidding. The fundamental obstacle to any rapprochement between Austrian and neoclassical economics is the fact that the latter cannot conceive of human action, but only of reaction to given circumstances.

What of the future? Austrian economists must evidently establish themselves as a third force outside the counterrevolution and the neoclassical establishment against which it is directed. This will be no easy task. Their numbers are small, their resources slender. The big foundations are closed to them. They have no academic foothold. Their only strategy can be to impress the world by the quality of their contributions. But this will hardly be enough. In the 1930s a hopeful flowering of Austrian economics was nipped in the bud; as Hicks put it, its "voice has been almost drowned in the fanfare of the Keynesian orchestra."[7] This must not happen again.

Owing to the current weakness of the Austrian position in the academic world, we must make optimal use of assets and exploit every opportunity. In this regard, I have three suggestions.

In the first place, two eminent contemporaries, Axel Leijonhufvud and Shackle, who do not, to my knowledge, regard themselves as Austrian economists, within the last six years made outstanding contributions that conform to what I have described as the main body of Austrian thought. It is for Austrian economists to make full use of the implications of their ideas.

Second, at times in the course of the counterrevolution, both sides present arguments with unmistakably Austrian implications of which their authors may be quite unaware. In such cases Austrian economists must appear on the scene at once to point them out. Otherwise the lesson will be lost. For example, when Luigi L. Pasinetti in his criticism of Robert Solow stated that "the two situations *a* and *b* that Solow compared differ not only by the single 'consumption good' he has hypothesised but also by *the whole structure of capital goods*",[8] the Austrian implications of this notion, are obvious. But neither of the rival sides appears to have taken much interest in them. In any case they go much beyond what is provided for in Hicks's neo-Austrian model.

The best opportunity for the rehabilitation of Austrian economics today is, I regret to say, to be sought in the permanent inflation the Western world has suffered since the Second World War. This is certainly not the fault of Austrian economists; there has been no lack of warnings from their side.

We live in a world in which prices can only rise and never fall, because the public has come to believe that a widespread fall of money wage rates in the face of a falling demand for goods and services would be intolerable. A world, however, in which all relative price adjustments have to be made against a background of continuously rising money prices and wages is one in which money is no longer a store of value: it can only depreciate, never appreciate. The process of inflation must accelerate once everybody understands what is happening.

Faced with this situation neoclassical economists, on the whole, have (predictably?) behaved badly. Some have distinguished between cost-push and demand-pull inflations as though we were dealing with a succession of historical processes of inflation and not one indivisible process. Some would have us believe that there is a choice between a little more unemployment and a little more inflation. The facts of the inflation now accelerating all over the Western world speak for themselves, though the econometricians may not understand the language. A mind for which the economic world is a complex system of given variables seems quite unable to grasp a kaleidic world. The facts of a world of accelerating inflation elude it.

Some neoclassical economists have shown themselves to be rather uninhibited inflationists. According to Kenneth J. Arrow:

The rates of inflation with which we have had to contend impose no insuperable problem or even major difficulty to the operation of the economic system, nothing comparable to the major depressions of the past. Individuals will learn and have learned to deal with inflation making their plans to take expected inflation into account. The economic system and the government will create and are creating methods of mitigating the effects. . . . Some analysts feel that inflation will inevitably accelerate, but others will note that in the past peacetime inflation has tapered off.

Second, we may have some reasonable hope that economic research and experimentation in policymaking, between them, will evolve more sophisticated means of managing the overall economy.[9]

Solow expressed an even more striking view: "In a monetary economy, it is natural to amend the definition of a steady state to require a constant rate of inflation; since everything else is growing exponentially, the price level ought to be no exception."[10]

Neo-Ricardians have been far more cautious about inflation. Hayek and Joan Robinson not merely agreed on the substance of the matter but actually, though no doubt unwittingly, used the same metaphor: "An inflationary economy is in the situation of a man holding a tiger by the tail."[11]

Faced with this terrible but challenging situation Austrian economists today have a triple duty. They must tell the public that:

1.   The real cause of the accelerating inflation lies in a change in the social climate that, engineered by the left intelligentsia, took place about a half-century ago and resulted in a taboo on downward adjustments of money wage rates.

2.   A market economy requires a money that can serve as a store of value, a money in terms of which prices are as likely to fall as they may be to rise. (An absolutely stable price level is impossible.) No such money exists today.

3.   None of the nostrums peddled by economists in many countries today involving price and wage controls will work, and they may well paralyze the market process.

NOTES

1.   G. L. S. Shackle, "Marginalism: The Harvest," *History of Political Economy*, Fall 1972, p. 587.

2.   For an excellent example of what I mean by neoclassical formalism, consider the following: "Implicit in such analyses there are certain recognizable formal uniformities, which are indeed characteristic of all scientific method. It is proposed here to investigate these common features in the hope of demonstrating how it is possible to deduce general principles which can serve to unify large sectors of present-day economic theory" (Paul A. Samuelson, *Foundations of Economic Analysis* [Cambridge: Harvard University Press, 1947], p. 7).

3.   Israel M. Kirzner, *Competition and Entrepreneurship* (Chicago: University of Chicago Press, 1973), p. 214.

4.   "L'individu peut disparaître, pourvu qu'il nous laisse cette photographie de ses goûts" (Vilfredo Pareto, *Manuel d'Economie Politique*, 2d ed. [Paris, 1927], p. 170).

5.   Sometimes the neoclassical formalists remember it in the formulation of their principles—more often they forget it in practice. Consider the following: "In every problem of economic theory certain variables (quantities, policies, etc.) are designated as unknowns, in whose determination we are interested. Their values emerge as a solution of a specific set of relationships imposed upon the unknowns

by assumption or hypothesis. *These functional relationships hold as of a given environment and milieu"* (Samuelson, *Foundations*, p. 7; italics mine).

6. Frank Horace Hahn, *On the Notion of Equilibrium in Economics: An Inaugural Lecture"* (Cambridge: Cambridge University Press, 1973), p. 14.

7. John R. Hicks, *Capital and Growth* (Oxford: Clarendon Press, 1965), p. 185.

8. Luigi L. Pasinetti, "Again on Capital Theory and Solow's 'Rate of Return,' " *Economic Journal*, June 1970, p. 429 (Pasinetti's italics).

9. Kenneth J. Arrow, "Capitalism, for Better or Worse," in *Capitalism: the Moving Target*, ed. Leonard Silk (New York: Quadrangle, 1974), pp. 105-113.

10. Robert M. Solow, *Growth Theory: An Exposition* (Oxford: Oxford University Press, 1970), p. 66.

11. Joan Robinson, *Economic Heresies* (London: Macmillan & Co., 1971), p. 95; Friedrich A. Hayek, *A Tiger by the Tail*, ed. Sudha R. Shenoy, Institute of Economic Affairs, Hobart Paper 4 (London, 1972), p. 112.

Selected Bibliography

Block, Walter. "A Comment on 'The Extraordinary Claim of Praxeol-
ogy' by Professor Gutierrez." *Theory and Decision* 3(1973):381-
82.
Böhm-Bawerk, Eugen von. *Capital and Interest.* Translated by George
D. Huncke and Hans F. Sennholz. South Holland, Ill.: Libertar-
ian Press, 1959.
Bresciani Turroni, Constanino. *The Economics of Inflation.* London:
George Allen & Unwin, 1937.
Buchanan, James M. "Is Economics the Science of Choice?" In *Roads to
Freedom: Essays in Honour of Friedrich A. von Hayek*, edited by Eric
Streissler, et al., pp. 47-64. London: Routledge & Kegal Paul,
1969.
de Roover, Raymond. *Business, Banking, and Economic Thought.*
Chicago: University of Chicago Press, 1974.
Fetter, Frank A. "The 'Roundabout Process' in the Interest Theory,"
Quarterly Journal of Economics 17(November 1902):163-80.
Grice-Hutchinson, Marjorie. *The School of Salamanca: Readings in
Spanish Monetary Theory, 1544-1605.* Oxford: Clarendon Press,
1952.
Dorfman, Robert. "A Graphical Exposition of Böhm-Bawerk's Interest
Theory." *Review of Economic Studies* 26(February 1959):153-58.
Hayek, Friedrich A. *A Tiger by the Tail.* Edited by Sudha R. Shenoy.
London: Institute of Economic Affairs, 1972.
———. *Collectivist Economic Planning.* 1935 Reprint. London: Rout-
ledge & Kegan Paul, 1963.
———. *Individualism and Economic Order.* London: Routledge &
Kegan Paul, 1952.
———. *Monetary Theory and the Trade Cycle.* Translated by N. Kaldon
and H. M. Croome. London: Jonathan Cape, 1933.
———. *Prices and Production.* 2d rev. ed. London: Routledge & Sons,
1935.
———. *Profits, Interest, and Investment and Other Essays on the Theory
of Industrial Relations.* 1939. Reprint. New York: Augustus M.
Kelley, 1969.
———. *Studies in Philosophy, Politics, and Economics.* Chicago: Univer-
sity of Chicago Press, 1967.

————. *The Counter-Revolution of Science: Studies on the Abuse of Reason*. Glencoe, Ill.: Free Press, 1955.

————. *The Pure Theory of Capital*. London: Routledge & Kegan Paul, 1941.

"Three Elucidations of the Ricardo Effect." *Journal of Political Economy* 77(March/April 1969):274-85.

Hicks, John R. *Capital and Growth*. Oxford: Oxford University Press, 1965.

————. *Capital and Time, A Neo-Austrian Theory*. Oxford: Clarendon Press, 1973.

————. "Capital Controversies: Ancient and Modern." *American Economic Review* 64(May 1974):307-16.

Hicks, John R., and Weber, Wilhelm, eds. *Carl Menger and the Austrian School of Economics*. Oxford: Clarendon Press, 1973.

Kauder, Emil. *A History of Marginal Utility Theory*. Princeton: Princeton University Press, 1965.

————. "Genesis of the Marginal Utility Theory: From Aristotle to the End of the Eighteenth Century." *Economic Journal* 63(September 1953):638-50.

————. "Intellectual and Political Roots of the Older Austrian School." *Zeitschrift für Nationalökonomie* 17(December 1957):411-25.

————. "The Retarded Acceptance of the Marginal Utility Theory." *Quarterly Journal of Economics* 67(November 1953):564-75.

Kirzner, Israel. *An Essay on Capital*. New York: Augustus M. Kelley, 1966.

————. *Competition and Entrepreneurship*. Chicago: University of Chicago Press, 1973.

————. *The Economic Point of View: An Essay in the History of Economic Thought*. 1960. Reprint. Kansas City: Sheed & Ward, 1976.

Knight, Frank H. " 'What is Truth' in Economics." In *On the History and Method of Economics*, edited by William L. Letwin and Alexander J. Morin, pp. 151-78. Chicago: University of Chicago Press, 1956.

Lachmann, Ludwig M. *Capital and Its Structure*. London: London School of Economics, 1956.

————. *Macroeconomic Thinking and the Market Economy*. London: Institute of Economic Affairs, 1973.

————. "Methodological Individualism and the Market Economy," In *Roads to Freedom: Essays in Honour of Friedrich A. von Hayek*, edited by Eric Streissler, et al., pp. 89-104. London: Routledge & Kegan Paul, 1969.

————. "Sir John Hicks as Neo-Austrian." *South African Journal of Economics* 41(September 1973):195-207.

————. *The Legacy of Max Weber*. Berkeley, Calif.: Glendessary Press, 1971.

Lutz, F. A., and Hague, D. C., eds. *The Theory of Capital*. London: Macmillan & Co., 1961.

Menger, Carl. *Principles of Economics*. Translated and edited by James Dingwall and Bert F. Hoselitz. Glencoe, Ill.: Free Press, 1950.

————. *Problems of Economics and Sociology*. Translated by Francis J. Nock. Urbana: University of Illinois, 1963.

Mises, Ludwig von. *Epistemological Problems of Economics*. Translated by George Reisman. Princeton: D. Van Nostrand, 1960.

————. *Human Action: A Treatise on Economics*. 2d rev. ed. New Haven: Yale University Press, 1963.

————. *Theory and History*. New Haven: Yale University Press, 1957.

————. *Theory of Money and Credit*. Translated by H. E. Batson. New Haven: Yale University Press, 1953.

Morgenstern, Oskar. *On the Accuracy of Economic Observations*. 2d rev. ed. Princeton: Princeton University Press, 1963.

Moss, Laurence S., ed. *The Economics of Ludwig von Mises: Toward A Critical Reappraisal*. Kansas City: Sheed & Ward, 1976.

O'Driscoll, Gerald P., Jr., "The Specialization Gap and the Ricardo Effect: Comment on Ferguson," *History of Political Economy* 7(Summer 1975):261-69.

Robbins, Lionel. *An Essay on the Nature and Significance of Economic Science*. 2d ed. London: Macmillan & Co., 1935.

Rothbard, Murray N. *Egalitarianism as a Revolt against Nature and Other Essays* (Washington, D. C.: Libertarian Review Press, 1974), pp. 2-3.

————. "In Defense of 'Extreme Apriorism.' " *Southern Economic Journal* 23(January 1957):315-18.

————. *Man, Economy, and State*. 2 vols. Princeton: D. Van Nostrand, 1962.

————. *Power and Market*. Menlo Park, Calif.: Institute for Humane Studies, 1970.

————. "Praxeology as the Method of Economics." In *Phenomenology and the Social Sciences*, 2 vols., edited by M. Natanson, pp. 311-39. Evanston: Northwestern University Press, 1973.

————. "The Mantle of Science." In *Scientism and Values*, edited by Helmot Schoeck and J. W. Wiggins, pp. 159-80. Princeton: D. Van Nostrand, 1960.

————. "Toward a Reconstruction of Utility and Welfare Economics." In *On Freedom and Free Enterprise*, edited by Mary Sennholz, pp. 224-62. Princeton: D. Van Nostrand, 1956.

————. "Value Implications of Economic Theory." *American Economist* 17(Spring 1973):35-39.

Schoeck, H., and Wiggins, J. W., eds. *Relativism and the Study of Man*. Princeton: D. Van Nostrand, 1961.

Yeager, Leland B. "Essential Properties of the Medium of Exchange." *Kyklos* 21(1968):45-68.

———. "Measurement as Scientific Method in Economics." *American Journal of Economics and Sociology* 16(July 1967):337-46.

CONTRIBUTORS

Edwin G. Dolan is Assistant Professor of Economics at Dartmouth College. His major scholarly publications include "Alienation, Freedom, and Economic Organization," *Journal of Political Economy* 79(September-October 1971):1084-94; "The Teleological Period in Soviet Planning," *Yale Economics Essays* 10 (Spring 1970):3-41; and *TANSTAAFL: An Economic Strategy for the Environmental Crisis* (New York: Holt, Rinehart & Winston, 1971).

Gerald Patrick O'Driscoll, Jr., is Assistant Professor of Economics at Iowa State University. His dissertation is entitled "F. A. Hayek's Contributions to Economics" (University of California, 1973). His recent publications include "The Specialization Gap and the Ricardo Effect: Comment on Ferguson," *History of Political Economy* 7(Summer 1975):261-69.

Israel M. Kirzner is Professor of Economics at New York University. His major works on economic theory include *The Economic Point of View* (Princeton: D. Van Nostrand, 1960); *An Essay on Capital* (New York: Augustus M. Kelley, 1966); and *Competition and Entrepreneurship* (Chicago: University of Chicago Press, 1973).

Ludwig M. Lachmann is currently Visiting Professor of Economics at New York University. His major writings include *Capital and Its Structure* (London: Bell & Sons, 1956); *The Legacy of Max Weber* (London: Heinemann, 1970); and *Macroeconomic Thinking and the Market Economy* (London: Institute of Economic Affairs, 1973).

Murray N. Rothbard is Professor of Economics at Polytechnic Institute of New York. Among his numerous publications in economics, history, and the social sciences are the following titles: *Man, Economy, and State*, 2 vols. (Princeton: D. Van Nostrand, 1962); *America's Great Depression* (Princeton: D. Van Nostrand, 1972); and *Power and Market: Government and the Economy* (Menlo Park, Calif.: Institute for Humane Studies, 1970).

Sudha R. Shenoy is Lecturer in Economics at The Cranfield School of Management at Bedford, United Kingdom. Her major writings on economics include "A Note on Mr. Sandesara's Critique," *Indian Economic Journal*, April-June 1967; *India: Progress or Poverty? A Review of Central Planning in India, 1951-69*, Institute of Economic Affairs Research Paper No. 27 (London) 1971. She has edited F. A. Hayek's major pronouncements on the theory of inflation and the economics of J. M. Keynes under the title *A Tiger by the Tail*, Institute of Economic Affairs, Hobart Paper no. 4 (London, 1972).

INDEX

Action: concept of, 5-6; vs. event, 5, 6; *see also* Human Action
Action axiom, 19-21, 24, 25, 27, 28, 31-32
Adler, Felix, 90, 95
Advertising, 9, 121-123
Affluent Society, The (Galbraith), 30
Aggregations, 6, 85, 133, 137-140, 149, 152, 154, 156-158, 191
Albertus Magnus, 59, 61
Allocative decision making, 118-120
Angel Gabriel model, 163
Antonino, Saint, 62, 64
Aquinas, Thomas, 59-63, 69, 71
Arbitrage, 155
Aristotelianism, 53, 68-71; *see also* Scholasticism
Arrow, Kenneth J., 221
Augustine, Saint, 54
Austrian circle, 167
Austrian economics: basic tenets, 42-43; as extraordinary science, 4; neo-Ricardian counterrevolution and, 215-223; prehistory, 52-74; postulates, 215-217; tasks, 6; *see also* Praxeology
Austrian paradigm, 4-5, 7-9, 12, 13
Axiomatic-deductive method, 21-22
Axioms, 7, 14, 28; epistemological status, 24; praxeology and, 19-29
Azpilcueta Navarro, Martín de, 56, 60, 65

Bailey, Samuel, 52
Balance of payments, 187

Baldwin, John W., 61
Bañez, Domingo de, 57
Bank credit, 179, 195-197, 199
Banking regulations, 179
Barter, 162, 169
Becker, Gary, 47
Behaviorism, 32
Bernardino of Siena, Saint, 58, 60, 62-64, 67
Bodin, Jean, 56
Böhm-Bawerk, Eugen von, 70, 154, 171, 194; capital theory, 134-136, 145-147
Bonaventure, Saint, 61
Bresciani-Turroni, Constantino, 176
Buchanan, James M., 47, 96
Buridan, Jean, 54, 58-59
Business cycle, 11-13, 174, 178, 186, 199-200; Keynesian analysis, 188-190; microeconomic analysis, 194; monetarist analysis, 190-193; monetary theory and, 202-204

Cairnes, J. E., 26
Cajetan, Cardinal, Thomas de Vio, 60, 62
Calvinism, 68
Capital: definition, 10; as fund, 134, 135
Capital and Time (Hicks), 41, 145
Capital combination, 147-150, 152, 198
Capital gains and losses, 157
Capital goods, 137-138
Capital heterogeneity, 147, 148, 150
Capital measurement, 149, 152-155; individual, 138-140; of national

232

Marshall, Alfred, 14, 69
Marshallian partial-equilibrium construction, 115, 116-117
Marx, Karl, 53
Materialists, 10, 133-135, 137-138
Mathematical formulations, 6-7, 9, 14, 21-24, 70, 170-171
Measurement, 157, 158
Medium of exchange, 162, 168-169
Menger, Carl, 69-71, 194, 217; on mathematical formulations, 23-24; monetary theory, 169; on tasks of economic explanation, 41-42; *Untersuchungen*, 75
Mercado, Tomás de, 57
Mercantilism, 52, 53
Methodological essentialism, 42
Methodological individualism, 118, 191
Methodology, 6, 7, 14, 40-51
Microeconomics, 8; approach to macroeconomics, 11; business cycle analysis, 194
Mill, John S., 190
Mises, Ludwig von, 115, 120; on action axiom, 24; on business cycle, 11, 194; on capital stock, 138; on econometrics, 33-35; on efficiency, 81; on free market, 80, 81, 86, 104; on historical events, 32; *Human Action*, 19, 170, 171; on human action, 70, 118, 119-120; on laissez-faire, 101, 104, 105; on liberalism, 105; on mathematical formulations, 7; monetary theory, 160-180, 194; on praxeologic axioms, 27; on praxeology, 19; on policy pronouncements, 79-82, 101-102; on purposefulness, 81, 86; regression theorem, 168-170, *Theory of Money and Credit*, 160, 166, 170, 179, 180; on time preference, 103; unanimity principle and, 101; as utilitarian, 104-106, 108, 109; on *Wertfreiheit*, 77, 79-82, 86

Molina, Luís de, 57-60
Monetarist school, on business cycle, 190-193
Monetary exchange, 172
Monetary expansion, 12, 163-164, 170, 172-178, 188, 191-192, 194-207; price and, 194-196; production structure and, 196-200; recession and, 205-206; resource allocation and, 195, 201-202, 204, 205; self-reversibility factor, 199-201; stagflation and, 204-207
"Monetary overinvestment" theory, 178
Monetary policy, 12, 190-194; capital structure and, 194, 205; price and, 185, 186, 188, 190-196, 200-201, 204; unemployment and, 188, 190, 192, 200, 202-205
Monetary theory, 11, 66-68, 160-184; business cycle and, 202-204; marginal utility in, 160, 161, 167, 168, 170; supply and demand in, 56-58, 160, 161, 163
Money, "objective exchange-value," 161
Money supply, 172-174; in cost inflation, 188; definition, 179-182
Montanari, Geminiano, 67
Morgenstern, Oskar, 115
Mutual determination, 171
Myrdal, Gunnar: on Austrian economics, 79; *The Political Element in . . .Economic Theory*, 77, 79-80; *Value in Social Theory*, 79; on *Wertfreiheit*, 77-79

National economy capital measurement, 140-141
National income measurement, 154
Neoclassical economics, 9, 126; critique of, 8
Neo-Ricardian counterrevolution, 215-223
New Left, 79

238